STORIES FROM OLD-FASHIONED CHILDREN'S BOOKS

ANDREW W. TUER

Augustus M. Kelley · Publishers
NEW YORK 1969

Published in the United States by
Augustus M. Kelley · Publishers
New York, New York 10010
First published in 1899 by The Leadenall Press Ltd
SBN 678 07507 7
Library of Congress Catalogue Card No. 75 75059
Printed in England by Redwood Press, Trowbridge, Wiltshire

The Proud Boy (p. 313.)

When alas! in a mean and dirty dark alley
Some women took hold of our poor little Sally;
Then instantly all her good clothes they were stripping,
And if she cried out, were preparing a whipping.

(p. 125.)

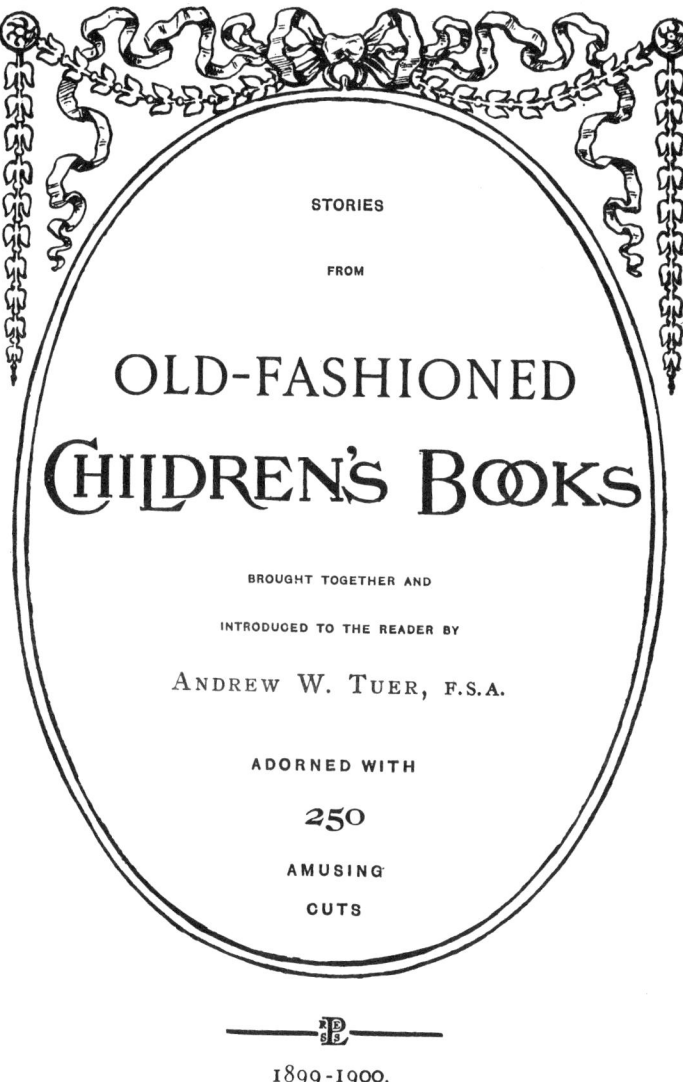

STORIES

FROM

OLD-FASHIONED

CHILDREN'S BOOKS

BROUGHT TOGETHER AND

INTRODUCED TO THE READER BY

ANDREW W. TUER, F.S.A.

ADORNED WITH

250

AMUSING

CUTS

1899-1900.
LONDON:
The Leadenhall Prefs, Ltd: 50, Leadenhall Street, E.C.
Simpkin, Marshall, Hamilton, Kent & Co., Ltd:

New York: Charles Scribner's Sons, 153-157, Fifth Avenue.

TO
THE
BEST
LOVED
WOMAN

INTRODUCTORY.

IN this collection of old-fashioned and long-forgotten children's-stories, the reader is spared much that is prosy and irrelevant. They are all—odds and ends as well—amusingly characteristic of times when our mothers' and fathers' mothers and fathers wore short frocks.

There can be few, if any, more interesting pursuits than the retrieving of old children's-books. At present the number of collectors is small, and those who know where to look may still pick up quaintly illustrated little treasures for a shilling or so. There is the joy of coming across such covetable rarities as the original editions of Charles Lamb's "*Poetry for Children*," in two volumes (1809); his "*Prince Dorus*" (1811); his "*Beauty and the Beast*," published without a title page in 1811*; "*The Elegant Girl*," a glorified child's book of verse,

---

* The earliest edition with a title appeared in 1813.

INTRODUCTORY.

oblong folio in size, with a dozen fascinating whole-page plates in colours; "*The Looking Glass, a True History of the Early Years of an Artist* [Mulready], 1805;" "*Dame Wiggins of Lee*," boomed by Mr. Ruskin; and "*Signor Topsy Turvey's Wonderful Magic Lantern; or, the World turned Upside Down.* By the author of 'My Mother' and other Poems. [Ann Taylor, helped by her sister Jane]. Illustrated with 24 Engravings [designed by their brother Isaac], 1810."

It will be discovered that the publishers of old children's-books were fond of using the text for advertising their wares. "Shall we order the coachman," asks a little girl ("*Mrs. Leicester's School*," p. 223), "to the corner of St. Paul's Churchyard [Harris's the opposition shop], or shall we go to the Juvenile Library in Skinner Street?" Of course mamma has a ready excuse for going Skinner-Streetwards. The motive of this acceptable puff from Mary Lamb, whose example the reader will see is conscientiously followed, must have been simply friendship.

The lady who thought it necessary to teach children that fishes have no legs, and who believed that sea-water when boiled becomes fresh ("*Parlour Teacher*," 1804, p. 50), probably did not follow literature for a livelihood.

It rather disturbs one to find that a paternal

INTRODUCTORY.

government's practice of destroying or "blacking out" objectionable matter is not new (vide p. 400).

We know that thrifty publishers made their cuts do duty over and over again: witness the unhappy king on p. 205. Children's books were very generally sold with the plates both plain and coloured, the coloured ones of course at a higher price. People who are fond of using the paint-box may like to see a wood-cut "depicted in lively colours." In a very fully illustrated and lately published volume—"*For-*

gotten Children's Books" *—I have described the method by which the cuts were coloured,

* (The Leadenhall Press, Ltd.—Six Shillings.)

INTRODUCTORY.

and therein also is shewn a genuine specimen of the old Dutch paper with leaf-gold background used for the covers. In other Dutch papers used for binding, the omission of the gold background was sought to be balanced by increased gaudiness in the patchy blobs of colour—laid on, by the way, with a brush by young children.

One hardly expects to find the discount system, or something very like it, in operation ninety years ago. In "*A Visit to London*" (1810), a dull book describing the principal public buildings, its publisher, Mr. Tabart, sandwiches in a whole chapter, headed *A Visit to the Juvenile Library*, in praise of his books which are separately named and criticised, and every one presented by the elders or bought by the youngsters of the party. The thirst of the little ones for Grecian, Roman and English history, spelling books, catechisms and class books of three hundred and sixty-five lessons, is prodigious and incredible. At the end of the chapter we learn that on receiving payment for the many purchases, " Mr. Tabart handsomely presented a book," the title of which was duly read aloud, to each of his patrons—mamma, governess and children. This he called "discount for ready money," which "mightily amused the whole party." In a list of his publications at the end of a charmingly

INTRODUCTORY.

illustrated "*Collection of Simple Stories*" (see p. 129), "Mr. Tabart respectfully acquaints the nobility, gentry and their friends in general that purchasers to the amount of one guinea will be entitled to a half-crown book gratis and so in proportion above that value."

Our grandmothers, to whom some of the little books in this collection were specially addressed, took delight in cutting out paper, an art demanding keen scissors and keener eyes, which was taught as a fashionable

INTRODUCTORY.

accomplishment. Ackermann published copies on " Bath Post " of landscapes and fanciful designs, many so elaborate as to look when finished like fine lace.

The illustration shews a portion only of one of these copies. The whole of the black work was laboriously cut away with scissors and knife, leaving a sort of white stencil, which, with a piece of paper behind coloured to accord with the subject, formed the picture.

On a higher plane were black paper profile portraits (silhouettes, or shadow likenesses) and groups of figures. The portraits were generally scissored out direct without preliminary sketch. Sometimes we find as a variant the portrait formed of the outside or surrounding paper—equivalent to the " counter " in engraved ivory and tortoiseshell work—laid over paper of another colour. On the next page are two mounted portraits cut together from paper blacked on both sides : one turned over to face the other gives the mildly jocular " Family Likeness."

There is a story, which we are not obliged to believe, of a professional silhouettist who was compelled by a dissatisfied client to cut many likenesses—one at each visit. At last the weary artist, in the presence of the sitter, placed the accumulated portraits one on top of the other, when, being all alike and exactly

INTRODUCTORY.

of the same size, they formed a solid block. I have explained elsewhere* how the shadow portrait originated. The groups were generally outlined on white paper; a piece of black paper was placed underneath and in cutting the scissors followed the outline. The black silhouette underneath was retained and

A FAMILY LIKENESS.

the white paper on top, on which the sketch had been made, was thrown away.

Good examples of figure cutting will be found at p. 392 in the hitherto unpublished illustrations to one of Gay's Fables, "*The Tame*

* "The Art of Silhouetting" in the *English Illustrated Magazine*, No. 82, vol. 7.

INTRODUCTORY.

Stag." About eighty of these minute groups (some of them appear amongst the miscellaneous cuts at the end of this volume) lately came into my possession. They have been preserved between the leaves of a little blank book, some bearing dates from 1796 to 1806. Beyond the versified fable of Gay's, the subjects of these charming trifles are unidentified. The little citron-morocco-bound volume is lettered on the front cover A.L.P. and on the back M.G. A.L.P. turns out to be the first wife of the fourth Earl Poulett of Poulett Lodge, Twickenham, but who M.G. was is unknown : it may be that the draughtmanship was due to Lady Poulett and the cutting out to M.G.

Pricking pictures with pins was another agreeable accomplishment. The pins were of several thicknesses, the broad lines and heavy shadows being pricked on paper with stout, and the finer work with thin pins. A toothed wheel with sharp points was used for outlines. For filling up large spaces two or more wheels were mounted on one axle. Without such labour-saving appliances, the more ambitious and microscopically minute pin-pricked pictures, specimens of which survive, could not have been achieved. Amongst ingenious variations giving employment to busy fingers were "pictures" constructed of innumerable little spirals made of long narrow slips of paper

INTRODUCTORY.

tightly rolled up and set on end side by side, the tops being gilt or tinted. Little misses also made wonderful scallop-edged handscreens, save-alls and letter-racks of bits of cardboard held together with silk thread and decorated with views and scroll-work borderings drawn and coloured with painstaking precision. Some of these pretty trifles they would present to their parents : for others they made their friends pay fancifully at bazaars.

None of the tales in this volume calls for special remark, except perhaps "*Joe Dobson.*" This amusing bit of versification was a prime favourite, whence it results that copies unthumbed and unscribbled upon are scarce. In the collection of children's books belonging to the Countess of Cavan is a carefully preserved copy of "*Joe Dobson,*" and an exceedingly pretty melody (p. 67) has been fortunately handed down in her family, which for the benefit of readers of these pages Lady Cavan has been good enough to commit to paper from memory.

The cuts which decorate the tales belong to them, but room has been found for others at the backs of title pages and in spaces which would otherwise be blank. The dozen or twenty scattered titled cuts, such as that on p. 8, are reductions of Adam Buck's gracefu work now so much in vogue.

INTRODUCTORY.

Perhaps it will be well not to try and swallow these little stories at a gulp. Better mark twain, read them and put the book away for a time.

No American books are included herein. My friend Mrs. Alice Morse Earle, of Brooklyn, N.Y., whose works on early Colonial life in America are familiar on both sides, is issuing a volume dealing with children's books, entitled "*Child-Life in Colonial Days*," which must find appreciative readers wherever our language is spoken.

For the contents of STORIES FROM OLD-FASHIONED CHILDREN'S BOOKS I have drawn chiefly on my own collection. For permission to make use of some of their cherished treasures, hearty acknowledgments are made to Lady Cavan, Mrs. E. Carthew, Mr. Joseph W. Darton, Mr. J. Mason Davenport, Mr. William Day, Mr. J. Evans, Mr. A. G. Farrow, Mr. F. Hockliffe, Miss H. De Lessert, Mr. Elkin Mathews, Miss Edith C. Pollock, Mr. George Potter, Miss Ravenscroft, Mr. A. Sindall and Professor Foster Watson.

SOME ACCOUNT OF THE AUTHOR TOMMY TRIP, AND OF HIS DOG JOULER.

[From *A Pretty Book of Pictures for Little Masters and Misses: or, Tommy Trip's History of Beasts and Birds. With a familiar description of each in verse and prose. To which is prefixed The History of Little Tom himself, of his dog Jouler, and of Woglog the great Giant.* Ninth Edition. London: Printed for J. Newbery, in St. Paul's Churchyard. MDCCLXVII.]

TOMMY TRIP, the author of the following sheets, is the only son of Mr. William Trip, of Spittle Fields, London. He is but short in stature, and not much bigger than Tom Thumb but a great deal better, for he is a great scholar, and whenever you see him you will always find him with a book in his hand and his faithful dog Jouler by his side. Jouler serves him for a horse as well as a dog, and Tommy when he has a mind to ride, pulls a little bridle out of his pocket, whips it upon honest Jouler, and away he gallops—*tantivy*. As he rides through the town he frequently stops at the doors to know how the little children do within, and if they are good and learn their books he then leaves an Apple, an Orange or a Plumb-cake at the door, and away he gallops again—*tantivy, tantivy, tantivy*.

You have heard how he beat Woglog, the great Giant, I suppose, have you not? But lest you should not, I will tell you. As Tommy was walking through a meadow on a moon-light night, he heard a little boy cry, upon which he called Jouler, bridled him and galloped away to the place. When he came there he found Woglog with a little boy under his arm whom he was going to throw into the water. Little boys should never loiter about in fields, nor even in the streets, after it is dark. However, as he had been a good boy in other respects little Trip was determined the giant should not hurt him; and therefore he called to him, " Here you great Giant, you Woglog, set down that little boy, or I'll make you dance like a pea on a tobacco pipe. Are you not ashamed to set your wit to a child?" Woglog turned round, attempted to seize little Trip between his finger and thumb and thought to have cracked him as one does a walnut, but just as his hand came to him, Jouler snapped at it and bit a piece of his thumb, which put the giant in so much pain that he let fall the little boy, who ran away. Little Trip then up'd with his whip and lashed Woglog till he laid down and roared like a town bull, and promised never to meddle with any little boys or girls again. After he had thus beat the great Giant, Trip put the little boy upon Jouler and carried him home to his father and mother, but upon the road he charged him to be a good boy and to say his prayers and learn his book and do as his pappa and mamma bid him, which this little boy has done ever since; and so must all other little boys and girls, or nobody will love them.

Little Trip is not only a very agreeable companion and a great scholar, but is also allowed to be one of the best Poets of the age, and that even by the Poets themselves, which in my opinion is an incontestible proof of his superior abilities. For if he did not as much exceed those Gentry as Apollo does the Muses, they who seldom make confessions of this sort, would never give up the point in his favour. He has now by him several dramatic pieces which are not culled from other authors, as the custom is, but all originals and well adapted to the English stage; and the following song composed by him when he was very young will sufficiently prove his superiority in lyric poetry.

I.

Three children sliding on the ice
  Upon a summer's day;
As it fell out, they all fell in—
  The rest, they ran away.

II.

Now had these children been at school,
  Or sliding on dry ground;
Ten thousand pounds to one penny
  They had not all been drowned.

III.

You parents who have children dear,
  And eke you that have none,
If you would have them safe abroad
  Pray keep them all at home.

TOMMY TRIP.

OF THE LION AND JACKAL.

The Lion is commonly called the king of beasts. . . The report of his being afraid of the crowing of a cock is found by experience to be entirely false. The Jackal is frequently called the lion's provider. It is said that when he seizes his prey, by his cries he gives notice to the lion, at whose sight he retires and when he has gone returns to eat what his master the lion has left.

OF THE LEOPARD.

Few beasts can with the Leopard vie
　His beauteous skin allures the eye,
His form, like Vice, serves to decoy
　Those whom his nature would destroy.

OF THE RHINOCEROS.

Should some fine lady view this beast
　His beauties ne'er could charm her,
Oh, how unlike Sir Foplin dressed
　Appears this hog in armour.

OF THE FOX.

So artful, so serious he looks and so sly
　At the goose when he casteth his eye on't,
That he seems like a gamester intent on his die,
　Or a lawyer surveying his client.

The Fox is remarkable for his craft and subtilty. When he is troubled with fleas he is said to take a piece of wool in his mouth and going by slow steps into a river, the fleas, leaping by degrees to avoid the water, assemble in the wool; after staying for a moment with only his nose above stream, he lets it go and is immediately quit of his troublesome companions.

TOMMY TRIP.

Of the Porcupine.
This creature shoots his pointed quills,
  And beasts destroys and men;
But more the rav'nous lawyer kills
  With his half-quill the pen.

Of the Bison or Wild Ox.
The bison though neither
  Engaging nor young,
Like a flatt'rer can lick
  You to death with his tongue.

The bison's tongue is long, hard and as rough as a file; with this alone he is said to be able to draw a man to him, and by only licking wound him to death. He smells like a musk cat; but though his flesh is in summer very fat it is too strong to be eaten.

Of the Crocodile.
The crocodile with false perfidious tears,
  Draws the unwary trav'ler nigh,
Who by compassion warm'd no danger fears
  But ah! th'unhappy wretch must die.

Of the Hawk and Kite.
The Hawk and Kite, both birds of prey
  Will kill and bear your fowls away,
And since your foes you cannot shun,
  Then cock your eye—and cock your gun.

Of the Game Cock and Pheasant.
The Game Cock rather than give way
  Will bravely fight and die;
But the poor Pheasant—tim'rous bird,
  Spreads both its wings to fly.

THE POLITE ACADEMY.

OF THE GOOSE AND THE DUCK.

This waddling, hissing, quacking pair
  Have but few charms for eye or ear,
But let the cook but spit and baste 'em,
  And every fool is glad to taste 'em.

The Goose lives on land and water. . . When provoked it hisses like a serpent. The Duck also lives on land and water, and will live on anything it can meet with. Its throat is very untuneable, but it seldom opens except at the approach of a shower.

[From *The Polite Academy for Young Ladies and Gentlemen*. London : R. Baldwin. 1762.]

OF BEHAVIOUR.

BEFORE you speak make a Bow or Curtesy, and when you have received your Answer make another.

Be careful how you speak to those who have not spoke to you.

Nothing shows the difference between a young Gentleman and a vulgar Boy so much as the Behaviour in eating.

Never touch your Meat with your Fingers.

Pick your Bones clean and leave them on your plate; they must not be thrown down.

Seldom blow your Nose and use your Handkerchief for that Purpose, making as little noise as you can.

Never spit in a Room.

Never sing or whistle in Company: these are the idle tricks of vulgar children.

Take care not to make Faces nor Wink.

Keep your Hands quiet, and use no antick Motions.

THE POLITE ACADEMY.

Never laugh immoderately at a Story told by another Person. Never laugh at all at what you tell yourself.

Never talk about any Thing but what you know.

DIRECTIONS FOR YOUNG LADIES TO ATTAIN A GENTEEL CARRIAGE.

TO MAKE A CURTESY.

HOLD yourself properly and easily upright.

Raise your Head with a free Air, not with a stiff Formality.

Let your Shoulders fall back with an easy Air.

Let your Arms fall easy to your Waist, and keep them straight to your sides, not putting them backwards or forwards.

Lay your Hands across and do not raise them too high, nor let them fall too low.

Let the Hollow or inside of your Hands be turned towards you.

Let your Fingers be a little open.

Bend your Wrists a little.

Turn with an easy Air towards the Person you are to compliment.

Step a little Sideways with either Foot.

Join the other to it.

Turn your Eyes a little downward.

Being thus placed bend softly and gradually into a curtesy.

Rise gently from it; and lift up your Eyes as you draw up your Head.

Come, Father's hope! Come, Mother's glory!
Now listen to a pretty story.

THE

LILLIPUTIAN MAGAZINE;

OR,

Children's Repository.

CONTAINING

WHAT IS WHIMSICAL, WITTY & MORAL

CALCULATED TO ENTERTAIN AND IMPROVE

THE MINDS OF YOUTH OF BOTH SEXES.

By TIMOTHY TEACHUM, & CO.

SIMON SIMPLE.
SALLY SPELLWELL.
POLLY PERT.

London :
Printed for W. TRINGHAM, *at No. 11 on the Left Hand Side of Fleet Ditch, leading to Blackfriars Bridge.*

The Mother's Hope.

The Father's Darling.

SIMON SIMPLE.

THE family of the Simples is as ancient a family as any in England, and their honours and dignities as great. From this family we have had at different periods, generals, admirals, bishops, statesmen and even kings and conjurers. The hero of the present tale comes of a younger branch of the noble house, whose father had never been at court but had always lived retired on his own estate without the assistance of place or pension.

Little Simon was the only child and consequently not a little made of by his indulgent Parents. When but quite an infant in his mother's arms he discovered great signs of an extraordinary capacity. Wonderful and surprising as this may seem, it is proved in the records of the family by sufficient witnesses. Some say he could walk before he could talk, but whether true or not is not material, as long as we are convinced that he could both talk and walk; for from the same valuable records we are informed that he said one day when the wind blew upon him, it's cold, and on another day in summer when the sun shone surprisingly fine, he said it was hot. As to walking very young, we have this account to prove it, that the nurse having let go his leading strings he walked quite to the stair head, and then tumbled all the way to the bottom. But whatever proof this may be of his abilities in his early part of life, there is not the least argument in favour of the nurse's prudence, and I am sorry to say that there are too many of her careless disposition existing at this very time, who too often are the cause of those being cripples all their life time whom nature had cast in the most perfect mould. However, Simon received as it happened no further

SIMON SIMPLE.

damage from this accident than scratching the skin off his forehead, although he cried as if he had been killed, as the saying is; but the nurse who was a wiseacre running downstairs catched him up in her arms and began to whip him with a vengeance, bauling out—You little urchin, you might as well have broke your neck, you might so. Another day when he could walk rather better, he had got close to the side of a pond where the ducks used to swim, and throwing in some bits of bread to please himself, straining rather too forward he fell in, when his good nurse who had left him to listen to a gossip's tale of mother Gadabout, happened to have a glimpse of him just as he was going in and arrived time enough to take him out alive, but it put her in a most violent passion. How could you, says she, how could master Simon dare to tumble into the pond; as sure as three beans make five, if I had not seen you till you had drowned, you would never have come out alive. Which was most certainly true, but the good woman had no doubt some other meaning in what she said, if one could but find it out. She had always a knack of being clever which the following account will no doubt justify. She had formerly a husband who was a woodcutter a very industrious, sober, honest man, when one day he had the misfortune to fall out of a high tree with his cutting-knife in his hand and break his neck. When the news was brought to his loving spouse, she lifted up her eyes to heaven, and said The Lord be praised it is no worse; he might have cut himself.

MISS SALLY SPELLWELL.

THE HISTORY OF MISS SALLY SPELLWELL.

MISS SALLY SPELLWELL was one of the prettiest little Ladies that ever con'd a Lesson. She was the Daughter of Mr. Spellwell, a country Curate, who died before she was born; and her Mamma had very little to support herself and Daughter with, but what she got by her Needle; but

being a very fine Workwoman she was employed by most of the Ladies of Distinction in the Place and for many

MISS SALLY SPELLWELL.

miles round, which enabled her to live comfortably and bring up her daughter very decently.

Mark this ye little Misses who read this Story, and be sure to be diligent and make yourselves Mistresses of your Needle, as it may sometime in your Life become necessary for your support. If you apply to those who knew your Family in better circumstances, they will say, Why does she not work at the Needle? What a cut that will be when you are obliged to say you don't know how!

MISS SALLY SPELLWELL had no Mistress but her Mamma, and indeed there could not be a better. As soon as ever she was able to speak, she was taught her Letters, and as she grew up was remarkable for her accuracy in Spelling, a Circumstance not so much regarded by the Ladies as it should be, but it is hoped that the example will have some influence for the future, for it's a great Pity (but 'tis too often the case) to see a fine Hand-writing in a Letter without a word of good English in it.

Miss Sally's Mamma, to help out, undertook to instruct six young Ladies in Reading and Needlework. And if she was sent for by any of the Ladies to teach them how to do some curious work, which they sometimes did at their own Houses, Miss Sally was such a proficient that she could supply her absence both in Reading and Working in an astonishing manner, which made her very much beloved by the pretty Ladies who boarded with her Mamma.

Miss Sally before she was six years of age had finished Two Samplers in a very curious Manner, containing the Lord's Prayer, the Belief and the Ten Commandments, with very pretty Ornaments. But what gained her the most Reputation was one which she had worked from a little POEM which was written by her father, and which her Mother had made her get by Heart as soon as she was able to read. This Sampler was ornamented with a variety of

MISS SALLY SPELLWELL.

Flowers, all marked in their natural Colours, and shaded with the greatest nicety.

This little POEM as I have said before, she had worked on a Sampler in so curious and neat a Manner that everyone who saw it admired it; her Mamma had it framed and glazed, and valued it more than any other Piece of Furniture she had in the House, and pretty presents had little Sally on its being seen by those Ladies who used to come to her Mamma; which made her still more fond of excelling in everything she undertook: and this is certain that Rewards will always follow those who strive to do well.

Miss Sally was now about twelve years of age, tall and genteel, with a Face which seemed as though it was designed for the residence of Beauty and Affability. At the same time such Modesty was observable in all her Actions that when the Parents of others had a mind to shame their Daughters for any Boldness of Behaviour, they would ask if they ever knew Sally Spellwell do so, which made some of them not a little angry with her, as they thought her good Behaviour was a Bar in the way of their Inclinations. Nobody could live more happy than Sally and her Mamma; for some years Peace and Contentment were their constant Companions, but alas! poor Sally was ordained to feel a severe Reverse of Fortune; her dear Mamma was taken ill of a Fever, and after a short Illness left this transitory World for the Eternal One.

Here was a stroke for one so young, who had never been a day from under the fostering wing of a tender and indulgent Parent: without Friends, without Connection, without that necessary knowledge to encounter a wide and wicked World. What could this Orphan do? How could she proceed? No one to advise with, no tender bosom to open the flowing of her woe-fraught Soul to.—Yet she must not fall a Victim to Despair. . . .

MISS SALLY SPELLWELL.

As Nature must be supported, she now turned her thoughts to consider what she must do for a Subsistance. She visited those Ladies who used to employ and encourage her Mamma, and solicited to be continued their Servant in the same Manner; but whether they did not think so well of her Abilities, or that she being entirely an Orphan they imagined she would become too troublesome to them, or what was the reason I will not pretend to say; but after the first Visit, she could never get into the presence of them again, nor ever had the least Employment.

Her Needle therefore became useless, and as to sewing she was entirely unfit for that; the only thing she next had to do was in a little room which she had taken to set up a School and teach young children to read.

In this Situation she lived for near Twelve months till her School was much increased; when an Accident happened which relieved her from all her poverty, and raised her up to that Dignity which so much Prudence, Virtue and Goodness deserved.

It happened that a Post Chaise with an old Lady and her Son in it, broke down just opposite the Cottage where Sally lived, and they were glad, as there was no Inn near, to take Shelter with her till another Convenience could be provided for them to travel in. The old Lady was surprised at the goodness of so mean a looking Place, but more so at the genteel and affable Behaviour of its young Mistress. Her curiosity led her to enquire into the History of Spellwell, which she with much Modesty informed her of, but when she mentioned the name of her Father, — Good Heavens! exclaimed the old Lady — MR. SPELLWELL! he was the intimate Friend and Fellow-Student with my Husband at the University, whom many a time have I heard him mention with the warmest zeal for his Welfare;

but could never learn what was become of him. For his sake, who alas! is dead and gone I will adopt you for my own. Tears of gratitude flowed from the eyes of the now-fortunate Sally, while strange emotions arose in the Breast of the young Gentleman.

In short, Miss Sally went with them to their Mansion, where in a short time with the full consent of his Mother she became her Daughter in law, by being married to her Son, a young Gentleman of such purity of Morals and good Understanding as is not everywhere to be found, and Miss Sally Spellwell rides in her own Coach and Six.

> If Virtue, Learning, Goodness are your Aim,
> Each pretty Miss may hope to do the same.

THE HISTORY OF POLLY PERT.

'TIS a very sad thing when little Folks fancy to themselves that a saucy pert Behaviour is Wit.

Poor POLLY PERT was very unhappy in this particular; every cant word or trifling expression which she had heard others laugh at she was sure to keep in her Memory, and discharge them like a Blunderbuss, alike out of time and place, and then she would laugh herself ready to split her sides, when nobody else could guess what it was about. Then she would be sure when anyone was talking to interrupt them by saying something in the middle of their Discourse, and if she did not know whom or what they were talking about, she would be sure to ask questions, and although she often got handsomely rebuked for her impertinent Curiosity, in two Minutes she was at the same Game again. Her Mamma and Pappa tried every Method they could think of to break her, but all in vain. They sent her to a Boarding School some miles off, thinking she would never have boldness enough to behave so among Strangers yet by the time she had been there a Week it was all the same to POLLY PERT. . . At length her Governess began to be quite tired of her and had some thoughts of writing to her Parents to send for her home; but a thought came into her head to put a Scheme in execution which might possibly go a little way towards curing her. Among other of her Impertinencies she had been observed to listen, to get at the knowledge of what she could not learn by asking. This is another thing which is very bad in any one, and deserves Punishment wherever it is found : 'twas by this mean Curiosity of Miss Polly they intended to find the means of making her ashamed, if possible, and break her of such scandalous Ways for the Future. The Governess got two of the eldest Boarders to be whispering together very loud near where she was but seeming not to know that she was nigh ; among the rest of the secrets that they were to pretend to talk about was a very great Curiosity which was in the Governess's little Closet where none was ever permitted to go but herself yet at the same time they were to pretend to have been there while she was out, and that it was the finest Thing they had ever seen. All this Miss Pert stood up on tiptoe to listen to, and as soon as they were gone she was almost upon the Rack to know what this Rarity could be and how she could get at the Sight of it. If they have seen it, says she to herself, why may not I ? If they were not seen, why should I be ? If the Closet door is open, why may I not look in ? And just then looking out of the window she observed the Governess walking with the same two young Ladies in the Garden. This she thought was a lucky time, and her evil genius prompted her to go immediately. She looked about as watchful as a Cat after a Mouse to see if anyone was in the way to observe her; but finding the coast clear she soon gained the Closet and in she went, when bang went the door and fastened her in. It was a spring bolt which was on the door, and they had so contrived with a String inside that she could not stir without touching it and the moment she did, down fell the bolt outside, and it was impossible to open it within. The bird was now caught, and she would have given a bit of her Tongue, though she valued it better than anything else she possessed, to have been ten miles off. There was a Window in the Closet, but it was not made to open; and if it had it was too high for her to have got out, besides there was a very deep Water ran at the bottom, so that she was certain she must be exposed. What to do in this case she did not know; however she was determined not to call out, and if she had it would have been in vain as it was determined before not to hear her. Night came on, but no Governess came to the closet, and poor Polly began to blame her own prying Disposition and wished she had never listened to what others were talking of. Ten o'clock came but no Governess; her Heart was now almost ready to burst. Alone and in the dark, locked in a Place where she could not pretend to have the least business in the World she trembled for fear they should think she wanted to take something which was not her own; and however bad her Behaviour was in other respects she was truly honest. Stung to the very Heart with these reflections she melted into sullen Sorrow, and actually cried herself to sleep, when she had nothing but the most terrifying Dreams. At length the Morning came.

Now it happened that the Governess had contrived it at a time when she knew that Polly's Mamma and Pappa were to come and see her; accordingly they did about Nine o'clock that very Morning when Miss was still in the closet. The Time began to draw near now when Polly was to face all her acquaintance. The Governess entered the Room where the Closet was, when going towards it, she heard her sigh very loud, upon which she called out "What's that?" "It's me," said Polly. "Oh dear," says the Governess, "there's Thieves in the house," and away she run calling out, Help, Thieves, Thieves! In came the rest of the Boarders with Miss Polly's Pappa and Mamma, with the Men Servants and Maid Servants, what a Posse! John the Footman stood close to the Door with a Blunderbuss in his hands, and Governess pulled up the Bolt, and there sat poor Polly Pert almost dead with grief and shame. Lifting up her eyes and seeing the Blunderbuss so close to her, she cried out "Oh, pray don't kill me, I am no Thief, I am only Polly Pert." "How, Polly Pert," said the Governess, "how came you in my Closet?" To this she could make no answer and seeing her Pappa and Mamma she was ten times more confounded, when her Pappa advancing lifted her up, saying "What Business my dear had you in your Governess's Closet; I suppose it was your idle Curiosity which I am afraid will never leave you; it might be imagined you had other views, and suppose you had been heard to stir in the Night you might have been killed before anyone knew who you were." Polly shuddered at the Thoughts of what might have been the consequences, but could not speak one Word. The Governess with the rest now thought proper to withdraw, and leave her with her Pappa and Mamma, who now took an opportunity to convince her of the Absurdness of her Conduct—which she owned she was truly sensible was wrong, and if they would be kind enough to forgive her what was passed and endeavour to make it up with the Governess, her future Behaviour she hoped should be unexceptionable and she would strive to make Amends for all her past Follies. This condescension and her promise of Amendment, melted their Hearts, and they embraced her with the utmost Tenderness, and Peace and Harmony soon took Place in the Family; and 'tis with the greatest pleasure I relate that Miss Polly fulfilled her Promise to the utmost of their Expectations; she took to Learning with the utmost Assiduity, grew extremely good-mannered and polite, so that she now was as much respected and beloved as she was hated and despised before.

FALSE ALARMS.

[From *False Alarms; or, The Mischievous Doctrine of Ghosts and Apparitions, of Spectres and Hobgoblins, exploded from the Minds of every Miss and Master.* London: J. Newbery, St. Paul's Churchyard 1770.]

My friend had the misfortune to have it reported that his staircase was haunted, and that the doors of his house were no sooner opened than evil spirits entered and put his bell-rope in the most violent agitation. The parson of the parish who was a sensible man, and who came to examine into this affair, imagined that some kitten, or other young animal, might get to some part of the rope, and put it into this agitation: but it was soon seen that such clearly was not the case.

A Methodist preacher came next, in order to discover the mystery and detect the deception, if any; but after various remarks and observations he concluded that an evil spirit of the cloven-footed kind had taken possession of the staircase, from which it would be exceedingly difficult to dislodge

FALSE ALARMS.

him, if at all practicable, without pulling down the house about his ears.

My friend's house was every day crowded with people to see the operation of the spirit on the bell-rope; but though his company increased his trade diminished, as it may well be supposed, that no people would chuse to purchase goods out of a house which was in the possession of a cloven-footed spirit.

The staircase was crowded with people on the day I called on my friend, when the bell-rope was in full motion, as it was a windy day the spirit was always found to be more active then than on calm days. I own I was at first a little surprised to see the bell-rope in such violent agitation without any apparent cause; and as I seemed very inquisitive into the business the company all crowded round me, not doubting but I was come to lay the spirit.

As I well knew the undulating motion of the bell-rope must arise from some natural cause, I had no doubt of soon being able effectually to lay this evil spirit. I observed that there were two doors opposite to each other in the passage which when both opened occasioned a very great draught of air.

The wonderful operations of this cloven-footed spirit were now fully discovered; for the wind in its way through the passage, partly making up the wall of the staircase, put the rope into a violent agitation which remained perfectly quiet on one of the doors being shut.

It was indeed laughable enough on this discovery to see how the company dropped off one after another, perfectly ashamed of their weakness and credulity.

RULES FOR BEHAVIOUR AT TABLE.

[From *The Honours of the Table, or Rules for Behaviour during Meals. For the Use of Young People.* London: Printed for the Author at the Literary Press, No. 14 Red Lion Street, Clerkenwell. 1788.]

OF all the graceful accomplishments, and of every branch of polite education, it has been long admitted, that a gentleman and lady never show themselves to more advantage than in acquitting themselves well in the honours of their table; that is to say, in serving their guests and treating their friends agreeable to their rank and situation in life.

When dinner is announced, the mistress of the house requests the lady first in rank, in company, to shew the way to the rest, and walk first into the room where the table is served; she then asks the second in precedence to follow, and after all the ladies are passed, she brings up the rear herself. The master of the house does the same with the gentlemen. Among persons of real distinction, this marshalling of the company is unnecessary, every woman and every man present knows his rank and precedence, and takes the lead, without any direction from the mistress or the master.

When they enter the dining-room, each takes his place in the same order; the mistress of the table sits at the upper end, those of superior rank next her, right and left, those next in rank following, then the gentlemen, and the master at the lower-end; and nothing is considered as a greater mark of ill-breeding, than for a person to interrupt this order, or seat himself higher than he ought. Custom, however, has lately introduced a new mode of seating. A gentleman and a lady sitting alternately round the table, and this, for the better convenience of a lady's being attended to, and served by the gentleman next her. But notwithstanding this promiscuous seating, the ladies, whether above or below, are to be served in order, according to their rank or age, and after them the gentlemen in the same manner.

When there are several dishes at table, the mistress of the house carves that which is before her, and desires her husband, or the person at the bottom of the table, to carve the joint or bird, before *him*.

Where there are not two courses, but one course and a remove, that is, a dish to be brought up, when one is taken away; the mistress or person who presides, should acquaint her company with what is to come; or if the whole is put on the table at once, should tell her friends, that "they see their dinner"; but they should be told what wine or other liquors is on the side board. Sometimes a cold joint of meat, or a salad, is placed on the sideboard. In this case, it should be announced to the company.

As it is unseemly in ladies to call for wine, the gentlemen present should ask them in turn, whether it is agreeable to drink a glass of wine. ("Mrs. ———, will you do me the honour to drink a glass of wine with me?") and what kind of wine present they prefer, and call for two glasses of such wine, accordingly. Each then waits till the other is served, when they bow to each other and drink.

If you dislike what you have, leave it; but on no account, by smelling to, or examining it, charge your friend with putting unwholesome provisions before you.

To be well received, you must always be circumspect at table, where it is exceedingly rude to scratch any part of your body, to spit, or blow your nose, (if you can't avoid it, turn your head), to eat greedily, to lean your elbows on the table, to sit too far from it, to pick your teeth before the dishes are removed, or leave the table before grace is said.

THE FAMILIAR LETTER WRITER.
(FOR YOUNG PEOPLE.)

[From *Newbery's Familiar Letter Writer, adapted to the Capacities of Young People.* London: Printed for E. Newbery, the Corner of St. Paul's Churchyard. 1788.]

LETTER FROM A YOUNG GENTLEMAN TO HIS COMPANION, RECOVERED FROM A FIT OF SICKNESS.

It gives me the most sincere pleasure to hear, that my dear Tommy is recovering his health so rapidly. Had you died, it would have been to me a most terrible loss; but it has pleased God to preserve my friend. I will take the first opportunity that offers to call and tell you how valuable your life is to

Your sincere friend and playfellow

ANSWER TO THE PRECEDING LETTER.

Your obliging letter, my dear Billy, is a fresh proof of your friendship and esteem for me. I thank God I am now perfectly recovered. I am in some doubt whether I ought not to consider my late illness as a just punishment for my crime of robbing Mr. Goodman's orchard, breaking his boughs, and spoiling his hedges. However, I am fully determined that no such complaints shall evermore come against,

Your sincere friend and playfellow

LETTER TO A YOUNG MAN, ON HIS TOO STRONG ATTACHMENT TO SINGING AND MUSIC.

Dear Cousin,

In the first place, my dear cousin, these pleasures of sound may take you off from the more desirable ones of sense, and make your delight stop at the ear, which should go deeper, and be placed in the understanding; for, whenever a good singer is in company, adieu to all conversation of an improving or intellectual nature. In the second place, it may expose you to company, and that perhaps not the best or most eligible. Hence your business and your other more useful studies may be greatly, if not wholly neglected, and very possibly your health itself be impaired. In the third place, it may tend, which it naturally does, to enervate the mind, and make you haunt musical societies, operas, and concerts; and what glory is it to a gentleman, if he were even a fine performer, that he can strike a string, touch a key, or sing a song, with the grace and command of an *hired* musician?

Letter of Advice to a young Lady, on her affecting manly airs.

Dear Polly,

It is with singular pleasure I view the alteration and improvement in your person, so visible within the space of a few months. The dawning of fine sense, and a good judgment, which discovers itself in your conversation, leads me to hope I shall see every perfection of my sister, your late excellent mother, revived in you. Yet one thing the duty of a tender uncle obliges me to blame in you, and that is a certain affectation that has lately stolen in on your behaviour, of imitating the manners of the other sex, and appearing more masculine than the amiable softness of a woman can justify. I have been particularly offended, permit me to tell you, my dear, at your new riding-habit, which is made so extravagantly in the mode, that one cannot easily distinguish your sex by it; for you look in it neither like a modest girl, nor an agreeable boy. Some conformity to fashion is allowable; but a cocked hat, a laced jacket, and a fop's peruke, strangely disfigure you.

[From "*The Blind Child*. By a Lady. London: E. Newbery 1793.]
"'Tis a glorious morning; the Spring returns in all its beauty."

A VISIT TO LONDON.

[From *Mental Amusement; or, the Juvenile Moralist*. Second Edition Revised. London : printed for G. Sael, No. 192 Strand ; and sold by M. Poole & Son, Chester. 1798.]

MR. THOMAS TRUSTY had for many years lived steward with a worthy gentleman in Bedfordshire, and from his fidelity and good sense was highly regarded and esteemed. His master having a daughter, an only child who had just left school, it was agreed that she should make a visit to her aunt Dillon, who resided in London, and that Trusty should conduct her. The day of departure being fixed, Miss Lucinda exclaimed to her maid—" Oh ! Jenny, how happy I shall be to see London ! what wonders we shall have to tell of on our return ! "

The journey and its fatigues were scarcely thought of when the travellers reached Highgate where having alighted and taken some refreshment, as the afternoon was fine and clear, they sauntered on towards the summit of the hill to take a distant glance at London and Westminster. On approaching the point from which both cities break at once upon the sight, Lucinda felt a mixture of surprise and delight that for some minutes rivetted her feet to the spot on which she stood. At length she softly uttered—" It does indeed surpass my utmost expectations ! Do not let us lose more time, Mr. Trusty ; I long to be in the midst of such a scene."—" It looks like a new world," said Jenny. The chaise now took them up and they descended the hill near Caen Wood, the seat of Lord Mansfield. Hampstead presented itself on the right, and the vale of Hornsey on the left. After passing through the pleasant street called Kentish Town, Lucinda soon reached the house of her

A VISIT TO LONDON.

expecting aunt in Fitzroy Square, where the travellers retired at an early hour to repose themselves after their journey.

Mrs. Dillon was extremely pleased with her niece Lucinda, and promised during her visit that she should enjoy as large a share as possible of town amusements.

The next evening Mrs. Dillon proposed going to the Opera; and as her niece had the advantage of having been taught Italian, it was expected that she would be highly entertained: but in this her aunt was mistaken. Lucinda thought she perceived, both in singers and dancers, something that appeared to "overstep the modesty of nature," and the limits of real grace. With the music she was much gratified, and with the house itself, which of course displayed much elegance, symmetry and taste. St. Paul's Cathedral and Westminster Abbey were next visited. Here, indeed, was a striking change of scenery, from the lively and voluptuous to monuments of departed genius, or grandeur mouldering in the dust.

On the following Sunday Mrs. Dillon took her young visitor through Hyde Park to Kensington Gardens: there she saw the young and the old, the citizen and the nobleman, all met together, to see and be seen. The concourse of carriages and horsemen that composed the moving scene appeared to excite no other idea in Lucinda but that of a race-ground. In this view, she said it exceeded anything she had ever seen in the north; but what most created surprise was that this parade took place on a Sunday. "I cannot think, my dear Aunt," said Lucinda, "but the examples of the rich and powerful influence others in a high degree. If *they* were to find a fitter place to spend their Sundays in, do you think that Hyde Park would be so much resorted to by their inferiors?" Mrs. Dillon scarcely knew what reply to make to reflections which at once displayed

A VISIT TO LONDON.

the goodness of her niece's heart, and did honour to the guardians of her education.

In short, London with all its gaieties, had little serious attraction for the heart of Lucinda: so after thanking her aunt with grateful warmth for all the kindness experienced during her stay in Fitzroy Square, she returned at the end of two months to her friends in the north, more gratified by parental caresses and the honest friendship of Trusty than with all the luxuries of a town life; and she repeated with strong emphasis the following lines, as she mixed in the family circle round her own fireside:

> "O, friendly to the best pursuits of mind,
> Friendly to thought, to virtue and to peace,
> DOMESTIC LIFE in rural leisure passed!
> To guide the pencil, turn the tuneful page;
> To lend new flavour to the fruitful year,
> And heighten Nature's dainties;
> Well-order'd HOME our best delight to make;
> And by submissive wisdom, modest skill,
> With ev'ry gentle, care-eluding art,
> To raise the virtues, animate the bliss,
> And sweeten all the toils of human life:
> This be the *female* dignity, and praise."

THE GENEROUS DAUGHTERS.

[From *The Children's Magazine for November* 1800. London:
J. Marshall, 4 Aldermary Churchyard, Bow Lane.]

Two little girls, Nancy and Jenny, picked up a purse containing two silver sixpences. Let us go to the fair and see the puppet show, said Nancy. No, said Jenny, let us rather buy meat and porter for our dear mother whose stomach sickens at eating nothing but potatoes every day, for a shilling will pay for both.

SONGS FOR LITTLE MISSES.

[From *Puerilia; or, Amusements for the Young.* By John Marchant, Gent. London : P. Stevens, 1751.]

Miss and Her Pin.

My Knot and my Hood
    It sticks in the Mode,
My Kercher in Order it places ;
    It fixes my Ruffles
    And other Pantoffles
In their Plaits it keeps all my Laces.

Miss working at her Sampler.

What Turns and Windings here !
    All ways the Stitches run ;
Some here are strait, and there
    Across and up and down.
Here I must work a Row
    Of tall Great A, B, C's ;
A Rank of Small below
    Again my Needle teaze.

SUMMER RAMBLES,

OR

CONVERSATIONS

INSTRUCTIVE & AMUSING,

for the use of

CHILDREN.

DEDICATED (by permission)

to

HER ROYAL HIGHNESS

THE

PRINCESS CHARLOTTE OF WALES.

BY A LADY.

London:
PRINTED FOR E. LLOYD,
HARLEY STREET, CAVENDISH SQUARE.
1801.

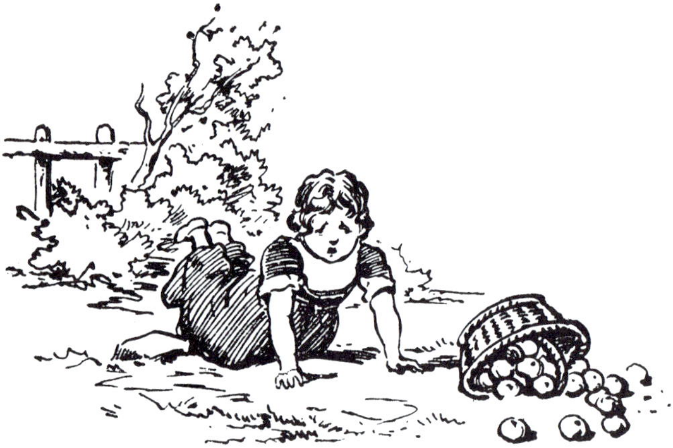

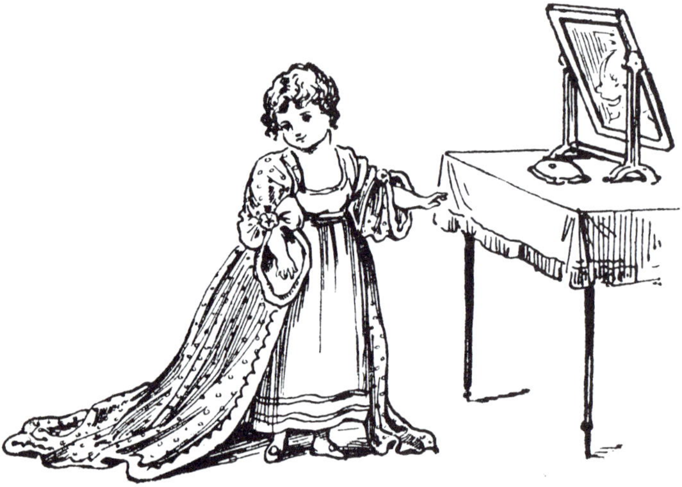

CONVERSATION I.

ANNA.

MAMMA! Mamma! pray look at what is going along the road, across the common; a little girl upon an ass, and a woman with a stick in her hand; see it stops, it will not stir a step, and she is beating it to make it move on.

MAMMA.

My love, I dare say they are going to the town which you see a great way off, to sell their eggs and butter, and their vegetables.

ANNA.

Vegetables! I do not know what they are; will you tell me?

MAMMA.

Yes, with a great deal of pleasure: pease, beans, potatoes, carrots, turnips, and cabbages are vegetables.

HARRY.

But why do they carry them to the town to sell them? I think it is very foolish; do they not want them at home, to eat for their dinner and supper?

MAMMA.

They want some of them at home, but they every year, plant and sow a great deal more than they can make use of.

HARRY.

Why do they take so much trouble? I think digging the ground is very hard work: I could not turn up the least bit when I tried with Robin's spade, though I put my foot upon it, and stamped as hard as ever I could. If I was in the place of that woman I would only plant and sow as much as I thought I should want for myself and my little girl, and some cabbage leaves for my poor ass.

MAMMA.

Then you would do very wrong, and you would be sorry, when too late, that you had been so idle; for you want a great many things besides your dinner, and even for that you would soon be tired of always eating vegetables without a bit of meat, and never to have a pudding, how should you like that, Master Harry? you who are so fond of pudding

SUMMER RAMBLES.

—and how wretched your garden would look, all lying waste except the little nook you had planted for yourself: besides you would be without clothes.

HARRY.

Why mamma! clothes would not grow in the garden.

MAMMA.

I know that very well, but still the garden would provide you with them and every other necessity if you would take the trouble to work in it. That woman's husband is a gardener, and I dare say that every little corner of his garden has something growing in it; in the spring of the year he turns up the ground and plants and sows; and when the things begin to grow the little girl and her mother help him to pull up all the weeds and do everything they can to assist him: then they have their poultry and their cows to take care of, so that they have a great many eggs and a great deal of butter as well as peas and beans and cabbages, more than they want themselves; and every week they fill their baskets and put them upon the ass and away they go to the town to sell them; the little girl is pleased to have such a ride, and the mother sells her things, and with the money she gets for them buys shoes and stockings and warm petticoats for herself and her children, and comfortable flannel waistcoats for her husband against the winter.

Now, Harry, if you had no money but what you could earn—(if you could suppose yourself in the place of that woman's husband, and that you determined to plant no more of your garden than you thought you should want for yourself) what would you do to procure all those necessaries I have been speaking of? You perceive that though they do not grow in the garden in the shape of shoes and stockings, the things that do grow there may be exchanged for money, and money may be exchanged for shoes and stockings, but laziness and indolence will produce nothing but want and wretchedness.

Harry.

I did not think of all that, but I see now that it is a very bad thing to be idle: pray Mamma what can I do that I may not be idle; I cannot dig, you know I am not strong enough.

Mamma.

Nor is it needful you should: your papa has money enough to pay people to work for him and a great many poor labourers live by what they get from him.

Harry.

Then *I* may be as idle as I please.

Mamma.

Indeed you may not; there are many other ways of employing your time besides digging or planting. You are too young at present to be of service to anybody; all you can now do is to attend to the instructions of your papa and your masters and learn against you are older, how you may be able to be most useful to your fellow creatures, and how to conduct yourself in order to gain the love and esteem of your friends and neighbours.

CONVERSATION XII.

Mamma.

I shall not take a very long walk to-day; the weather is growing chilly, and the wind is quite cold on this bleak place. Do you observe that little boy with his faggot upon

SUMMER RAMBLES.

his shoulder! He is without a hat, and has neither shoes nor stockings upon his poor feet.

Harry.

May I give him my old hat, Mamma? I have two hats and only one head.

Mamma.

That is very true, and he has a head but no hat; I dare say he will be very glad to have one of yours, for if it should rain (as I think it will very soon) he will be wet and cold.

ANNA.

But he may go home with his faggot, and keep himself warm, instead of running out in the rain; would not that be better?

MAMMA.

Perhaps he may not be able to avoid going out, and that is very likely: I know who he is, and where he lives and I can assure you that he and his sister are two of the best-disposed children I ever met with in my life; their mother is a poor widow, who lives down by the mill, and she has another little boy and girl much younger than those I speak of; she is a cripple and cannot go out of her house; she can only sit and spin and the two elder children do everything for her and go out for everything she wants; the boy gathers wood sufficient to serve them, though he is obliged to go many miles to get it; the farmers are very kind to him, because they know he is so dutiful to his mother, and so good to his little brother and sister, and they sometimes give him potatoes and turnips, and a little corn to make a brown loaf; and then he runs home so joyful, and so happy that he neither minds the rough road, nor the cold, nor anything else.

ANNA.

How came you to know so much of them, Mamma? did you go to see them without us? I do not remember ever having been there.

MAMMA.

You were neither of you with me when I went to their house, and you will wonder when I tell you that it was at night, and that I went to see Sally safe home.

ANNA.

Who is Sally? Is she the good boy's sister?

SUMMER RAMBLES.

Mamma.

Yes, she is—but I will tell you how it happened. Your papa and I had dined last winter at Mr. Wilson's, and the evening was so very fine and pleasant, though very cold, that we preferred walking home over the fields and through the wood, to having the chaise, so we wrapped ourselves up very comfortably and walked on till we came to the middle of the wood, where you and I have often stopped to observe how very thick the trees and bushes grow; and there your papa first thought he heard a child cry, and a moment after we heard it lamenting very bitterly. "What shall I do? What shall I do?" "Where are you?" asked your papa. "Here I am," said the poor thing. "Pray, pray come to me, I cannot find my way out of the wood." The voice was quite near us, but the bushes were so thick that we had a great deal of trouble to find the child; at length, however, we got to the place, and there stood a clean, tidy little girl, with a pitcher of milk, and a small basket of potatoes, but she was so frightened that she could hardly tell us how she came there, or whom she belonged to. When she had a little recovered herself, and we had promised to see her safe home, she told us her name and that she lived by the side of the mill; that her mother was a cripple and had nobody to do anything for her but her brother and herself, and that there were two little ones to take care of; that her brother had that afternoon been taken very ill, and they had nothing in the house to eat; and her little brother and sister were beginning to cry that they were hungry, and her mother said, "What shall I do for these poor children till to-morrow?" so she told us she thought she would take the pitcher, and the basket and go to farmer Jackson's for some milk and some potatoes; and that if she went the nearest way (that is, through the wood) she would be able to get back again before night; she could not bear, she said, to hear her little brother and sister cry; so away she went, and got what she wanted, but coming home she lost the right path and had rambled about in the wood till she had got quite into the thickest part of it, and it grew dark, and she thought she would be obliged to stay there all night; and she was crying because she thought how frightened her mother would be at not seeing her return, and how hungry her poor little brother and sister would be, who could get nothing to eat.

Anna.

What a good girl she must be!—but what would she have done if you and papa had not heard her?

Mamma.

Indeed, I do not know. We went home with her, and rejoiced her poor mother, who was very uneasy, but had nobody to send to seek her; and the little ones were crying for Sally and the milk, so that the poor woman did not know what to do.

We gave them a little money, and left them very happy, for I told Sally she might come every morning and have her pitcher filled with milk at our house without having to go through the wood to fetch it.

Anna.

Then she had not got it to pay for, and that was another good thing.

Mamma.

Certainly she had not, and the money she had to spend in milk has for months past served to buy other things, and I am very thankful that God Almighty has blessed me with plenty, and that I have it in my power to relieve my poor neighbours and help to make them comfortable and happy.

A NEW RIDDLE.

And now, my children, we must make haste to get home, for I am very cold; we must have a good fire, and our books, and our pictures, and all our other winter amusements, for our summer rambles are at at end.

[From *A New Riddle Book*. By John the Giant-Killer, Esquire. York: T. Wilson, 1804.]

> GREAT virtues have I
> There is none can deny,
> And to these I shall mention an odd one;
> When apply'd to the tail
> It is seldom I fail
> To make a good boy of a bad one.

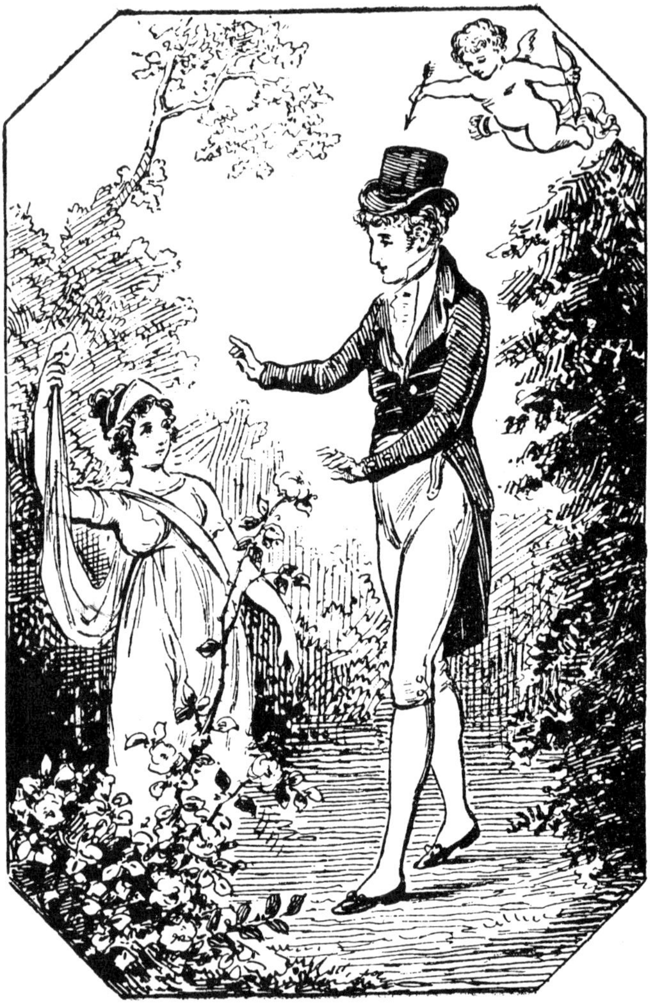

THE
RENOWNED HISTORY
OF
PRIMROSE PRETTYFACE,

WHO

BY HER SWEETNESS OF TEMPER AND LOVE OF LEARNING
WAS RAISED FROM BEING THE

Daughter of a Poor Cottager

TO

Great Riches

AND

TO THE DIGNITY OF THE

Lady of the Manor.

SET FORTH
FOR THE BENEFIT AND IMITATION OF THOSE PRETTY LITTLE

Boys & Girls

Who by learning their Books and obliging Mankind,
Would to Beauty of Body add Beauty of Mind.

Adorned with Cuts by BEWICK

YORK:
Printed for T. WILSON *&* R. SPENCE
1804
(Price Sixpence)

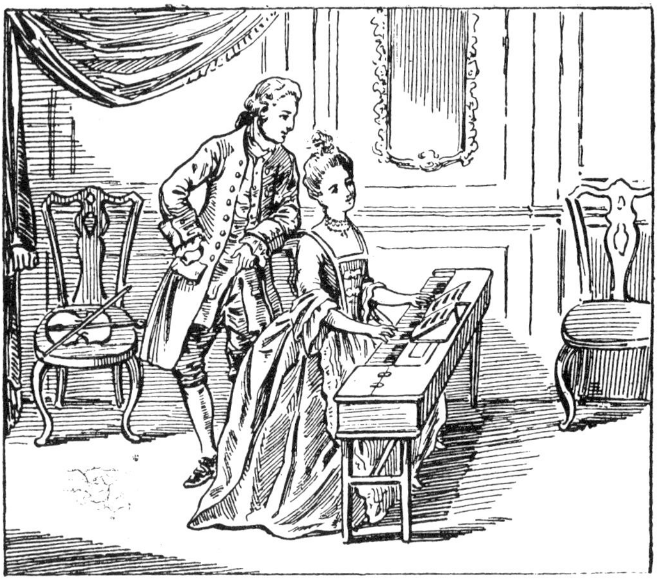

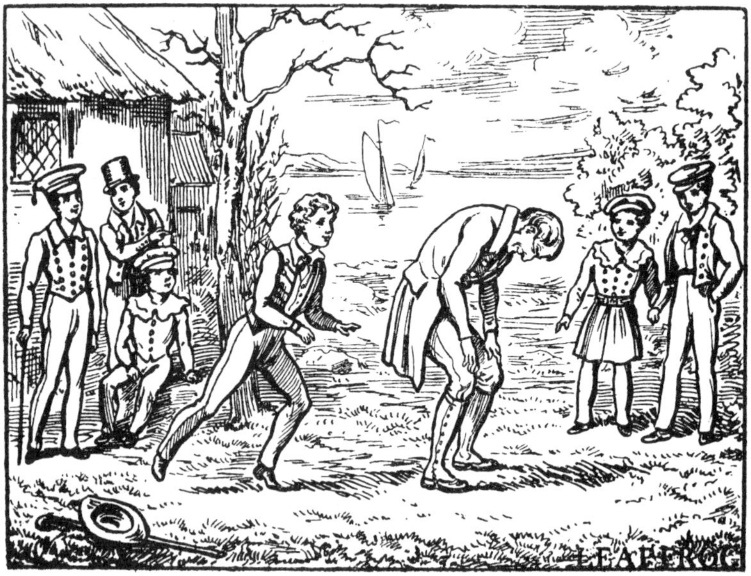
LEAPFROG

PRIMROSE PRETTYFACE.

THE RENOWNED HISTORY OF PRIMROSE PRETTYFACE.

WHEN Primrose Prettyface became old enough to go to service, she was taken into the family of Squire Homestead in the next village. It was her business there to sweep and dust the rooms and do such other matters as came within her sphere, which were often much increased by the carelessness or wantonness of their son Jemmy. This young gentleman being the darling of his papa and mamma was so humoured in everything that, according to the old proverb, he was one of those who are better fed than taught. If they had company at dinner he would be pawing the dishes that stood next him and licking his fingers. Then call out for such and such particular bits of a fowl; and when it was given him, truly it was not so nice and white as that papa had on his plate. Well then, to be sure, the dear boy must have papa's, and papa take his. Presently while the servant was attending some of the company he would call for beer and when it was brought begin scolding because the servant forgot to give it him in the painted cup. So that with his throwing down the wine, pulling the victuals about, greasing people's clothes and other such disagreeable actions, many people left off visiting at their house. He was very unlucky and would tell fibs, and sometimes swear and call names shockingly. In these things he was not a little forwarded by keeping company with the son of one of his father's tenants. This lad had taught him almost everything that was bad. Evil communications corrupt good manners, says my copybook, and this indeed is often verified to the cost of many who will not take advice in time. Jemmy was continually

PRIMROSE PRETTYFACE.

in mischief, and when he had done any, to screen himself would tell fibs and lay it on other people.

Squire Homestead had frequently observed to his lady that the best apple-tree was often robbed, but by whom he could never discover. Little Jem who stood by, said he believed Primrose Prettyface did it, for he often saw her in

the garden near that tree. Upon this she was called into the room, and interrogated concerning it. Prim, who had been very little used to accusations of this kind, cried very much when she was asked how she dared to do it. However, drying up her pretty eyes, she declared she had never taken an apple off any tree in the garden without the knowledge of her fellow-servants; but in particular she had never

PRIMROSE PRETTYFACE.

touched that tree because she had heard her master say he liked the apples and would have them saved for his friends and himself. Jemmy still insisted on the truth of his accusations, and Squire Homestead bid her go out of the room for an impudent baggage as she was. Primrose Prettyface knowing herself innocent, cried sadly, while Jemmy triumphed in his wicked contrivances. But this triumph was of very short duration, he being found out, and when he least thought of it too.

One day when Squire Homestead had a great deal of company, Jemmy came running into the room without taking the least notice of the Gentlemen and Ladies present. His uncle who had just then been looking out of the window, but turned round at hearing Jemmy make a great stamping in coming upstairs, observed his rude manner of entering the room, and asked somewhat sharply, Where was his bow? Jemmy looked much confused, but neither spoke nor moved. I say, sir, said his uncle, where is your bow? After some hesitation, he replied, in the barn, and roared like a town bull. The company not knowing what he meant burst into a loud laugh. However, Jemmy continued crying, and said, Jack Dobbins was as much in fault as he; and added, indeed he would never do so any more. His uncle, however, suspecting something at the bottom, seized hold of him (see how silly he looks!) and asked him how he dared to do so? Come, continued he, tell the truth, and you shall be forgiven; but if you say a word that is not so, you shall be sent for a drummer as sure as you are alive. After much sobbing and crying, out came the truth at last. Jemmy with his hopeful companion Jack Dobbins had been in the garden, and not content with pulling the fruit had broke a bough off the tree Squire Homestead so much valued, and which but a few days before Primrose Prettyface had been falsely accused by Jemmy of robbing. The bough they had hid in the barn; but the apples Jack Dobbins carried home for his own use.

At this discovery Squire Homestead was very angry, and would have thrashed him soundly had not the company interposed and begged him off. His uncle too reprimanded him severely, and the more so because of the fibs he had told of Primrose; nor would he be satisfied till she was called into the room, and he had begged her pardon before the whole company. When Primrose was gone, he told Jemmy how wicked it was to keep such company as he did, who had taught him to rob even his own father's garden, and then added to the crime by telling a lie and laying the blame on an innocent person: besides his stripping the tree in that manner was proof of a greedy disposition. He finished his advice with the homely but good counsel which he said his old grandmother gave him when he was a boy,

> Of a little, take a little,
>   You're kindly welcome too:
> Of a little, leave a little,
>   'Tis manners so to do.

EASY LESSONS.

[From *The Parlour Teacher*. London: W. Darton and J. Harvey, 55, Gracechurch Street. Price 1s. 1804.]

THE doc-tor of the vil-lage sent for all the poor chil-dren, and all the poor men and wo-men who had not had the small-pox and in-oc-u-lated them with the cow-pox, for he had found out that who-ev-er had once had that dis-ease nev-er had the small-pox; and by this kind act he sav-ed much pain and trou-ble if not man-y val-u-a-ble lives.

EASY LESSONS.

The sea con-tains man-y things to be ad-mir-ed; rocks, weeds, or plants, and fish-es in great var-i-et-y. Fish-es have no legs, be-cause they can swim, and do not walk, so that fins ans-wer all the pur-pose of legs. Man-y fish-es have sharp teeth; most of them have scales; some have sharp thorns at their sides, on their backs or on their heads; and others have ve-ry hard shells.

All sea-wa-ter is salt or brack-ish, which be-comes fresh when boil-ed. As the sea is al-ways in mo-tion, sea-wa-ter soon cor-rupts if it stands in a ves-sel: in-deed stand-ing or stag-nat-ed wa-ter soon spoils, but the wa-ter in riv-ers does not spoil be-cause it is kept runn-ing or in mo-tion, by means of springs, foun-tains or the rain.

Do not hurt live things, for they can feel; do not catch flies, nor pull off their legs. There was a rude boy, and he took a poor bird as she was sit-ting on her eggs, from off her nest, and tied a piece of string to one of her legs, and led her about till she died. Now if he had not done so there might have been four or five young birds hatch-ed from the eggs, and they might have liv-ed to fly a-bout from tree to tree, and would have sung ve-ry sweet-ly at morn and ev-en-ing : in-deed if they had been night-in-gales they would have sung by night.

THE PAINTER'S PANEGYRIST.

[From *Juvenile Pieces designed for the Instruction and Amusement of the Youth of Both Sexes*. By John Evans, A.M., Master of a Seminary for a limited number of pupils at Pullin's Row, Islington. London : B. Crosby and Co., Stationer's Court, Paternoster Row. 1804.]

A FEW years ago I visited London, and resided during my stay in a relative's house. A gentleman lived in the family, of whom I had frequently heard, and for whose character, though I had never seen him, I conceived an high esteem. I was introduced to him on my arrival in town, and experienced great pleasure and satisfaction in his company. He was a solitary widower, and spoke often of his wife and children, in a strain characteristic of conjugal and paternal tenderness.

One trait in this gentleman's character, even a stranger on a slight interview, might discover. The love of PAINTING was his darling passion; and its ascendancy over him sensibly affected his conduct. It was not unlike Aaron's rod, which swallowed up those of the magicians. I have observed him using many little innocent arts to make the nature and utility of PAINTING the leading topic of conversation. Whenever he succeeded, his countenance was illumined with gleams of joy

THE PAINTER'S PANEGYRIST.

During my residence in town, I told the Connoisseur, that paintings gave me exquisite pleasure, and that with the most agreeable emotions I had surveyed the annual exhibition at Somerset House. He enquired instantly whether I practised myself, and expressed a wish of seeing my juvenile productions. "I feel," said I, "a predilection for the art—devote much of my time to the study of it, and with my parents' consent shall embrace that line of profession."

THE PAINTER'S PANEGYRIST.

The information pleased him, and he again repeated his desire of seeing some of my sketches. I had but few with me, and those I put into his hands. When he returned them, he with candour observed—"They possess considerable merit, and though not void of blemishes, yet these blemishes the improvement of your present good taste will effectually correct."

The day previous to my departure from the metropolis, just after breakfast he took me aside into his apartment. Having shut the door, he furnished me with a seat, and thus addressed me :

"The choice of an employment my friend, involves your future felicity. Many destitute of an intelligent adviser engage in occupations for which they are by no means fitted. I much approve of the choice you have already made. You are blessed with a genius for PAINTING. Cherish that genius with sedulous care. For want of the soul's being moulded by the hand of Nature for this noble art, how few of its *amateurs* attain to eminence ! In rewarding merit the present age is not backward; and the reign of George the Third is distinguished for its attention to the fine arts. You will require the tuition of an accomplished master. Should your parents refuse to advance a competent premium I will afford every necessary aid. Nothing on my part shall be omitted to ensure your celebrity in your profession, and to render you a useful member of society. Be ambitious of rising above the common herd of mankind—of attracting the notice of a generous public—and of having your name transmitted with honour to an impartial posterity :

> For who would sink in dull oblivion's stream ?
> Who would not live in songs of distant days ?
> —WOLCOTT.

THE PAINTER'S PANEGYRIST.

The Connoisseur (scarcely giving me time to thank him for the generous proposal) now took up his golden-headed cane which lay across the table and pointing to the several parts of the room, described the ornaments with which it was decorated. On the mantel-piece stood the busts of RAPHAEL, TITIAN and GUIDO. Having mentioned the persons they represented, he specified the place of their birth—the times in which they flourished—and the *chefs-d'œuvre* which had immortalized their names. On this last topic he eloquently expatiated. He not only extolled those masters of the pencil but reprobating their critics who had asserted their famous pieces to be defective—he almost averred they were faultless. Demosthenes declaimed not more vehemently against the ambition of the Macedonian monarch than this good man did at (what he termed) the *insolence* of criticism. The Encomiast then pointed to a single bust which graced an elegant pedestal elevated a foot above the rest. "This," says he, "is the bust of SIR JOSHUA REYNOLDS." He favoured me with a brief account of that eminent artist; and wound up the whole with an apostrophe in his praise.

We next surveyed the different pictures with which the apartment was embellished. They were so numerous as to occupy almost the whole wainscot, and so arranged as to have a peculiar effect on the beholder's imagination when he first entered the room. To whatever part the eye glanced, you perceived a group of portraits, landscapes or historic pieces. On each of these the Panegyrist descanted. "See," exclaimed he, with a glow on his visage, and a sprightliness in his eye, "how boldly are they sketched!—how vivid the colours!—how delicate the finishing!"

I was, however, astonished that one picture passed unnoticed, which struck me beyond any of the rest, and seemed full as worthy of praise as those upon which he had bestowed his encomiums. It represented a young woman, about thirty years of age, seated in an elbow chair. Graceful was her appearance, neat her attire, sprightly and intelligent her countenance. Her features were engaging. I think I never beheld a face so thoroughly expressive of female loveliness. The moment I saw her she reminded me of the beauteous rose in all its glory. In her arms she held a sweet infant on whom she smiled with maternal fondness; and on her knee leaned a lovely boy, apparently near four or five years old. The little boy was drawn in the attitude of looking up into his mother's face with an interesting earnestness, and his innocent features glowed with the warmth of filial affection. I interrupted the Connoisseur by begging him to explain this delightful picture, and assign his reason for passing it over in silence. I immediately perceived the question agitated his mind, and his eyes were suffused with tears. "Alas!" said he, in a faltering voice, "it is the dear wife of my youth, and two sweet children—now—no more!" The three last words were scarcely articulated. He sat down and wept bitterly. That they were to him *no more* wrung his tender heart. I approached him, and taking him by the hand, said, "My dear Sir, abandon not yourself to grief. These misfortunes are incident to frail mortality. Our best tears are due to departed worth, and may be shed frequently o'er the tomb of the deceased. Sorrow not, as those who are *without hope*. Though to you they return not, yet the Christian religion assures you, that you shall again meet each other, *never more to be separated.*" These consolatory hints, though imperfect, proved a cordial to revive his spirit. He gradually recovered. Wishing not to open wounds which seemed far from being closed by the lenient hand of time, I enquired no further into particulars.—Poor man! I was not surprised at thy amiable sensibility.

HENRY.

[From *A Cup of Sweets that can never Cloy; or Delightful Tales for Good Children.* By a London Lady: J. Harris, successor to E. Newbery, corner of St. Paul's Churchyard. 1804.]

HENRY was the son of a merchant of Bristol; he was a very good-natured, obliging boy, and loved his papa and mamma, and his brothers and sisters, most affectionately; but he had one very disagreeable fault, which was, that he did not like to be directed or advised.

He was the most amiable boy in the world, if you would let him have his own way: but the moment he was told not to stand so near the fire, or not to jump down two or three stairs at a time, not to climb upon the tables, or to take care he did not fall out of the window, he grew directly angry, and asked if they thought he did not know what he was about—said he was no longer a baby, and that he was certainly big enough to take care of himself.

A lady, who visited his mamma, and who was extremely fond of him, met him in the hall on new year's day, and gave him a seven-shilling piece to purchase something to amuse himself. Henry was delighted at having so much money, but instead of informing his parents of the present he had received, and asking them to advise him how to spend it, he determined to do as he liked with it, without consulting anybody; and having long had a great desire to amuse himself with some gunpowder, he began to think (now he was so rich) whether it might not be possible to contrive to get some. He had been often told of the dreadful accidents which have happened by playing with this dangerous thing, but he fancied *he* could take care, *he* was old enough to amuse himself with it, without any risk of hurting himself; and meeting with a boy who was employed about the house by the servants, he offered to give him a shilling for his trouble, if he would get him what he desired; and as the boy cared very little for the danger to which he exposed Henry, of blowing himself up, so as he got but the shilling, he was soon in possession of what he wished for.

A dreadful noise was, some time afterwards, heard in the nursery. The cries of children, and the screams of their maid, brought the whole family upstairs : but, oh! what a shocking sight was presented to their view on opening the door! There lay Henry by the fireside, his face black, and smeared with blood; his hair burnt, and his eyes closed : one of his little sisters lay by him, nearly in the same deplorable condition; the others, some hurt, but all frightened almost to death, were got together in a corner, and the maid was fallen on the floor in a fit.

It was very long before either Henry or his sister could speak, and many months before they were quite restored to health, and even then with the loss of one of poor Henry's eyes. He had been many weeks confined to his bed in a dark room, and it was during that time that he had reflected upon his past conduct : he now saw that he had been a very conceited, wrong-headed boy, and that children would avoid a great many accidents which happen to themselves, and the mischiefs they frequently lead others into, if they would listen to the advice of their elders, and not fancy they are capable of conducting themselves without being directed; and he was so sorry for what he had done, and particularly for what he had made his dear little Emma suffer, that he never afterwards did the least thing without consulting his friends : and whenever he was told not to do a thing, though he had wished it ever so much, instead of being angry, as he used to be, he immediately gave up all desire of doing it, and never after that time got into any mischief.

FIDO.

PAULINA going to spend the afternoon with her little cousins, arrived at their door at the very instant that they were dragging out a poor little dog, once so great a favourite, that it was fed with every kind of nicety, and reposed, when it was inclined to sleep, on a beautiful silk cushion.

"What are you going to do with poor Fido?" inquired Paulina.

"Oh, the nasty thing!" replied her cousin Emily. "Pray look how ugly it is grown—I would not keep it in the house on any account—I am going to give it to those boys you see at the gate: I do not care what they do with it; my brother Charles has given me a most beautiful little creature—come in, and I will shew it to you."

"Stop, stop, for pity's sake!" exclaimed Paulina. "Pray do not give poor Fido to those boys, to be worried and tormented to death; let me have him: I will carry him home to my hospital, and will take care of him as long as he lives."

Fido had unfortunately strolled into the kitchen (where certainly neither young ladies nor their dogs can have any business), when the cook was very busy in getting ready for dinner, and (I hope without intending such a piece of cruelty) she had thrown a quantity of boiling water over the poor little creature's head and back, and scalded him in so terrible a manner, that no one thought he could have lived through the day.

FIDO.

Emily was so angry with the cook, and shed so many tears when she beheld the agony of her favourite, that one would have thought she had the best heart in the world, and that she had a very great regard for it; but as soon as it was recovered, and she saw it had lost one eye, and that all the side of its head, and its whole back, was without hair, she could not bear the sight of it: it was turned out of the parlour, and kicked about by everybody, glad to pick up any bone it could meet with, and to sleep in a corner on straw, instead of the silk cushion it had been accustomed to; and at length, had not Paulina arrived in time to save it, would have been given to half a dozen unfeeling boys, who would soon have destroyed it.

Paulina was very little pleased with her cousin Emily on this occasion, for her own disposition was very different; she was so humane, so kind to everybody and every creature in distress, that she was beloved by all who knew her; she had quite a little hospital of sick and lame animals and birds; a dog, which had had its leg broken by being caught in a gin; a cat with one ear, the other having been bitten off by a large mastiff; and a blind squirrel: she had a little goldfinch in a cage, which had had its wings torn off by a cat, and as it could no longer fly down from its perch to drink, and return when it liked, she had contrived a little ladder, on which it could hop up and down without any difficulty; a blackbird, almost frozen to death, which she had picked up in the snow, but which never recovered the use of one of its legs, sung very merrily, however, in its cage; for it was well fed and taken care of; and one or two blind cocks, which she had bought from boys who had been fighting them, and were going to throw at them, by way of *finishing the fun* (as they called it); and several lame hens, become so by some accident or other, lived comfortably in her little poultry-yard, for she took care to feed all her pensioners herself, and never trusted the care of them to any other person.

Paulina had great pleasure in procuring every comfort she could for her poor animals; and her papa and mamma, to encourage her kind and humane disposition, increased her pocket-money, that she might be able to purchase barley for her poultry, and seed for her birds: her brothers also, who were at school, often sent her presents for that purpose. As she grew up, her humanity was shewn to her fellow-creature in distress, as much as it had been in her childhood to the dumb creation; and as God had given her the means of doing good, she freely indulged herself in acts of kindness, for which she received a thousand thanks and blessings wherever she appeared; she was beloved by all her neighbours, both poor and rich, everything prospered with her, and she was happy and contented, and she deserved to be.

MORAL PLAYTHINGS.

[From *Moral Playthings, or Tales for Children.* By M. Monget. London: Didier and Tebbett, 75, St. James's Street. 1806.]

"Envy not your neighbours' good lot, but banish jealousy, wish for their prosperity, and strive to merit like good fortune."

MORAL PLAYTHINGS.

"Under her mother's eyes, she, a soldier's daughter, every day had lessons from the music master, the drawing master, then a little geography, then dancing."

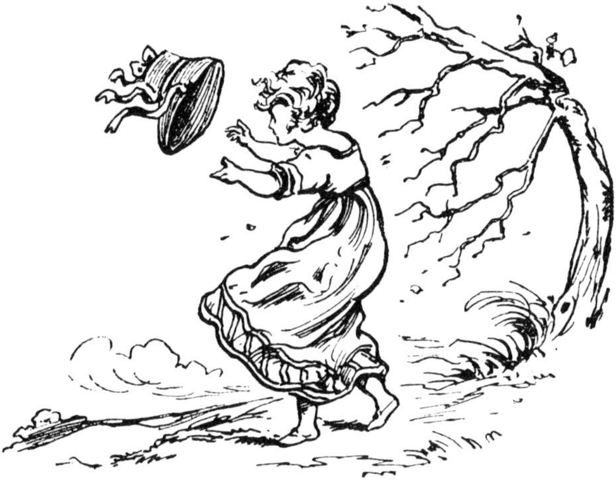

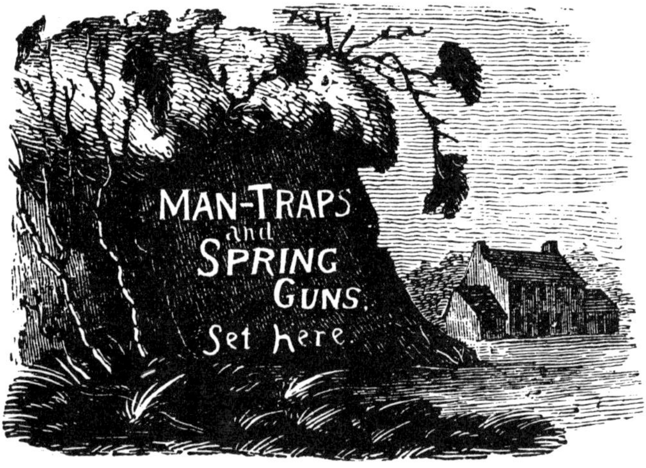
MAN-TRAPS
and
SPRING
GUNS.
Set here.

Cobler! stick to your last;

OR,

The Adventures

OF

Joe Dobson

Exhibited
In Sixteen Elegant Copper-Plate
Engravings

By B. A. T.

London:
Printed for J. HARRIS, *successor to* E. NEWBERY,
*At the Original Juvenile Library, corner
of St. Paul's Church Yard*

Price One Shilling plain, & Eighteen-pence coloured

1807

Mamma, don't make me beg in vain,
Pray read that pretty book again.

Joe Dobson.

Joe Dobſon was an Engliſhman, In days of Robin Hood; A country farmer eke was he, In

JOE DOBSON.

for - eft of Sher - wood, In for - eft of Sher - wood... Joe beft...

JOE DOBSON.

Joe Dobson was an Englishman
  In days of Robin Hood,
A Country Farmer eke was he,
  In Forest of Sherwood.

JOE DOBSON.

Joe Dobson said unto his Dame,
  I vow that I could do
More household work in any day
  Than you can do in two.

JOE DOBSON.

She soon replied, I do declare
  Your words you shall fulfil,
To-morrow you my place shall take
  I'll to the plow and mill.

JOE DOBSON.

Next morning came, they sallied forth
    Each sure of doing well,
She with her stick, He with a pail,
    The rest I soon will tell.

JOE DOBSON.

Away went Joe to milk the cow,
  His business to begin,
She tossed the pail and kicked his leg
  The blood ran down his shin.

JOE DOBSON

But see him now sit down to reel
   The yard his rib had spun,
But puzzled and perplexed was he
   He swore it was no fun.

JOE DOBSON.

Next job to boil the pot he went—
　　The fire he had forgot;
He ran with chips and burnt his head,
　　Oh! grievous was his lot.

JOE DOBSON.

Away went Joe to wash the cloaths
But sore against his will,
The water scalded both his hands
Bad luck pursued him still.

JOE DOBSON.

He went to hang the cloaths to dry—
 It was a lovely day,
But oh, alas ! a Magpie came
 And stole his wig away.

JOE DOBSON.

Away went Dobson in despair
  At losing thus his wig ;
The Magpie flew with rapid flight
  And left it on a twig,

JOE DOBSON

Good lack! quoth he, I must dispatch
   And haste the bread to make,
But stooping down to knead it well
   His back did sorely ache.

JOE DOBSON.

Loud crowed the Cocks, the Turkeys screamed,
    The Geese and Ducks now quacked,
Enraged for food, which Joe forgot,
    He was by all attacked.

JOE DOBSON.

An effort then poor Dobson made
    The little pigs to feed;
The old Sow tripped him in the mud
    In spite of all his heed.

JOE DOBSON.

The old Dame now with speed returned
    Quite stout and blithe was she,
And found poor Joe all bruised and ill
    Fatigued as he could be.

JOE DOBSON.

Now Mrs. Dobson, tidy soul,
  Soon set all neat and right,
Prepared the meat and drew the ale
  They bravely fared that night.

JOE DOBSON.

Whilst they partook this dainty meal
   Joe sullenly confessed
He was convinced that wives could do
   The household business best.

𝔇angerous 𝔖ports:

A Tale

ADDRESSED TO CHILDREN

WARNING THEM AGAINST

WANTON, CARELESS OR MISCHIEVOUS

EXPOSURE TO SITUATIONS

FROM WHICH ALARMING INJURIES SO OFTEN PROCEED

Second Edition

By JAMES PARKINSON

"Who knows but one of my Stories may, one day,
save the life of some child?"—OLD MILLSON

LONDON:
Printed for H. D. SYMONDS,
Paternoster Row,
By LAW & GILBERT, St. John's Square, Clerkenwell
1808
Price Two Shillings & Sixpence

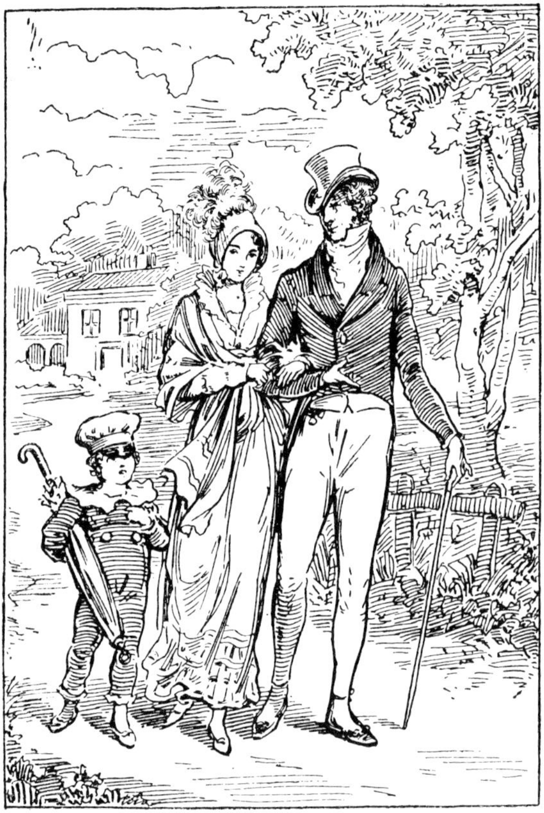

DANGEROUS SPORTS.

It is not necessary to mount a horse to be exposed to danger from him since several children have had their skulls beat to pieces from the kick of a horse, in consequence of their sillily plucking the hairs of its tail. Indeed of such different tempers are these animals that he must be more bold than prudent who ventures within reach of their heels. So ferocious are they sometimes, that two dreadful instances have occurred lately; in one of which the hand of a gentleman was seized by a horse and terribly ground by his teeth. In the other, an enraged horse seized the arm of a poor man which he did not loosen until the bystanders had broken the bone of his nose by beating him; and the arm was so injured as to be obliged to be cut off.

* * * * * *

A young gentleman passing a dog slightly touched it with a switch he carried in his hand, upon which the ferocious animal turned and seized him; and in spite of the exertions of those around him continued his hold until the bowels of the youth appeared at the wound: I need hardly say that the poor youth died within a few hours.

* * * * * *

Always be careful to avoid any dog which you see running along, looking heavy and lowering, seemingly inattentive to everything, his eyes looking red and watery, and his tail hanging between his legs, lest it should be mad. If at any time you should be bitten by a dog, though ever so slightly, endeavour to ascertain whose dog it is and immediately apprise your parents of the circumstance; since they will be the fittest to carry on the enquiry farther; and even if the dog should have been mad, can prevent its being of the least ill consequence to you, if you give them early information.

*   *   *   *   *   *

Never leave your penknife open, especially on a desk, since being likely to glide down, it may fall with its point into your thigh, or wound you just by the inner ankle, where the artery runs very near the surface.

*   *   *   *   *   *

It is said that a little girl found her frock on fire, when she tried to tear off the skirt, but this she could not do; she then after ringing the bell violently flew to the sideboard, hoping to find water in the decanter, with which she would have been enabled to have directly extinguished it, but failing here and finding the flames by rising were communicating with the upper clothing, she sat herself on the hearth carpet and directly folded the ends of the carpet over the burning

DANGEROUS SPORTS.

part by which the flames were smothered and extinguished; the carpet at the same time protecting her arms from the flames. Should such an accident happen to you, that is the exact conduct I would wish you to adopt.

* * * * * *

Never stand opposite to anyone who is spinning his top, nor sufficiently near to his side to receive it on your head should it hang in the string.

* * * * * *

A foolish practice is that of jumping unnecessarily from high places; this is frequently done without the idea of any danger: but consider when you alight on your feet after such a jump with how severe a shock you meet the ground. Frequently by this shock is one of the bones of the legs broken, and even when this is not the case, the shock affects the ends of the bones at the knee or hip-joint so severely that their surfaces polished like glass, sustain very considerable injury; from which such diseases follow as may occasion the loss of a limb or of life.

* * * * * *

Think before you taste, and taste before you swallow. For want of attending to this simple rule I knew two poor children lose their lives. One from thoughtlessly tasting something he found in a bottle, and which was aqua fortis had his mouth and throat so burnt that he died in the greatest agonies. The other was a little girl, who playing alone in a parlour, perceived a bottle of liquor standing on the sideboard. On tasting the liquor she found it pleasant, and putting her mouth to the bottle drank so freely that when her mother came into the room she found her senseless on the floor. The liquor she had drank was brandy, and in a very few hours she died.

* * * * * *

Very lately a most dreadful accident happened in the

DANGEROUS SPORTS.

country. The guards of the mail coaches always travel with loaded pistols and a blunderbuss. In a room at an inn, some of the pistols had been left by one of the guards, and had remained there several days when a little boy about eleven years of age took up one of the pistols and carried it into the garden as a plaything. On his return to the house he met his sister, towards whom he presented the pistol and snapped it several times. At last most unexpectedly and unfortunately it went off and its whole contents were lodged in her stomach: she survived only a few hours during which she suffered the most excruciating torments.

CHRISTMAS HOLIDAYS.

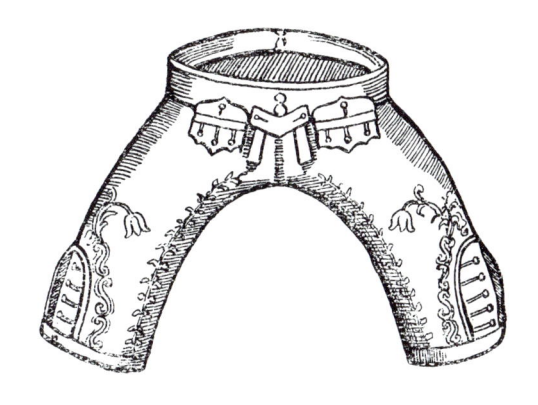

[From *Christmas Holidays, or Anecdotes of Mrs. Truegood's Scholars*. By Humphrey Teach'em, esq. London: Robert Bassam, 53 St. John Street, West Smithfield.]

TOMMY stole the cakes and put one into his sister's box to make his mother believe she had done it. The cake was found and her mother ordered the servant to take the little girl upstairs and undress her for punishment. Master Lovetruth tearfully confessed he had seen Tommy put the cake into his sister's box, and Tommy also told him that he had hidden the others in the rack of hay which stood in the stackgarth at the back of the orchard. The cakes were found and Tommy confessed. He was immediately stripped and flogged, and then sent to bed without any supper. To add to his punishment a pair of new breeches which his father had brought him from town were taken from him.

THE COCK-CHAFER.

[From *Original Poems Intended for the Use of Young Persons.* By Mrs. Richardson. On a plan recommended by the Rev. Dr. Isaac Watts. London: Vernor, Hood and Sharpe, 31 Poultry. 1808.]

A DIALOGUE.

GEORGE.

ONLY look at this chafer, transfix'd on a pin ;
It will do your heart good to see how he will spin :
He's been at it this hour, and I've had so much fun !
I think 'twill be nigh-time before he has done.

PHILIP.

It will do your heart ill, George, such sports to pursue—
Suppose that a giant should do so by you ;
And, running a sword through you, take a delight
In beholding your torture, convulsions and fright ?

GEORGE.

Suppose ! What a curious idea is that ?
Why a chafer is harder to kill than a cat :
You can scarcely destroy him whatever you do ;
And I think, Philip, I'm as good natur'd as you.

PHILIP.

I think that you are, when to think you take time
But the want of reflexion brings many a crime.

THE COCK-CHAFER.

GEORGE.

A crime, too! Indeed—I that fancy admire:
So you think it crime a poor chafer to tire?
The world will have plenty of crimes at that rate;
But you only so style it to make a debate.

PHILIP.

Indeed, George, I speak as I feel the impression:
In my mind, wanton cruelty's no light transgression;
And whatever the creature—cat, dog, worm or fly,
I should think it a fault if I calmly stood by,
And saw but another afflict and torment them,
Without an endeavour, at least, to prevent them

GEORGE.

Come I'll take the pin out then—there now, will that please you?
I perceive, Philip, what I have done seems to teaze you.

PHILIP.

It does, my dear George, for you must destroy him;
The wound you have made would for ever annoy him.

GEORGE.

Poor thing!—there he's dead; and now pray if you've leisure,
Inform me, good Philip, what you would call pleasure.

PHILIP.

You need ne'er for amusement, George, be at a loss;
Bows and arrows are pleasant to shoot at a boss;
Then there's cricket, or trap-ball, and kites for fair weather;
And of evenings a book, when returning together:

THE COCK-CHAFER.

With races in winter, and football and skating,
And many more pastimes than I've been relating;
You'll find for your leisure there's ample employment.
In pursuits where you need not repent the enjoyment.
Then give me your hand, George, before that we part—

GEORGE.

With thanks, my dear Philip, my hand and my heart,
You have taught me a lesson I ne'er shall forget,
And shall think while I live that I'm much in your debt;
For all barbarous sports I now feel an aversion,
And in nought but what's harmless will seek for diversion.

Ride on Pickback my darling!

DR. GOLDSMITH'S

Celebrated Elegy

on that Glory of Her

SEX,

Mrs. Mary Blaize.

Published
Nov. 1, 1808, by J. Harris, corner St. Paul's
Churchyard.

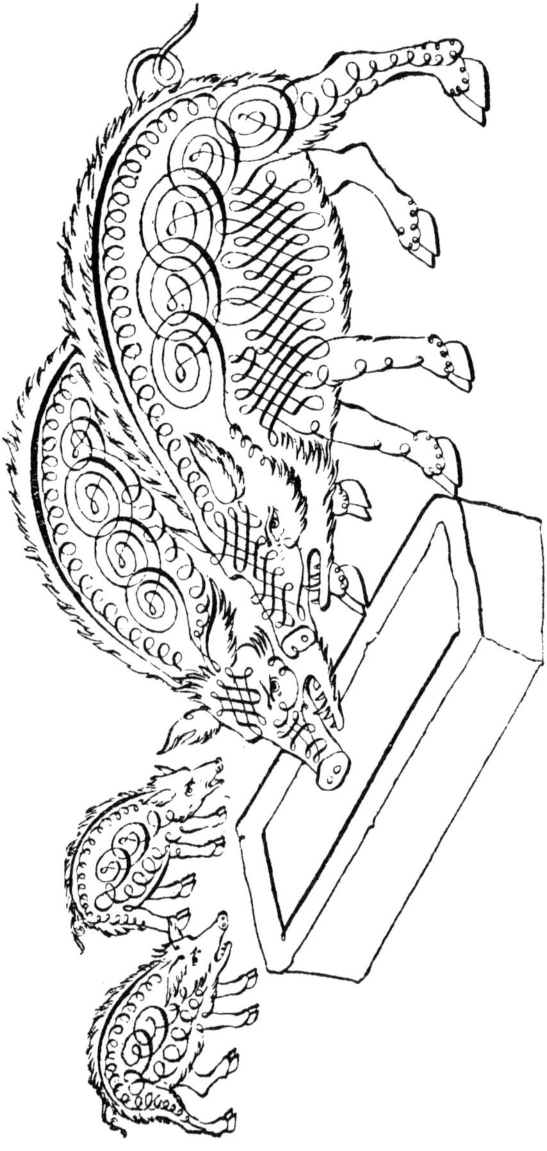

MRS. MARY BLAIZE.

Good people all with one accord,
Lament for Madam Blaize,
Who never wanted a good word—

MRS. MARY BLAIZE.

From those who spoke her praise.

MRS. MARY BLAIZE.

The needy seldom passed her door,
And always found her kind;
She freely lent to all the poor—

MRS. MARY BLAIZE.

Who left a pledge behind.

MRS. MARY BLAIZE.

She strove the neighbourhood to please,
With manners wondrous winning;
And never followed wicked ways—

MRS. MARY BLAIZE.

Unless when she was sinning.

MRS. MARY BLAIZE.

At church in silks and satins new,
With Hoop of monstrous size;
She never slumbered in her Pew—

But when she shut her eyes.

MRS. MARY BLAIZE.

Her love was sought I do aver,
By twenty Beaux and more;
The King himself has follow'd her—

MRS. MARY BLAIZE.

When she has walked before.

MRS. MARY BLAIZE.

But now her wealth and finery fled,
Her hangers on cut short all;
The Doctors found when she was dead,—
Her last disorder mortal!

MRS. MARY BLAIZE.

Let us lament in sorrow sore,
For Kent Street well may say,
That had she liv'd a twelvemonth more—
She had not dy'd to-day!

CRIES OF LONDON.

[From *London Cries for Children.* London: Darton and Harvey, Gracechurch Street; and W. Darton, Junr., 40 Holborn Hill, 1806.]

IN the Gazette GREAT NEWS to-day
The enemy is beat they say—
But what, alas! will that avail?
Since war we still have to bewail.
Yet all are eager to be told
The news that new events unfold.

CRIES OF LONDON.

Little folks will lend an ear
When this pair approaches near;
Their buns are found so very nice
They are always eager for a slice.
But if flour should rise anew,
To hot cross buns we bid adieu.

CRIES OF LONDON.

'Tis very proper to be known
Whatever may come from the throne.
This Gracious Speech, 'tis said, contains
Something that will assuage our pains;
But must new taxes yet continue
Still to increase the revenue?

CRIES OF LONDON.

Stern winter is no sooner gone,
And nature's milder garb put on,
Than young and tender cresses grow,
Where smooth streams and rivulets flow.
These at once to town we bring
And announce th'approach of spring.

CRIES OF LONDON

Sixpence a peck these peas are sold,
Fresh and green, and far from old;
Which as times go cannot be dear,
And don't forget the time of year.
See for yourselves, they are clean and round,
As any peas that can be found,
Just come growing from the ground.

CRIES OF LONDON.

Delicious to the taste are found
These tempting cherries, sound and round.
Nowhere better will you meet,
For like sugar they are sweet;
But if you should incline to buy,
Be so kind first one to try.

CRIES OF LONDON.

[From *The Cries of London as they are daily exhibited in the Streets*. London: J. T. Ward and Co., 3 Bread Street Hill, 1808.]

OLD CLOATHS!

COATS or preeches do you vant,
 Or puckles for your shoes;
Vatches too me can supply,—
 Me monies vont refuse.

CRIES OF LONDON.

Sweep O!

Soon up the chimney then he goes,
   And thro' the soot does creep—
When at the top, out pops his nose,
   And he aloud cries sweep!

Cucumbers!

All fresh and nice as green turf
   That sparkles after rain,
Which would induce imprudent men
   To eat to give them pain.

Walnuts!

When winter makes all things look sable,
   Walnuts often grace the table,
And after dinner relish fine,
   Immersed in a glass of wine.

Dust O!

With noisy bell here comes old Dan,
   Who makes all dust his pelf—
He'll gather all the dust he can
   'Till he is dust himself.

Sweet Lavender!

Ye ladies who are fond of health,
   And prize your beauty rare,
Will find in Lavender a wealth,
   When taking of the air.

Fine Windsor Beans.

If Beans and Bacon can allure ye,
This man will faithfully assure ye,
His beans will better hit your taste
Than the most sumptuous rich repast.

THE LILY:

A

𝔅ook for Children:

containing

TWENTY-TWO TRIFLES IN VERSE,

ADORNED WITH CUTS.

The lily loves the humble vale
And reads a silent moral tale.

London:
PRINTED FOR J. HARRIS, ST. PAUL'S CHURCH-YARD
1808

Have I not learned my book, Mamma?

I could not learn my book Mamma.

THE ROD.

Little George would not be dress'd,
   He pouted, scream'd and cried;
Repulsed the maid, if she caress'd
   And all her threats defied.

He gave her many a fruitless blow,
   To keep off soap and water;
But, at last was made to know
   'Twas wrong that he had fought her.

For when the rod appear'd in sight,
   His passion soon was cool'd,
His face was wash'd, and all was right;
   And George was quickly rul'd.

THE DISCONTENTED CHILD.

A most unhappy child I am,
I must not play with Will or Sam,
Nor in bad weather run about,
Nor at large go in and out.
If in the stable I am caught
I'm reprimanded for the fault;
And if I take the porter pot,
Oh then I'm called a little sot.
If I with servants chuse to walk,
Or leave my book to hear them talk,

THE DISCONTENTED CHILD.

I'm quickly from the kitchen sent,
Though harm, I'm sure, is never meant.
If ever I a fault deny
I'm told—*how sad it is to lie*.
They say it is so mean a plan
I never shall become a man.
Though with the groom I've often ridden,
That pleasure also is forbidden.
If ever to defend my right
I slily with my sisters fight,
There's such a clamour, such a noise,
And so much preached to naughty boys
That oft to frighten them, I say,
"If I am beat I'll run away."

THE SCHOOL.

Thus foolishly this boy complained,
And all instruction he disdained,
He grew so daring and so idle,
That once he rode without a bridle;
The pony threw him on his head,
And for three weeks he kept his bed.

Such will be the fate of those
Who every good advice oppose.

THE SCHOOL.

THERE was a little girl so proud,
She talked so fast and laughed so loud,
That those who came with her to play
Were always glad to go away,
In bracelets, necklace she did shine;
Her clothes were always very fine.
Her frocks through carelessness were soiled;
In truth she was already spoiled.
Her mother died; she went to school,
And there obliged to live by rule.
Though oft before the time for bed,
A cap with bells disgraced her head.
Tickets—for *idleness* she had,
And these sometimes would make her sad.
So when she'd been at school a year,
And Christmas holidays were drawing near,
Her greatest faults were all amended
And to her learning she attended.

THE CONTRAST.

When false indulgence warps the mind,
The discipline of school we find
Most efficacious to correct
The ills arising from neglect.

THE CONTRAST.

On the cold stones a boy was laid;
  Whilst tears bedewed his pallid cheek,
"*Oh pity me!*" was all he said,
  From weakness he could hardly speak

THE CONTRAST.

A bigger boy was passing by,
　　Whose garb bespoke abundant wealth;
He saw the tear, he heard the sigh,
　　And the pale cheek devoid of health.

Unmov'd he heard—"*Oh pity me!*"
　　Pity ne'er touched his callous heart;
He bade the child that moment flee,
　　Or he would force him to depart.

" Away young rascal, instant go,
　　" Or I will make you feel my stick;
" 'Tis all a lie—your tale of woe:
　　" And I am sure you are not sick.

" You look so young, you ought to work,
　　" And not sit idling here all day;
" But in this place you shall not lurk,
　　" Thus filling up the common way."

Then on his head he laid the cane,
　　The little boy soon felt the smart;
And growing bolder from the pain,
　　Told him *he would not then depart.*

Just now, advancing came a youth
　　His satchell hung with careless grace;
And innocence and heav'n-born truth
　　Both shone resplendent in his face.

The unequal contest soon he heard;
　　He pulled th'opponent by the nose
Called him a coward, most absurd,
　　For ridiculing infant woes.

The coward slunk in fear away ;
　The champion hooted as he ran ;
Now tell me readers—tell me pray,
　Which will make the braver man ?

THE CROWD.

" My dear little girl, now keep close by my side,
Or in this great crowd we shall surely divide.
I've here got you fast, so take hold of my gown,
And then the rude people will not push you down ;
For the Lord Mayor's fine coach it is passing along,
Which makes all the people now eagerly throng."

But Sally she foolishly stared so about,
And when the crowd lessen'd, she ran in and out,
Then carelessly stopping to look at some toys,
Was jostled and laughed at by many rude boys.
The mother soon missing her little girl's hand,
Became so alarmed she hardly could stand;
And for two anxious hours was searching the street,
In hopes that her lost little girl she should meet;
Who indeed had become quite an object of pity,
And had wandered along almost out of the city,
When alas ! in a mean and a dirty dark alley
Some women took hold of our poor little Sally;
Then instantly all her good clothes they were stripping,
And if she cried out, were preparing a whipping.
But a gentleman hearing a bustle so odd,
And seeing some women had got a great rod,
He, luckily passing that moment close by,
Soon heard with astonishment Sally's loud cry.
He ordered the women to put down the child;
Then spoke to the trembler in accents so mild,
That whilst he attended poor Sally's redressing,
She, terribly frightened, her faults was confessing;
And having escaped from so cruel a beating,
Oh, think of the joy of the mother at meeting.
And the poor little girl ever after took warning
From what she had suffered on that fatal morning.

THE REMEDY.

Louisa was a pretty child,
Her temper flexible and mild.
She learnt her lessons all with ease,
And very seldom failed to please.

THE REMEDY.

But still Louisa had a fault :
So fond of tasting sugar, salt,
Or anything, in short, to eat,
Puddings, pies, or wine or meat ;
And as she was so often sick,
Mamma soon guessed the foolish trick.
And, planning for her little daughter,

By stratagem she fairly caught her.
Unseen, Louisa would remain,
And all the dirty glasses drain ;
Or carefully some closet shut,
Until a slice of cake she cut.
The dinner done, one winter's day,
And guests removed, their cards to play,

MUSIC.

Louisa stole where they'd deserted,
And by her usual pranks diverted,
Here see this foolish, greedy lass
Draining the bottom of each glass,
Eating the parings of the fruit,
And scraping a pine-apple root;
When, lo, a tumbler caught her sight,
Which gave Louisa new delight,
For it appeared half full of wine,
So sparkling, and so clear and fine,
She drank it quick, and hardly tasted,
Nor one drop of the liquor wasted.
Had you at that moment seen her face,
So much distorted by grimace,
How she stamped and cried and spluttered
Complained, grew sick, and faintly muttered,
Then sought the nursery and her bed;
And glad thereon to lay her head,
You soon, I think, had understood
The wine Louisa thought so good,
Was mixed with physic by her mother
And slyly placed there by her brother.

And from the sickness she endured
Her love of tasting soon was cured.

MUSIC.

" My dear little Lucy, now sit down and play,
   Don't refuse your mamma, if she ask;
'Tis very provoking, you always cry, *nay*;
   And music appears like a task.

MUSIC.

" Consider the expenses your parents bestow
   On this part of your good education ;
And your refusal perverseness doth show ;
   Which is ever a source of vexation."

Thus reasoned a friend, both indulgent and kind,
   To Lucy, who heeded her not ;
For when called on to play she was never inclined ;
   And murmured out " *I have forgot.*"

But much she regretted these childish neglects,
   As she grew up to woman's estate ;
And when others excelled, her many defects
   Were repented when it was too late.

THE DISAPPOINTMENT.

[From *A Collection of Simple Stories*. London: F. G. Tabart & Co., 12, Clifford Street, New Bond Street.]

> OH, why do I so frequent hear
>   My little darling heave the sigh?
> And why does now the starting tear
>   Bedew my little Fanny's eye?

THE DISAPPOINTMENT.

My love, I guess the cause I own,
   And must I then the truth declare,
It is because the rain pours down,
   You cannot go and see the fair.

The mother took her daughter's hand,
   And led her weeping to the door;
Where, shivering, she observed to stand
   A little beggar, cold and poor.

Mammy, she said, is cold and bad,
   Beneath a hedge she now does stay;
And nothing, scarcely, she has had
   To eat and drink this many a day.

Oh, give me but one bit of bread
   To take unto my crying brother,
I would not taste one crumb of it,
   But give it all to him and mother.

Oh, take this shilling, it is mine,
   Then pretty little Fanny said,
I do not want my playthings fine,
   'Twill buy for you both meat and bread.

Why that you had from good papa
   To buy a doll with flaxen hair.
Oh, never think of that, mamma,
   I do not wish to see the fair.

RIDING THE DONKEY.

See Frederic pulling donkey's ears;
How very patient he appears:
While stroked by all their little hands,
Meek animal, how still he stands.
Ride on, my boys and girls, ride on,
And when the joyful sport is done,
Remember what to you I tell,
Be sure to feed poor donkey well.

THE SPINNING WHEEL.

PRAY, dearest mother, come to play,
And put your spinning wheel away,
   I'm sure your work is done:
Oh, take me now upon your knee,
I've nobody to play with me,
   For brother George is gone.

Don't let your wheel go round and round,
I am quite tired of the sound,
   And you are tired too:
You wish to put it by, I see,
So come along and play with me,
   My dearest mother, do.

GOING TO SCHOOL.

The holidays o'er, and with them all their joys,
See, with sorrowful faces, appear little boys,

Who from friends are preparing to part ;
Yet some, better than others, contented and good,
Would not stay from their school, if they might or they could,
    Though they feel quite as much at their heart.

Thus observe little Henry, see his rosy face,
No tears of ill-temper could ever disgrace
    His looks so expressive and mild ;
He is loved by his mother, his sisters and friends ;
His play and his studies together he blends,
    He's a good and a sensible child.

Now see, onward he goes, and, still hiding his tears,
He looks back to mamma, who so anxious appears
    To keep her dear Henry in view ;
Delighted in her little darling to find
So gen'rous a heart and so steady a mind,
    Well determin'd his duty to do.

RURAL SCENES.

The Coach.

[From *Rural Scenes, or A Peep into the Country for Children*. London : printed for Darton, Harvey & Darton, Gracechurch Street. Price Half-a-Crown.]

Ah ! what comes here, rumbling so fast over the gravel and stones ? The Colchester stage, heavily laden for London, just stopping at the sign of the Swan, for the horses and Coachey to drink. Come, master coachman, make haste and finish that pot of porter, for your little inside passengers

RURAL SCENES.

(**who are** going home to see their friends for the Christmas holidays) cannot imagine why you are stopping so long. Master Dickey would have put his head out of the window several times, to bid you cut up your horses a little more, if Patty, his little sister, had not pulled him back again by the sleeve: "For, Dicky," said she, "we should always be kind to the poor animals that drag us so willingly, and as for a

few minutes sooner or later, it is not worth while to make them suffer for it, poor things. Though I am sure I long to kiss papa, and mamma, and brothers, and sisters as much as you do, and to give papa the nice shirt that I have been making for him, and the purse, and the watch chain, and the——"

"Huzza! there we are off again," said little Dick.

RURAL SCENES.

The Stage Waggon.

WHILE the old waggoner is stopping to drink, poor Jack the soldier is bidding his wife good bye.—She has come a long way with her children to see him once more: and now is going home again in the waggon. She does not know whether she shall ever see him again.—Jack was obliged to leave his country life, and his good master, and his plough and his comfortable cottage, and his poor wife and little ones to go and be a soldier, and learn to fight, because *other people* would quarrel.

PLEASING INSTRUCTOR.

Music and the Bird.

[From *The Pleasing Instructor; or a Packet of Pictures for all Good Children.* London: printed by & for Hodgson & Co., Juvenile Press, No. 10 Newgate Street. Sixpence.]

A LITTLE tame bird came and perched on the top of a pianoforte, on which a gentleman was playing a merry tune.

The vibration—that is, the shaking of the strings, made the boards of the piano tremble, and thereby tickled its feet very much. It was frightened, yet had not sense enough to hop off, and enjoy the pleasure of the music without the pain of being too near it.

> How pleasing soever things look in the face,
> Still nothing is right that's not in its right place.

PLEASING INSTRUCTOR.

Visiting the Ball-Room.

MASTER WEBB was one evening permitted to attend a dancing party. As he entered the ball-room everyone was surprised at the grace and elegance with which he bowed; and when the ball was over, his behaviour had pleased his parents so much that they made him a present of a copy of "Hodgson's Children's Guide to Good Breeding."

> Never think you've learnt enough,
> Whilst your conduct's coarse and rough.

PLEASING INSTRUCTOR.

THIS man, from a very fine gentleman, was reduced to a plain cottager, partly through his extravagance and folly. He had been much addicted to the sports of hunting and shooting, and he still retained a strong desire to be constantly out after his pleasures instead of attending to his little garden, and making his afflicted wife as comfortable as possible. She often begged of him to return early, and he as often promised that he would, but did not keep his word.

> How hard it is with vice to part,
> When once 'tis cherish'd in the heart!

THE DANGERS OF THE STREETS.

[From *Tales uniting Instruction with Amusement: consisting of The Dangers of the Streets; and Throwing Squibs. Ornamented with Engravings.* London: Printed for J. Harris, successor to E. Newbery, at the Original Juvenile Library, the corner of St. Paul's Churchyard.]

EDWARD AND GEORGE MANLY were brothers. Edward was nine years old, very sensible and prudent for his age, and as cautious in walking the streets of London as a man of forty.

Whenever he had to cross a street, he always looked to see whether any carriages, horses or bullocks were coming up; and if he saw any such at a small distance he stopped till they were gone by and then crossed quietly. He knew that if he attempted to run across while they were near and his foot happened to slip on the dirty pavement, he would very probably be run over and either killed or much hurt; and he thought it much more comfortable to sleep in a whole skin than to be carried home with an arm or a leg broken.

In like manner, whenever he saw scaffolding up against a house, he took care not to look up at it as he passed near for fear of dirt or lime falling into his eyes and blinding him. And if he saw men at work on the scaffold he would not pass under it, lest a brick or a plank should fall on him and do him some terrible mischief. In such case he either walked outside in the middle of the street, if there were no carriages to prevent him, or crossed to the opposite side of the way; for he thought it much better to dirty his shoes a little than to have his bones broken.

Yet it was not through cowardice that Edward took such care of his person: he was not a coward; he was a boy of

THE DANGERS OF THE STREETS.

real courage, and one day boldly attacked and beat a lad taller and older than himself who had insulted his sister Ellen and snatched a toy from her hand. But he had learnt from his father that it is folly and madness, not courage, to run into danger without necessity, when there is neither honor nor profit to be gained by it.

His brother George, who was about a year younger than he, was of a very different disposition. He was thoughtless

and giddy, would run across streets when carriages were driving up at full speed, and often very narrowly escaped being run over. In turning corners, he never looked to see if any person were coming against him but hurried on without care or caution, and was frequently thrown down in the dirt by persons passing hastily along.

One day as Edward and George were going on a visit to their aunt Selby who lived in a distant part of the town, they came to a narrow street where the flagway was barely

THE DANGERS OF THE STREETS.

wide enough for one person to walk; and the streets were very slippery after a shower of rain.

When they had gone about half way up the street, Edward who always looked before him, saw a great waggon coming down loaded with a huge pile of timber, which was fastened and held up only by a slight chain.

"George," said he, to his brother, "let us stop till that waggon has passed by. If the chain should break, and the timber fall on us, it would crush us to pieces." Accordingly Edward himself stopped, and for greater safety, placed himself on the step of a door, with his back close against the door: and there he determined to stay until the waggon was passed.

But George did not act with the same prudence. Unluckily for him, a noise in the street had prevented him from hearing the good advice that Edward gave him. And as poor Georgy never thought or looked before him he hurried on without minding the waggon.

While he thus ran heedlessly forward a man happened to be coming against him on the narrow footway just at the moment when the waggon approached. Here, instead of stopping to let the man pass by, as he ought to have done, George attempted to pass the man by giddily skipping along the outside edge of the slippery flagway.

But see the dreadful consequences of his giddiness and folly! His foot slipped; he fell under the loaded waggon; the wheel passed over one of his legs, and shattered it in a most shocking manner.

Thus mangled and racked with pain, he shrieked most piteously and repented of his folly when too late. He was taken up by his brother and some charitable persons of the neighbourhood who laid him on his back upon a window shutter and carried him home in that manner crying and lamenting all the way.

His father sent in haste for a surgeon: the surgeon immediately came, examined his leg and found it so terribly shattered that he declared he could not cure it but must cut it entirely off at the knee.

George now roared worse than before at the thought of losing his leg. However, as nothing else could be done to save his life, he was forced to submit. The surgeon took out his instruments, cut the flesh all round with a sharp knife, cut through the bone with a saw, and thus poor George's leg was taken completely off.

It was several months before the wound was healed. All that time George was confined to his bed unable to go out on parties of amusement with his schoolfellows, or even to stir about the room. At length a wooden leg was made for him: with that he now hobbles about as well as he can; and at every step he repents of his giddiness and says to himself, "Ah, how cautious children ought to be in walking the streets!"

THROWING SQUIBS.

MR. TINDALL had a little son named Tom who was very naughty and never minded his book but delighted in running about the streets and playing with blackguards. He was very fond of lighting bonfires, and throwing squibs and crackers, and took particular pleasure in throwing them at people passing by, but more especially at women and girls.

His father more than once told him of the danger of playing with squibs, related to him many accidents caused by unlucky boys throwing them, and desired him never to touch one: he even whipped him once or twice for lighting squibs and crackers contrary to his orders; but all this was

THROWING SQUIBS.

not sufficient to prevent Master Tom from indulging his mischievous inclination.

Once, on a rejoicing night, Tom having a shilling and seven penny pieces lying by him, which he had long hoarded up for the purpose, laid out the whole in squibs and crackers, and went to divert himself with a crowd of little blackguards in flinging them at every person who happened to come in his way.

While he was amusing himself with this wicked sport, a gentleman came in sight, who was riding on a very spirited horse; and the animal appeared greatly alarmed by the squibs, starting and snorting every instant at the blaze and the report. Tom thought this was rare fun, and resolved to have as much of it for his money as he could, so he quickly lighted one of the largest of his squibs, and flung it directly into the horse's face.

The poor animal, that was already very much terrified,

THROWING SQUIBS.

now took fright to such a degree as to be no longer manageable. He galloped off at full speed, threw down a nurse with a baby in her arms, rode over an elderly gentlewoman and two boys, hurt them all very much, and at last stumbling on a bad spot in the pavement, dashed his rider on the flagway. The gentleman was severely bruised by the fall; but as he had no bones actually broken and was not killed outright, Tom disregarded the mischief and still considered the whole as mere fun.

The wicked young villain was determined to continue this cruel and dangerous diversion so long as his stock of squibs lasted; and he only regretted that the number was not greater.

Just as he was lighting another, his own father happened to pass by, on his way home from an evening visit in the neighbourhood. Tom was so bent on mischief that he did not perceive that it was his father but flung the squib right into his face; and it burst directly in Mr. Tindall's eyes.

A crowd immediately gathered round the unfortunate man; and one gentleman who had seen Tom throw the squib ran after him with his cane uplifted, to give him a good beating. But Tom, who was well acquainted with all the narrow alleys in the neighbourhood, escaped from the gentleman's pursuit and went to continue his sport in another street, as he had yet four or five squibs remaining.

Here, however, Master Tom was in some degree rewarded for the mischief he had done. For, as he held the remaining squibs all together in his hand, and was hastily lighting one, to fling into a carriage full of ladies, it burst before he had time to throw it, set fire to the others, and they all at once blew up into his own face. His hand was terribly burned, one whole side of his face was dreadfully scorched, and his left eye was entirely blinded.

In this condition Master Tom was led home by some of

THROWING SQUIBS.

his blackguard companions. A surgeon had already been called in to his father's assistance, and did everything in his power to relieve both the father and the wicked son. Tom's hand and face were cured in some time, but he never recovered the use of his left eye and remains to this day blind on that side.

This, however, was not the worst of the mischief. His father was so much hurt in both eyes that all the surgeon's skill could not restore the sight of either, and he continued wholly blind from that unlucky night to the hour of his death. Indeed it was not long before a sad end was put to poor Mr. Tindall's misfortunes: for the loss of his sight and the thought of his son's wickedness grieved him so sorely that he broke his heart in a few months and died.

As Mr. Tindall was not a gentleman of independent fortune, and had only supported himself by writing, he had not a single guinea remaining in the house when he died. His goods were sold, and after paying the expenses of his burial, and some debts due to his baker, butcher and other persons, there was not money enough left even to put Tom apprentice to any decent trade, so that he was in danger of being obliged either to go to the workhouse or to beg about the streets.

Just at this time it happened that Gregory Grime, a master chimney-sweeper in the neighbourhood, lost one of his apprentices who fell from the top of a chimney and was dashed to pieces on the pavement in the street below. Gregory had heard of Tom's distressed condition, and thinking it would be no great harm if so wicked a rogue should fall in the same manner and break his neck, he offered to take him apprentice without any money.

As Tom had very little to eat and saw little chance of getting more, he was obliged to consent to Gregory Grime's proposal. So Gregory took him home, pulled off his decent

THROWING SQUIBS.

clothes, dressed him in a coarse shirt and breeches, with a woollen night-cap and a pair of old shoes, and at once converted him into a chimney-sweeper.

Instead of a good bed, such as he used to sleep in at his father's house, Tom now lies upon straw without sheets, and with only an old ragged blanket to cover him. He seldom has anything but coarse bread for his meals and hardly enough of that: he is obliged to rise early in the morning before he has slept half the necessary time, to go about the streets in rain and cold, without coat, waistcoat or stockings, crying "Sweep ho! Soot ho!" and is glad when he can get a dry crust of bread or a morsel of cold meat, in any of the houses where he is employed to sweep the chimneys.

All these misfortunes have been brought on him by his own folly and wickedness in throwing squibs. He often bitterly laments his ill-conduct, and wishes he had followed his poor father's good advice. If he had done so, he might now have been at a genteel boarding school, with both his eyes safe, instead of being a chimney-sweeper, and blind of one eye. Let his punishment serve as a lesson to other boys, and teach them how wicked and dangerous it is to play with squibs.

THE BAD FAMILY.

[From *Lessons for Children: or Rudiments of Good Manners, Morals and Humanity.* By Mrs. Fenwick, Author of "The Life of Carlo," "Mary and Her Cat," "Visit to the Juvenile Library," etc., etc. Part the First. London: printed for M. J. Goodwin, at the Juvenile Library, No. 41, Skinner Street. 1809.]

THERE is a certain street in a certain town (no matter for its name) in which there are two handsome houses of equal size. The owners of these houses have each six children, and the neighbours have named one the BAD FAMILY, and the other the GOOD FAMILY.

In the bad family there are three boys and three girls; and the servants who are always much teased and vexed when they live where there are naughty children, speak of them

THE BAD FAMILY.

thus:—The eldest they call FIGHTING HARRY, the second GREEDY GEORGE, and the youngest IDLE RICHARD; the eldest girl is nicknamed CARELESS FANNY, the next, LYING LUCY, and the youngest SELFISH SARAH.

Master Henry, indeed, well deserves his title, for he thinks it a mighty fine thing to be a great boxer, and takes great pride and pleasure in having a black eye or a bloody nose. This does not proceed from courage; no, no: courage never seeks quarrels, and is only active to repel insult, protect the injured, and conquer danger; but Harry would be one of the first to fly from real danger, or to leave the helpless to shift for themselves. He knows that he is very strong, and that few boys of his age can match him, so he picks quarrels on purpose to fight, because his great strength and his constant practice make him almost sure to conquer. All his school-fellows hate him, for such a boy can neither have a good temper, a good heart, nor good manners. It is a pity he should be sent to school, for learning is thrown away upon him: he will be fit only to live with men that sweep the streets, or drive carts or waggons, for with such coarse and vulgar habits gentlemen will not endure him in their company.

George, the second boy, is always thinking of eating and drinking. He follows the cook from place to place, to know what nice things she has got in her pantry. When there is any dainty on the dinner-table, his greedy eyes are fixed on it from the moment he sits down, till he is helped, and then he grudges every morsel that any-one else puts into his mouth. In his eagerness to get more than his own proper share, he crams great pieces into his mouth till he is almost choked, and the tears are forced from his eyes. He will get slily into the store-room, and steal honey, sugar, or raisins; and in the pantry he picks the edges of the tarts and pies, and does a number of other mean tricks. When there is company at dinner, he watches the parlour-door till they leave it, and before the servants have time to clear the table, he sips up all the drops of wine that are left in the glasses, and will even eat the parings of apples and pears that lie on the dessert plates. If he has an orange or a cake, he runs into some dirty hole to eat it, for fear his brothers and sisters should ask for a piece. If he has any money given him, he spends it all at once, and crams and eats till he can scarcely move.

This greedy boy is always watched and suspected. No one will trust him in a garden, for he would eat till he made himself sick, or tear down the branches of the trees to get at the fruit. Nor can he be allowed to pay any visits, for the manners of a glutton give great offence to well-bred people. He has a sallow, ugly look, and is always peeping and prying about, like a beast watching for its prey.

Idle Richard, the third son of the bad family, is a great dunce. Yet he is very capable of learning well, if he chose to take the trouble, but he is fond of idleness and of nothing else. In the morning when he is called, though he knows it is time to get up, he will lie still, and after he has been called again and again, he is never ready in time for breakfast. At his meals he lolls upon the table, or against the back of his chair, and is just as slow and drawling in his manner of eating as in his learning. When he is sent to school, instead of looking at his book, he is gazing all round the room, or cutting bits of stick with his knife; sometimes he lays his head down on the desk and falls asleep, and then pretends to have the headache to excuse his idleness. His master is obliged often to punish him, and then for an hour or two he will learn very well, but next day he gets back to all his idle tricks, and does nothing; so that he is far below many boys that are much younger than himself. When other children go to play, he sits still or lies down upon the ground: he can take no pleasure, for he

THE BAD FAMILY.

hates the trouble of moving, and there he sits yawning and pining for want of something to do. When he walks, he drags his feet along, as if they were too heavy to lift up. His clothes are always dirty, for he will not brush them : his eyes are dull and heavy : he looks like a clown, and speaks like a blockhead. Idle Richard is a burthen to himself, and scorned by everybody.

Miss Fanny has got the title of Careless, because she minds no one thing that she ought. If she goes out to walk, she is sure to lose one of her gloves, or lets her bonnet blow off into the mud, or steps into the midst of some filthy puddle, because she is staring about, and not minding which way she goes. At home, when she should go to work, her needle-book, or her thimble, or her scissors cannot be found : though she has a work-basket to put all these things in, they are never in the right place.

At dinner she does not observe how her plate stands on the table, and perhaps her meat and all the gravy tumble into her lap. If she has a glass of wine, she spills it on her frock : if she hands a plate of bread and butter to anyone, she is sure either to drop the plate, or to let the bread and butter fall upon the carpet. She wears very coarse clothes, for she cannot be trusted with good ones. At night when she undresses to go to bed, she throws her frock on a chair or the ground, instead of folding it neatly up, so that it is tumbled and not fit to put on the next morning. If she writes, she throws the ink about her clothes ; if she tears a hole in her frock, she does not take a needle and thread to mend it directly, but pins it up ; then perhaps the pin pricks her half-a-dozen times in an hour, and tears three or four more holes in the frock. If she has a book lent to her, she will let it fall in the dirt, or drop the grease of the candle upon the leaves. She is always a slattern, and always dirty ; she is a disgrace to herself, and a burthen to her friends.

THE BAD FAMILY.

What a shocking name the next is—Lying Lucy! It is dreadful to think that anyone should deserve to be so called, but this wicked little girl deserves it, for she has no sense of honour, and seldom speaks the truth. Even when she does say what is true, on account of her having told falsehoods so long, people know not how to believe her; for who can depend upon the word of a LIAR. If she would forbear for a whole month to tell a lie, there would be hopes of her amendment, and then her word might be taken. But till she leaves off this shameful practice, she must expect to be shunned, and pointed at with scorn wherever she goes.

Selfish Sarah loves no one but herself, and no one loves her. She will not let her brothers, or sisters, or any other child play with her toys, even if she is not using them. She hoards up her playthings, and cannot amuse herself with them, for fear another should touch them. If she has more sweet cake or fruit than she can eat, she puts it by, and lets it spoil and get mouldy, rather than give it away; or if she sees a poor child begging in the streets, without shoes, stockings, or clothes to cover him, she will not part with a halfpenny to buy him a bit of bread, though she is told that he is starving with hunger. She never assists anyone, never feels for distress or pain that befalls anyone, nor is ever thankful or grateful for what is done for her. She covets everything she sees, yet takes no real pleasure in anything.

The parents of these odious children never look happy, nor enjoy comfort. The brothers and sisters never meet but to quarrel, so that the house is always in an uproar. Each abuses the other's vices, yet takes no pains to cure his or her own faults. The servants hate them, the neighbours despise them, and the house is shunned as though it had some dreadful distemper within. They live without friends; for no prudent persons will suffer their children to visit where they can learn nothing but wickedness and ill-manners.

THE GOOD FAMILY.

WHAT a different picture the other house presents to our view! The parents of the Good Family are always cheerful and happy, the children love each other and agree together; the servants are content and eager to oblige, and visitors delight to come to the house, because they pass their time there with both pleasure and profit.

MANLY EDWARD, the eldest son, is a fine youth, who makes himself the friend and protector of his younger brothers and sisters. Edward has true courage, for he will meet any danger to help the helpless, to rescue the oppressed, or in defence of the injured; yet he tries to avoid all quarrels, and is very often the peace-maker among

THE GOOD FAMILY.

those who are engaged in a dispute. His manners are gentle and graceful. He shuns the company of rude vulgar boys, yet insults no-one by seeming to hold them in contempt. It is not fine clothes or money that he pays respect to, it is virtue and good manners, and if the poorest boy in the school has the most of these good qualities, he gains the most of Manly Edward's love and esteem.

STUDIOUS ARTHUR, the second son of the good family, does not learn quickly, but what he wants of that power, he makes up by diligence. As he finds he cannot get his task by heart so fast as some other boys, he therefore fixes his whole thoughts on his book; and no calls to go to play, nor any sort of thing, can draw him from his lesson, till he has learned it perfectly. Arthur is seldom seen without a book in his hand; and if he goes out to walk, he puts one in his pocket, to be ready, if he should chance to have a few minutes to himself. He never wastes any time, and by that means he gains a great deal of knowledge. He is so attentive, that he never forgets what he reads and learns. Arthur will, no doubt, become a very wise man, and already he often finds the knowledge he has gained of great use to him. His parents commend him, his friends admire him, and his school-fellows respect him.

WELL-BRED CHARLES, the third son, is also a charming boy. He is greatly remarked for his perfect good manners. He never forgets to behave with politeness wherever he is. In the company of his parents and their friends, he is attentive to supply the wants of every-one. He listens to the discourse, and when he is spoken to, he answers at once in a lively, ready, and pleasant manner, but is never forward and talkative. When he has a party of playfellows, his mirth is not noisy and boisterous. He does not think, as some rude children do, that all play consists in screaming, shouting, tearing clothes, and knocking things to pieces; but finds

THE GOOD FAMILY.

plenty of sport for his little visitors without doing any of these things, and makes them as merry as possible. When cakes or fruit are sent into the play-room, he helps his guests all round before he touches any himself. He places them in the seats nearest the fire, or in fine weather, where they can see the most pleasant prospect. As good manners always arise from a good temper and a kind heart, which desires to make others happy, so they are sure to promote good humour and happiness. The play-parties of Charles therefore are never spoiled by disputes and quarrels. His visitors come with delight, and leave him with regret.

Well-bred Charles is constantly attentive to the ease and comfort of those about him. He pays great respect and deference to people who are old. He never uses coarse words, nor bad language, and always speaks civilly to servants. He does not enter the parlour with dirty hands and face, nor ever greases his clothes, for he knows that dirty habits are offensive disgusting things, and therefore he carefully avoids them.

Some children put on their good manners with their best clothes, and think they need only behave well before company, but the politeness of such children is stiff, awkward, and troublesome, and they always forget themselves, and return to some of their vulgar habits, before they leave the company. It is the constant practice of good manners at all times and in all places, that renders them easy, becoming, sweet, and natural, like those of Well-bred Charles.

The daughters of this good and happy family are no less worthy of praise than the sons. The eldest girl, whom we may call PATIENT EMMA, has the misfortune to suffer from illness. Sometimes she has severe pain, yet she bears it with patience and fortitude. She even tries to hide what she feels, that she may not afflict her kind parents; and the

THE GOOD FAMILY.

instant she has a little ease, she becomes as cheerful as anyone. She submits without a murmur to take what medicines the doctors prescribe for the cure of her illness. She is not so foolish as to expect to find a pleasant taste in physic, but she expects that it will be of service to her; and she would rather have a bitter taste in her mouth for a few moments, than endure days, weeks, and months of pain of sickness. As peevish, fretful tempers often bring disease on the body, so a patient, even temper not only lessens all suffering, but helps to cure the diseases of the body; Miss Emma therefore will perhaps in a short time regain her health, and should such an event happen, what joy it will give to all who know, pity, and admire this excellent little girl!

GENEROUS SUSAN thinks all day long how she can add to the happiness of others. It is her greatest pleasure to relieve distress, to do good, and to promote the comforts of all around her. She watches the looks of her parents, that she may fly to oblige them. If they are going out to ride in the coach, and there is not room enough for all the children, she will give up her place that one of her brothers or sisters may go. She will at all times leave play, or decline paying a visit, to attend on Emma, her sick sister. She sits whole hours by her bedside to watch her while she sleeps, and is careful neither to stir hand nor foot, lest she should disturb her slumbers. When awake, she reads to her, talks to her, or sings to her, if that seems most to amuse her. She would gladly bear the pain herself, if it were possible so to relieve poor Emma. When Susan has any money given to her, she does not treat herself with sweetmeats or toys, but buys something that will be useful to her brothers or sisters. At other times she will buy a pair of shoes for a poor child that goes barefooted, or purchase a book for some little boy or girl to learn to read in. Her mamma often gives her old frocks and gowns to

THE GOOD FAMILY.

bestow on some distressed family; and then Susan works with all her might for several days to mend and make them up in the most useful manner: for she has been told that a poor woman, who has two or three children to take care of, and goes out to daily labour, has not time to work with her needle, and perhaps does not know how to do it properly. When Susan has mended or made three or four little frocks, and sees the children neatly dressed in them, she feels more delight and pleasure, than if she had twenty dolls of her own clothed in silks and satins. Generous Susan has the blessings of the poor, and the love of all her family.

MERRY AGNES, the youngest child of the whole, is a fine healthy, lively, sprightly, laughing little girl, who feels no pain, and has no cause for sorrow. She is a kind of plaything for her elder brothers and sisters, who all delight in her good humour. They never tease, torment, and try to put her out of temper, as some children do to those who are younger than themselves, but they commend her goodness and strive to improve her. When they tell her not to do anything, she obeys them at once, for she sees that they are all gay, smiling, happy children, because they do what is right. If she wants to have what is not proper for her, she can bear to be denied, and skips away just as merry as before. This little girl will become very clever, for her brothers and sisters take pleasure in teaching her what they have been taught, and she attends to their lessons, and improves by their advice. She knows that they are all good, and she wishes to be like them.

It is a fine sight to see this good family all together; for among them there are no sour looks or rude words, no murmurs, no complaints, or quarrels. No: All is kindness, peace, and happiness.

FOOLISH FEARS.

CLARA HAMMOND had a silly habit of screaming when she saw a spider, an earwig, a beetle, a moth, or any kind of insect, and the sound of a mouse behind the wainscot of the room, made her suppose she should die with fright. The persons with whom she lived used to pity her for being afraid, and that made her fond of the silly trick, so that she became worse daily, and kept the house in a constant tumult and uproar; for she would make as much noise about the approach of a poor insect not much larger than the head of a pin, as if she had seen half-a-dozen hungry wolves coming with open jaws to devour her.

Clara Hammond was once asked by Mrs. Wilson, a very good lady, to go with her into the country; and Clara was much pleased at the thought of going to a house, where there was a charming garden and plenty of nice fruit. But the country is a sad place for people who encourage such foolish fears, because one cannot walk in a garden or field without seeing numbers of harmless insects.

Mrs. Wilson, with her coach full of guests, arrived at her country house just before dinner, and as soon as that meal was over, Clara begged leave to go out into the shrubbery. It was a charming place; and Clara was quite delighted with the clusters of roses and all the sweet smelling shrubs and flowers that seemed to perfume the air. But as she was tripping along, behold on a sudden a frog hopped across the path. It was out of sight in a moment, yet Clara could go no further, she stood still and shrieked with terror. At the same instant she saw a slug creeping upon her frock, and she now screamed in such a frantic mannner that her cries reached the house. The company rushed out of the dining parlour, and the servants out of the kitchen. Mrs. Wilson was foremost, and in her haste to see what was the matter she stumbled over a stone, and fell with such violence against the tree, that it cut her head dreadfully; she was covered with a stream of blood, and was taken up for dead.

It was soon known that the sight of a slug and a frog was all that ailed Miss Clara, and then how angry and scornfully did everyone look at her, to think that her folly had been the cause of such a terrible disaster. Clara Hammond had not a bad heart, and when she heard Mrs. Wilson's groans of pain whilst the doctors were dressing her wounds, she wept bitterly, and sorely repented her silly unmeaning fears.

Mrs. Wilson was in great danger for many days, and Clara crept about the house in the most forlorn manner, for no one took any notice of her, and she dared not go out in the garden, for fear still of meeting some mighty monster of a snail, or something equally alarming. At length Mrs. Wilson grew better, and then she sent for Clara to her room, and talked to her very kindly and very wisely on the folly of fearing things which had not the power to hurt her, and which were still more afraid of her than she could be of them; and with reason, since she was stronger, and had far more power to hurt and give pain, than a thousand frogs or mice had. Clara promised that she would try to get the better of her fault, and she soon proved that her promise was sincere.

One day she was with Mrs. Wilson in her chamber, and this good lady being fatigued and sleepy gave Clara a book of pretty stories to divert her, and begged the little girl would make no noise while she slept. Mrs. Wilson lay down on the bed, and Clara sat on a stool at some little distance. All was as still as possible: and after some time as Clara chanced to lift her eyes from her book, she saw not

FOOLISH FEARS.

far from her a spider, who was spinning his web up and down from the ceiling. She was just going to scream, when she thought of the mischief she had already done to Mrs. Wilson, and she forbore. At the same moment, as she turned her head to the other side, a little grey mouse sat on the table, nibbling some crumbs of sweet-cake that had been left there. Clara now trembled from head to foot, but she had so much power over herself that she neither moved nor cried out. This effort, though it cost her some pain at first, did her good; for in a minute or two she left off trembling. Her fear went away by degrees, and then she could observe and wonder at the curious manner in which the spider spun long lines of thread out of his own mouth, and made them fast to each other and the wall just as he pleased, and could also admire the sleek coat and bright eyes of the little grey mouse on the table. Clara's book slipped from her lap, and as she stooped to catch it, that it might not fall on the floor, she was seen by the two visitors, who instantly fled away to their retreats in the greatest fright possible. Neither spider nor grey mouse appeared again that day: and ever after Clara Hammond had courage and prudence, and took care not to do mischief to others, nor deprive herself of pleasure, by the indulgence of foolish fears.

GAMMER GURTON'S GARLAND.

[From *Gammer Gurton's Garland: or the Nursery Parnassus. A Choice Collection of Pretty Songs and Verses, for the amusement of all little good children who can neither read nor run.* London: Printed for R. Triphook, 37, St. James's Street, by Harding and Wright, St. John's Square. 1810.]

THE OLD WOMAN THAT WAS TOSS'D IN A BLANKET.

THERE was an old woman toss'd in a blanket
   Seventeen times as high as the moon;
But where she was going no mortal could tell,
   For under her arm she carried a broom.

Old woman, old woman, old woman, said I,
   Whither, ah whither, ah whither so high?
To sweep the cobwebs from the sky,
   And I'll be with you by and by.

THE SONG OF THE THREE WISE MEN OF GOTHAM, WHO WENT TO SEA IN A BOWL.

Three wise men of Gotham
Went to sea in a bowl,
And if the bowl had been stronger
My song had been longer.

THE SURPRIZING OLD WOMAN.

There was an old woman, and what do you think
She lived upon nothing but victuals and drink;
And tho' victuals and drink were the chief of her diet,
This plaguy old woman could never be quiet.

She went to the baker to buy her some bread,
And when she came home, her old husband was dead;
She went to the clerk to toll the bell,
And when she came back her old husband was well.

The Old Man and his Calf.

There was an old man,
    And he had a calf;
    And that's half:
He took him out of the stall,
And put him on the wall;
    And that's all.

    The man in the moon
    Came tumbling down,
And asked his way to Norwich.
    He went by the south,
    And burnt his mouth,
With supping hot pease porridge.

To make your candles last for aye,
You wives and maids give ear, O!
To put 'em out's the only way,
Says honest John Boldero.

The rose is red, the grass is green
Serve King George, our noble king:
Kitty the spinner will sit down to dinner,
    And eat the leg of a frog;
All good people look over the steeple,
    And see the cat play with the dog.

CRICKET IN 1812.

If all the world was apple-pie,
   And all the sea was ink ;
And all the trees were bread and cheese,
   What could we do for drink ?

      I'll sing you a song
      Nine verses long,
         For a pin ;
      Three and three are six,
      And three are nine ;
      You are a fool,
         And the pin is mine.

CRICKET IN 1812.

[From *The Book of Games; or, a History of Juvenile Sports, practised at a considerable Academy near London.* London : Richard Phillips, No. 7, Bridge Street, Blackfriars. 1812.]

THREE good strong sticks of about two feet in length are driven into the ground at about four inches asunder. In the top of each is cut a little notch, and a small piece of wood is laid across from one to the other. The upright sticks are distinguished by the name of *stumps ;* the cross one by that of the *bail*. This wicket—for that is the name by which it is called—is placed about the middle of the field. The players divide themselves into two parties, and toss up, as in many other games, for the first innings. One party, who is out, bowls the ball from the distance of about thirty yards, towards the wicket, which it is the business of the *bat's man* to defend. If he is fortunate enough to give it a good stroke he immediately sets off to run as far as the line at thirty yards distance, where the opposite party stood when they bowled ; and if he can touch it with his bat and get home to the wicket before one of the adverse party has

CRICKET IN 1812.

knocked off the bail with the ball, he reckons one. If the ball has been struck to such a distance that he thinks he shall have time for a second run, he may go on again, and reckon as many notches as he takes runs to the appointed place and back again during the time that he remained *in*, but if his adversary strike off the bail either in bowling, or while he is running, or catch the ball when he had struck it and before it touched the ground he is *out*, and is obliged to resign the bat to one of his own party, till they each have their innings; and then the opposite party come in.

The bat's man is the only *player* of the party that is *in*, who is engaged, but all of the other party are employed—one in bowling, the others in trying to stop or catch the ball when struck, and endeavouring to knock off the bail with the ball while the bat's man is running, and those who are thus engaged are called the *seekers-out*. When all the players have had two innings, the game is finished, and that party is winner which has gained most notches.

AMUSING ALPHABET.

L.

The Lion.

[From *The Amusing Alphabet for Young Children beginning to Read.* London: Printed for R. Taylor & Co., Shoe Lane. 1812.]

HERE is a great lion! the king of beasts! and look how that little lamb skips around him. He could eat up the lamb in a moment, but he is too noble and generous to hurt the poor harmless lamb because it is in his power. Oh! what a noble animal! So you, my dear child, when

AMUSING ALPHABET.

you catch a bird, or butterfly, or any little creature, remember the lion, and do not hurt it because you have caught it; but let it go again and be happy, and then everybody will call you a good child and love you.

T.

THE TRUANT BOY.

HERE is a schoolroom, and all the little children sitting round and learning their lessons. They are all good children. But look, there is one boy in the corner crying. He is a naughty boy, and going to be whipped, because he

AMUSING ALPHABET.

played the truant and did not come to school with the rest. His mamma told him to go to school like a good boy; but he ran away to play, instead of going as he was bid : so he is whipped for being idle. School is the place where children all go together to learn their books ; and when they have done their lesson they all play together, and are very happy when they are good; but when they are idle they are punished. When you are old enough, my dear child, you will go to school, and I am sure you will read your book well, and then you will be happy, and have a great many playfellows.

First Steps in Life (1).

First Steps in Life (2).

THE
PARENT'S OFFERING:

OR

Tales for Children.

By

MRS. CAROLINE BARNARD.

—◇◆—

LONDON:
Printed for M. J. GODWIN,
Juvenile Library, no. 41 Skinner Street

1813.

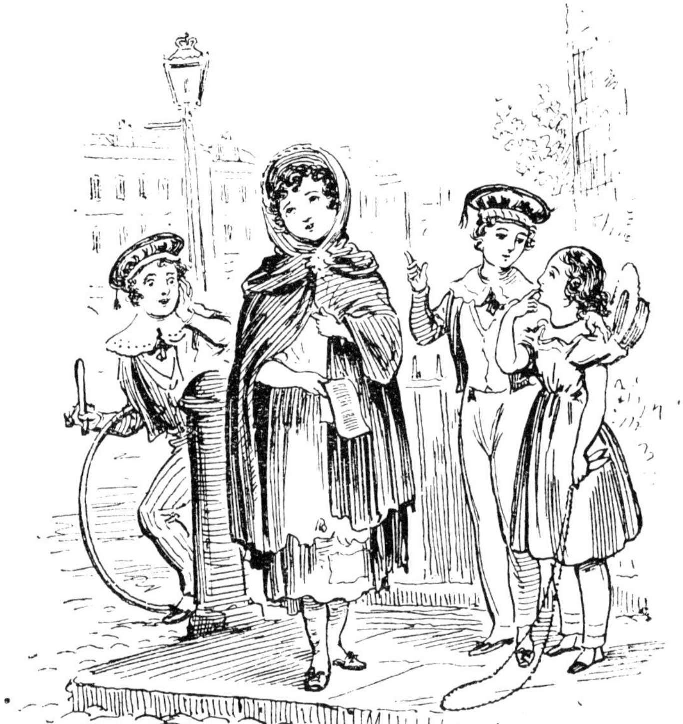

THE PARENT'S OFFERING.

THE KIND TUTOR.

I WAS born at my father's country-seat in Somersetshire, the heir of a large estate, the hopes of my family and the idol of my mother. My father went abroad when I was an infant and is but just returned to England, so that the care of my youth was entirely left to my mother. Almost the first thing I recollect was my sorrow at the departure of a favourite nursery-maid who was sent away because she had ventured to punish me for striking one of her fellow-servants. When she got to the lodge at the end of the park, and turned into the road, I lost sight of her entirely, and then I began to cry and scream, and to insist that mamma should send for her back again. In vain my poor mamma endeavoured to appease me, and told me it was impossible. The more she said, the more I cried. At last mamma was tired out with me and rung the bell for nurse. Here nurse, said she, try what you can do with the child for I am tired to death with him, and I cannot make him happy. For Heaven's sake, stop his crying if you can.

Blessings be good unto us! said the fat old lady, beginning with her old-fashioned sayings, "What was the matter with the sweet cherub? Who was it has affronted my pretty boy? Come to its own nurse, and no one shall dare to vex him; and he shall have everything he wants—a darling! Come and feel in old nurse's pockets, and hear a pretty story—come."

But I was too much accustomed to all this jargon of nonsense to feel its effects. I struggled and shrieked the louder.

THE PARENT'S OFFERING.

Oh stop his cries, stop his crying, for pity's sake! said mamma; and she threw herself back on the sofa and burst into tears. I had never seen mamma cry before. I stopped the horrid noise I was making and stared at her with surprise. I saw old nurse trudge off, and return in a great hurry with a glass of water, and at the same time hold something to mamma's nose, and I heard her say—Indeed, my lady, you should not have the child so long; you have quite turmoiled yourself, my lady. I thought to myself—Then it is *I* who have made poor mamma ill. I believe I was frightened, for I did not make another sound, but went up to mamma and took her hand and kissed it. I do not know how long mamma was ill, or anything more about it; for I was then taken to bed directly.

My health became very delicate; I was constantly ill. I took no pleasure in any of my playthings, though my nursery contained toys enough to have made half the little boys in the kingdom quite happy. Though I was a great boy and had been in breeches two years, I was constantly being petted up in my mamma's or in my old nurse's lap. I never went out except in the carriage, for mamma was afraid of my walking, for fear it should fatigue me.

On the birth-day that I was six years old, mamma made me a present of a beautiful little pony, with a little bridle and saddle:—and now I never either walked or went in the carriage, but rode out every day with a servant on each side of me; one to hold me and the other to lead my pony. I was very much pleased at first with this because it was something new; so I rode every day, and all day long, till very soon I became as tired of my pony as the rest of my pleasures. One day as I was slowly riding on being led a foot-pace and yawning incessantly I passed a boy's playground; it was full of boys who seemed very busy and very happy. They were all engaged at some play or other; not

THE PARENT'S OFFERING.

one was idle. In one corner some little fellows were stooping down in a ring playing at marbles; at another part of the ground a great tall boy was flying a kite, and some little ones standing round him jumping and hallowing as it mounted in the air. Not far off a party were eager in the heat of a game at trap-ball and on the most even part of the green a set of bigger ones with their coats and waistcoats thrown off were in the middle of a cricket match. The boy who was in was playing very well, and was sending the ball to a great distance. I longed to try and play, for I fancied I could do just the same, though I never handled a cricket bat in my life.

Lift me off—lift me off, I said, impatient to dismount the pony. I want to go and play at cricket.

Indeed, my lord, said James, your lordship mustn't go into that there playground among them there rude boys: your lordship will be hurt. Your mamma will never forgive me.

Let me down, Thomas, for I will go; let me get down, I say.

In vain the poor servants tried to dissuade me; down I would get, and on the playground I ran.

Hullo! what's that little fellow getting in my way for? called out the boy who was in. Get out of the way you little rascal, or you'll be knocked down with the ball.

Give me the bat, I called out, I want to play and will play. I am Lord Henry ———, and you must do what I tell you; give me the bat.

At this the boys began to laugh and point at me. Some called me names. Give *you* the bat, said one of them, yes, I'll give it you, and he lifted it up, and was preparing to strike me with it, but James ran up and prevented him. I began to set up a loud cry, when a good-natured boy came up to me with a bat in his hand, and said, Come, you shall

THE PARENT'S OFFERING.

have a try if you've a mind; only leave off blubbering and I will lend you my bat.

Oh, yes, come, said they all, let's see what sort of a hand his little snivelling lordship is at cricket.

I snatched up the bat very proudly and was going to shew off and play very finely, when I found it was so heavy I could scarcely lift it, much less strike a ball with it. I threw it down in a great passion, and set up one of my tremendous roars.

Take me away, Thomas—take me away, James—take me home to mamma.

The servants hastened up to me and carried me off in their arms: the boys all following after me, hissing and hooting all the way I went.

And now, are you not almost tired of hearing of my follies and passions? Well, have patience, I am soon coming to a pleasant part of my history.

I did not see so much of mamma as usual; for she was very often so ill she could not leave her room, and I was not allowed to go to her for fear of making her headache worse.

One day as I was standing at my nursery window I saw a carriage drive up to the door. It was my uncle come to pay mamma a visit. He staid some time at our house; and he used to have very long conversations with mamma, and used to make her cry very often. I do not know what they talked about, for they spoke in a low voice; but I could perceive they were talking about me and I used to try and listen to hear what they said. Once I heard my uncle say, Indeed, my dear sister, consider he is more than six years old; he should really be at school by this time. He knows nothing. His father will be disappointed in him. Besides, consider your own health.

Then I heard mamma say, I cannot, I cannot indeed,

THE PARENT'S OFFERING.

my dear brother, I cannot send him from me. And this was all I could hear.

The morning my uncle was going away he took me on his knee, and said to me, My dear Henry, listen to me. You have got a new friend coming to live with you; he is a very wise, good man; he will be called your tutor: if you are sensible enough to be obedient and kind to him, he will soon grow very fond of you and he will make you much happier than you are now. Nobody can be happy till they have learned to be good, and this kind tutor will teach you to be good and happy. God bless you and give you grace to become so.

My uncle jumped into his carriage, kissed his hand to me and was out of sight in a minute.

One day, after my uncle had been gone some weeks, my maid Susan took hold of my hand and told me to come with her. I had not seen mamma for nearly two days. Susan led me quite to the other end of our great house and took me into the furthest room, quite at the end of a long gallery, a great way off my nursery which adjoined mamma's room.

Here, said she, when she had shut the door, this is your new nursery and here you are to remain; here you are out of your poor dear mamma's hearing, and you may scream and roar ever so loud, and she will not be disturbed with your passions. Your poor mamma is very ill indeed, and it's all your doing, you naughty child. She is quite worn out, and you'll be the death of her at last.

It was to no purpose I cried out that I wanted to go to mamma:—Pray take me to mamma. The doors were only shut the closer, and the less chance there was of my being taken into her sick room.

Oh, said Susan, one day (I shall never forget her face while she was speaking) I've heard a fine piece of news—

good news for your lordship and good news for us all. There's a certain person coming who will soon teach your lordship another story than to sit moping in a corner all day long; then I take it there'll be lessons to learn and copies to write, and a good caning into the bargain now and then when it's wanted. Oh, it will be a good thing, my little master, when you are taken into tight hands; aye, aye, Mr. Hartley will set all to rights, I'll warrant me.

In this manner did Susan make the idea of my tutor terrific and odious to me and I dreaded his arrival as if he had been a sea monster coming to devour me. I saw by the smiles and mysterious faces of the servants that some event had happened, and at last I was told my uncle had called to see me and had brought with him Mr. Hartley, my tutor.

I was now dressed very nicely, and told that I was to go down into the drawing-room. In spite of the dread I felt for my tutor, I was happy at being taken downstairs once more, and going to see my uncle, of whom I was very fond; and above all at getting away from my nursery and from Susan. Without any resistance therefore I suffered myself to be dressed and taken down. When I got into the drawing-room I ran up to my uncle and threw my arms round his neck. I believe he was very much pleased with my doing this, for he pressed me to his bosom very closely.

He said to me, My dear Henry, do you remember the kind friend I promised to bring to you? Here he is. Go and shake hands with him.

I made no answer but clung closer to my uncle, and hid my face in his coat. I heard a voice say, Do not be afraid to look at me, Lord Henry; I am your friend.

Oh, fie, Henry, said my uncle, do not be so childish, or I shall be quite ashamed of you—and Mr. Hartley will think you are a baby.

Still! I remained unchanged in my position. I heard my

THE PARENT'S OFFERING.

uncle and tutor whispering together, and shortly after they talked aloud about a great many things, but not a word about me. As soon as I found they took no notice of me, I began to move. I just ventured to look round and take a sly peep at the stranger—then quickly hid my face again. This I did several times, but no notice at all was taken of me.

One morning I was taken down to the library, as Susan said, to begin my "schooling." I found my tutor there alone. He was sitting at a table, with several large books before him. I supposed that these were all books out of which I was supposed to learn to read; and as I hated the thoughts of reading or learning I determined I would not do either;—so I kept for some time in a corner of the room and did not go near Mr. Hartley, or his table, or his books.

To my great surprise, Mr. Hartley took no notice of me at

THE PARENT'S OFFERING.

all: he neither spoke nor looked at me, but continued turning over the leaves of his book with great attention. I expected every instant he would call me to him—but no such thing—he rested his head on his hand, and did not speak a word. As he turned over the leaves I thought I saw pictures in his book, and I crept softly behind his chair and peeped over his shoulders.

There I saw in his great book nothing but beautiful pictures of birds, and beasts, and insects of all sorts and kinds. I was very fond of things of this sort, and never did I see anything that excited my curiosity so much; but I longed to see them more comfortably; for I was standing up on the bar of my tutor's chair, straining my little neck to peep: and my tutor turned them over so quick, I could hardly see them.

For the first time I ventured to speak to my tutor. I said to him in a timid voice, May I look at those pictures?

I will show them to you with great pleasure, said he. Will you come and sit by me, and see them?

Yes, I will, said I, joyfully; and he seated me by him, and told me the names of them all, one after another. There were lions and tigers, and a rhinoceros, and a giraffe, and hyaenas, and birds of all sorts and colours. I had never seen anything half so beautiful before.

When we had got about half-way through the second book, the bell rang, and Susan came to fetch me to dinner.

Go away, Susan, said I, pettishly; I don't want any dinner; I can't come.

Hearken to me, my little boy, said my tutor. I have shewn you a great many pretty pictures, and I have a great many more still to show you, and besides I have got a pretty story to read to you about them all; but I read and shew pictures only to good boys who are docile and obedient.

THE PARENT'S OFFERING.

I will be good, said I. Take me to dinner, Susan. And I went away directly.

Thus ended my first day's *schooling*, that I had dreaded so much.—Oh, how impatient I was for the time to come that I might go again to my tutor and his pictures!

The next morning came at last. Oh, make haste, Susan, said I, make haste and take me down.

Hey, what !—bless me—how unaccountable, how surprising! said Susan, as she combed my hair. In a hurry to go down to lessons, forsooth. There must be something at the bottom of all this. I can't make it out, not I.

I went, or rather ran down to the library, burst open the door, placed the chair myself by my tutor's side, and then exclaimed, Now for the pictures!

Now for the pictures, echoed my tutor with equal exultation; and he went on to shew me all I had not seen the day before.

Then according to his promise he took another great book, and while I was examining the picture he read me an account of the animal I was looking at. I listened to him with great delight, and if he stopped for a minute, I remember I exclaimed, Oh, go on, read some more, pray read more. I believe my tutor was pleased at this; for he always smiled and read on again directly.

At last he stopped in the middle of a very interesting anecdote about a wolf and a lamb. I was burning to know the fate of the poor little lamb, when my tutor stopped short and shut his book.

More of this another day, said he.

Oh, was the poor little lamb killed? said I. Do tell me, my dear tutor.

You shall hear that when you come to me to-morrow. The sun shines. I must take my walk while it is fine.

Won't you take me with you, said I, I will be very good.

THE PARENT'S OFFERING.

I should have great pleasure in your company, my dear Lord Henry, but I shall walk faster than you ride. Besides I would rather not walk with the servants who must attend your pony.

Oh, I do not want my pony or my servants; I would rather walk with you alone, and then we can talk about the wolf and the lamb as we go along.

Come along then, said he.

My tutor then took hold of my hand, and led me through some pretty fields and lanes, talking to me all the way, and shewing me a great many of the insects and birds that I had just seen in the pictures.

So we went on, and I became every day more fond of my tutor. He made quite a different boy of me, but I was not yet quite happy, for I had not yet seen mamma.

One day I thought to myself I would ask my kind tutor to allow me to go to mamma. He never refused me anything that was proper for me; or if it was improper he explained to me why it was so. I therefore went up to him with my old petition.

Pray, dear Mr. Hartley, said I, when do you think I may be allowed to go and see my dear Mamma?

My dear Lord Henry, said he, I will make interest for you, and I think you will then be allowed to see her this very evening. Your friends, my dear boy, have thought it necessary hitherto to keep you from your poor mother because they knew you to be once a perverse fretful child. But I will tell them what I really think to be the case, and what will give them all joy and comfort—that Lord Henry is an altered child—that he will carry nothing but peace and comfort to his fond mother.

I threw my arms round my tutor's neck, and burst into tears. Oh, tell them this, my dear kind tutor! tell them this and let me see mamma.

THE PARENT'S OFFERING.

Mr. Hartley told me to compose myself, and then left the room. I suppose he went, as he had promised, to make interest for me, for in a little time in came my good nurse.

Come my sweet one, said she—you are to come and see dear mamma at last, but be sure now you fall into none of your *figaries ;* and he shall have some cake when he comes out of mamma's room if he behaves well.

I remember I felt very indignant at this speech of nurse's, and thought she might as well leave off talking to me as if I were a baby.

Hush, hush! said nurse (holding her finger to her nose) you must be very quiet my dear.

When the door opened I saw mamma lying on a sofa, and my uncle sitting by. I crept in on tip toe with my finger to my lips. I think my mamma and uncle were pleased to see me come in so softly for they looked at one another and smiled.

I shall never forget what I felt when I got close up to mamma, and saw how she was altered since I had seen her. Her cheeks and lips, which used to be so very rosy were quite white, her eyes dim and sunk in her head; and she looked terribly thin.

When mamma put her arms round my neck and kissed me, I felt her cry, for her tears wetted my cheeks and hands. I felt quite inclined to cry too, but was afraid nurse would call me to account; so I swallowed and choaked and prevented my tears from coming. Mamma then made signs for me to sit upon the pillow by her; and there I sat, and mamma smiled and looked at me, but she did not speak. I believe she was too weak to talk.

I then whispered in her ear, and asked her when she would be well, and she said gently—Soon, love! I could ask no more questions, for I was then taken away with a promise of coming again.

THE PARENT'S OFFERING.

The next time I went to see mamma, she seemed much better, and I talked to her a great deal, and told her how much I loved my tutor, and what nice things he taught me, and what pretty books he had got; and I do believe that my talking made her better, for I saw the colour come into her cheek as I spoke—and she cried and laughed with joy.

After this mamma got better and better every day; and I grew daily more good, more happy and more fond of my tutor.

Mamma grew quite well, and came down stairs and rode in her carriage the same as ever. My tutor said to me one day—

Look Henry, look at your fond and indulgent mother. A little while ago she was on the brink of the grave. You, her only child, had almost broken her heart; but God in his mercy has saved her to you. Oh, be grateful to him for this blessing! Cherish your mother! and by your good conduct and filial attention repay her for all her cares and prove in future the comfort of her life.

These were the words of my kind tutor. They made an impression on my heart. I have remembered them ever since, and I hope and trust I shall never forget them.

The Elegant Girl;

or

Virtuous Principles the true Source

of

Elegant Manners.

Illustrated by Twelve Drawings with Lines to each.

1813.
Entered at Stationers' Hall, and
Published for the Proprietor by S. INMAN,
7 Lamb's Conduit Street, London.

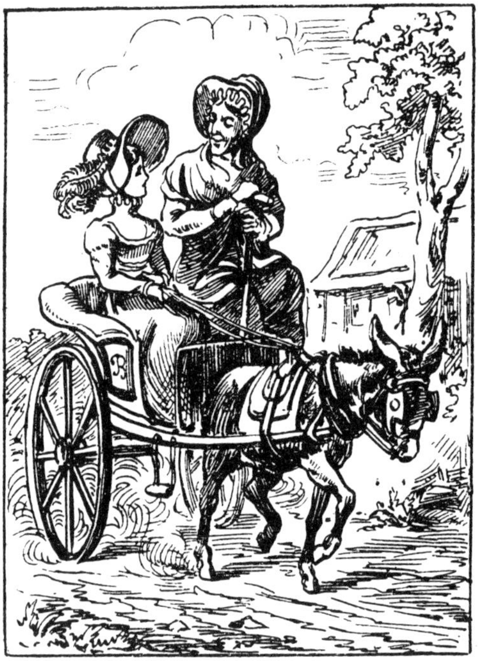

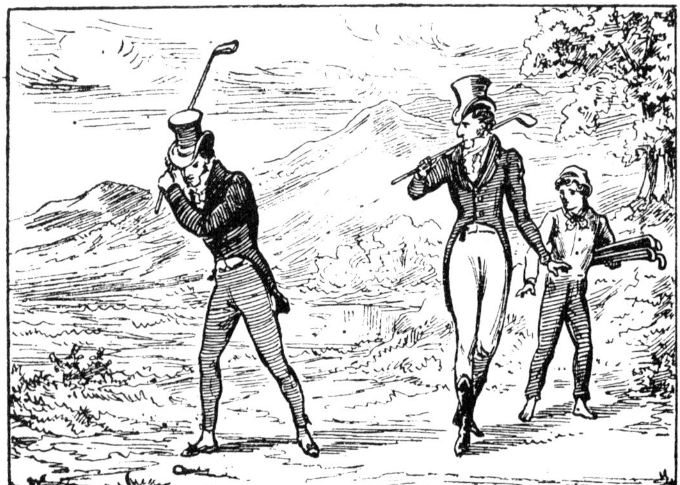

THE ELEGANT GIRL.

Devotion's lovely form we see
As lowly bending on her knee,
Her Bed just left, the little maid
Implores her Great Creator's aid
T'obey *his* own Almighty Will
And all *her* duties to fulfil.

THE ELEGANT GIRL.

Her prayers said, she soon is drest,
Not caring " what becomes her best,"
Her aim is of a nobler kind—
By study to improve her mind,
To turn the leaf of history o'er
And arts and sciences explore.

THE ELEGANT GIRL.

But what a picture here is given!
O Charity, meek child of Heaven!
May all the rich thy virtues feel
And learn this lesson at each meal;
To clothe the naked, feed the poor—
Nor drive the beggar from their door.

THE ELEGANT GIRL.

Her Master pointing to the book,
Attention marks her steady look,
His lesson is not thrown away,
By science taught with taste to play
She'll charm ere while the list'ning throng
And sing with modest grace her song.

THE ELEGANT GIRL.

Though first the humble copyist stands
And lessons learns from other hands,
Improvement soon will nurture hope,
And time will give her talents scope
The glowing landscape to design
Or paint the human face divine.

THE ELEGANT GIRL.

Look at the group beneath the tree,
What can so interesting be?
The little schoolmistress we find
Instructing here the infant mind;
Her conduct they can best approve
Who virtue and religion love.

THE ELEGANT GIRL.

The lady here holds out her hand
And says "Temptation you'll withstand,
This fruit with you my child, I'm sure,
Will on the table rest secure,
You'll touch it not without my leave,
Laura her mother won't deceive."

THE ELEGANT GIRL.

To visit a poor cottage dame,
One summer's evening Laura came,
Of viands brought a little treat
And placed her bottle at her feet;
Whilst Dash her faithful dog appears
With anxious looks and listening ears.

THE ELEGANT GIRL.

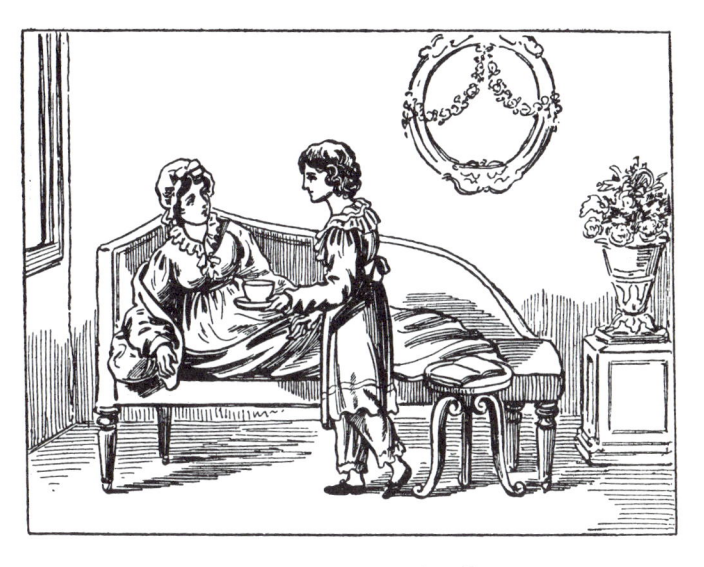

Languid and pale her mother lies,
She speaks not, but her speaking eyes
In language plain, express the pleasure
She feels, in having such a treasure;
A daughter, who in early days,
Maternal tenderness repays.

THE ELEGANT GIRL.

To innocence what charms belong.
The dance delightful as the song,
Whilst bounding light on agile feet
Her steps the measured cadence meet;
With pleasure beams the Mother's eye
As o'er the strings her fingers fly.

THE ELEGANT GIRL.

In sickness when the poor you see
Will you their ministering angel be?
Will you their thirst and pain assuage,
And read to them the sacred page?
Dry up the Widow's scalding tears,
Exalt her hopes, and calm her fears.

THE ELEGANT GIRL.

Here Laura, by her mother led,
With pleasure sees before her spread,
Proofs of a Parent's kind regard.
Gifts for the Poor, her own reward,
For Laura felt and understood
The luxury of doing good.

MAMMA'S PICTURES.

[From *Mamma's Pictures, or the History of Fanny and Mary*. London : Darton, Harvey & Darton, 55, Gracechurch Street. 1813.]

PAPA was so kind as to put up a swing for them in the garden: it was fastened to the branch of a large tree; and while Fanny ran about and made nosegays, her mamma lifted Mary into the swing and pushed it for her till she went up quite high in the air.

VERSES FOR LITTLE CHILDREN.

[From *Verses for Little Children : Written by a Young Lady for the Amusement of her Junior Brothers and Sisters.* London : Darton, Harvey & Darton, 55 Gracechurch Street. 1813.]

MY FATHER.

Who taught me on a stick to stride,
Or on his fav'rite nag to ride,
And guide the bit on either side?
                      My Father.

ANNA.

And while her wheel goes quickly round,
   With heartfelt joy she sits and sings;
No tiresome languor there is found,
   Her moments fly with fairy wings.

BEASTS, BIRDS AND FISHES.

[From *Beasts, Birds and Fishes. From Original Poems with Pictures for Children.* London: Printed for Darton, Harvey & Darton, Gracechurch Street and Published as the Act directs Nov. 1, 1813.]

The Dog will come when he is called;
The Cat will walk away.

The Monkey's cheek is very bald:
The Goat is fond of play.

BEASTS, BIRDS AND FISHES.

The Parrot is a prate apace
Yet knows not what she says:
The noble Horse will win the race
Or draw you in a chaise.

The Pig is not a feeder nice,
The Squirrel loves a nut.

BEASTS, BIRDS AND FISHES.

The Wolf would eat you in a trice,
The Buzzard's eyes are shut.

The Lark sings high up in the air :
The Linnet on the tree.

The Swan he has a bosom fair,
And who so proud as he;
O yes, the Peacock is more proud
Because his tail has eyes.

The Lion roars so very loud
He'd fill you with surprise;
The Raven's coat is shining black,
Or rather raven grey.

The Camel's bunch is on his back,
The Owl abhors the day.

The Sparrow steals the cherry ripe,
The Elephant is wise.

The Blackbird charms you with his pipe,
The false Hyena cries.

The Hen guards well her little chicks,
The useful Cow is meek.

The Beaver builds with mud and sticks,
The Lapwing loves to squeak.

The little Wren is very small :
The Humming Bird is less.

BEASTS, BIRDS AND FISHES.

The Lady-bird is least of all,
And beautiful in dress.
The Pelican she loves her young,
The Stork his father loves.

The Woodcock's bill is very long,
And innocent are Doves.

The spotted Tiger's fond of blood,
The Pigeons feed on peas.

The Duck will gobble in the mud :
The Mice will eat your cheese.

A Lobster's black, when boil'd he's red :
The harmless Lamb must bleed.

The Codfish has a clumsy head :
The Goose on grass will feed.

The Lady in her gown of silk,
The little Worm may thank.
The sick man drinks the Ass's milk.

The Weasel's long and lank :
The Buck gives us a ven'son dish
When hunted for the spoil..

The Shark eats up the little fish :
The Whale produces oil.
The Glow-worm shines the darkest night
With lantern in its tail.

BEASTS, BIRDS AND FISHES.

The Turtle is the Cit's delight;
It wears a coat of mail.

In Germany they hunt the Boar;
The Bee brings honey home.

The Ant lays up a winter store,
The Bear loves honey-comb.

The Eagle has a crooked beak :
The Plaice has orange spots.

The Starling if he's taught will speak :
The Ostrich walks and trots.

The child that does not these things know,
He may be thought a dunce;
Then up my Lads in knowledge grow,
As youth can come but once.

AMUSING PICTURE BOOK.

[From *Harrison's Amusing Picture and Poetry Book*, containing *Seventy Engravings*. J. Harrison, Devizes.]

> Unhappy youth what hast thou done,
> Why urge thy steed so fast?
> Alas! I hear him scream and groan;
> Ah me! he breathes his last.

THE ROSE.

[From *The Rose, containing Original Poems for Young People. By their friend Mary Elliott. Accompanied with Engravings.* London: William Darton, 58 Holborn Hill.]

CRICKET.

But look on the Green
What an active scene
Presents itself to the eye;
The cricketers stand
With bats in their hand
Their skill and power to try.

THE ROSE.

One feeling alone
These happy boys own—
Good humour is never asleep;
No squabbles we hear,
By which it is clear
That each his temper can keep.

ELLEN'S FAIRING.

The day so often wished to come
  Is here, and all the young look gay;
In laughing groups they rush from home,
  To view the neighbouring Fair's display.

FAMILIAR REPRESENTATIONS.

What youthful bosom felt more light
    Than Ellen's, as she viewed the purse,
In which were lodged three shillings bright,
    To buy a doll to dress and nurse.

A stool with carpet covered o'er,
    Which well her new-formed plan would suit;
For it would keep from earthen floor
    And rest her father's gouty foot.

[From *Familiar Representations with Suitable Descriptions and Useful Observations in Prose and Verse. Beautified with various Engravings.* London: Printed for John Chappell, Hayden Square, Minories.]

THE EVIL OF GOING TOO NEAR THE FIRE.

    JULIA did as she had done
        On many days before;
    And from her eldest brother's books
        The printed pages tore.

FAMILIAR REPRESENTATIONS.

But as she o'er the fender reach'd
   The lighted coals below;
The paper burnt her muslin frock
   And burnt her person too!

Such blisters on her arms appear'd
   Such scars upon her face!
As neither doctor can remove
   Nor time itself erase.

And what excruciating pain
   She suffered for her play;
Which made her promise not to do
   The same another day.

THE HISTORY OF A GOLDFINCH.

[From *The History of a Goldfinch, with neat coloured plates.* London : W. and T. Darton, 40 Holborn Hill.]

A FOOLISH, silly boy—I hope no little girl would have thought of such a thing, or if she did I should be ashamed of her—took it into his head that a poor bird which had fallen into his power would look *very pretty* after his feathers were plucked off. To work he went, the poor bird did not complain, and he plucked every feather except the wings ; and to make the bird look the prettier as he called it, he got some warm paste and with it stuck a piece of red cloth upon the poor creature's head, and then let it go. Whilst he was admiring the victim of his cruelty, his father, who abhorred it, seeing him very attentive to the wicked work that he had been about, called him and questioned him in a kind manner, how he could be so cruel to an innocent creature that never injured him ? The boy, "did not," he said, " think any harm in it : he thought it looked pretty," and added that " he had not hurt the bird." Upon this, the father called him in the same mild way, for had he scolded, it would not have been so effectual, and plucking some of the hair from the young gentleman's head asked *if it hurt him ?* The boy cried and said that it hurt him very sadly indeed. The father then plucked some more, the pain of which made the boy cry very loud. " Now then," says the father, " learn in future to be more tender to your fellow creatures ; for if such a small portion of hair which I have plucked from your head has occasioned you such pain as to make you cry so bitterly, what must you think of the

THE HISTORY OF A GOLDFINCH.

pain which the poor little defenceless bird was put to, when without any provocation you plucked the feathers from its whole body! Go from my presence, you cruel wicked boy,

and never let me see your face till you are sensible of your monstrous crime!"

This punishment had such effect upon the son that, as he himself not long since told me, he never could abide to be cruel to little innocent creatures ever afterwards.

Ride on a Horse to Banbury Cross.

THE STORY

OF

LITTLE MARY

AND HER CAT.

IN WORDS NOT EXCEEDING

Two Syllables.

LONDON:
WILLIAM DARTON & SON
Holborn Hill.

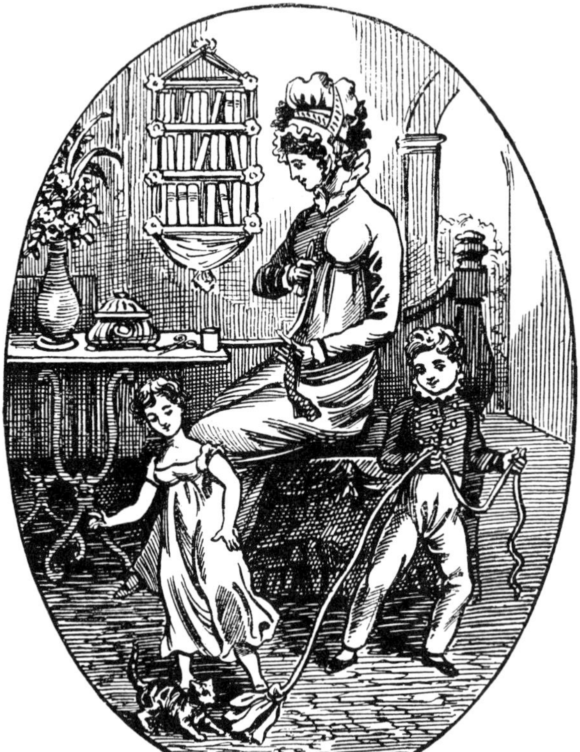

THE STORY OF LITTLE MARY AND HER CAT.

THERE was once a pret-ty lit-tle girl cal-led Ma-ry. Some-times Ma-ry would read to Nurse Brown, and some-times Nurse would tell stor-ies to her or sing old songs, such as she had learn-ed from the books that are sold at Mr. Dar-ton's shop on Hol-born Hill, where all kinds of books that can a-muse or in-struct chil-dren are to be bought.

As Ma-ry was once tak-ing a walk, she found a half-starv-ed lit-tle kit-ten. A cru-el boy had thrown it in-to a pond, to see how it could swim; and the poor lit-tle creature had crawl-ed out of the wa-ter just as Ma-ry came by. The boy ran a-way

LITTLE MARY.

and Ma-ry took the kit-ten home with her. Muff, the cat, had nev-er seen a kit-ten be-fore, and at first could not tell what to make of it; the kit-ten took Muff for its mo-ther, and ran up to him in a great hur-ry; but Muff ran back-ward half a-fraid, and hid him-self un-der a ta-ble. When the kit-ten had been fed, it lay down to sleep be-fore the fire. Muff came and look-ed at it, and af-ter some time he lay down by it, and at last be-gan to clean it, for it was ver-y dir-ty. From that time Muff was quite fond of the kit-ten; he play-ed with it in the most gen-tle man-ner; it al-ways lay at night in his basket: they eat out of the same plate, and Muff would oft-en sit still, and let the kit-ten eat first as if he was a-fraid it would not have e-nough.

Ma-ry had an un-cle who was go-ing a great way off in a ship. He did not ex-pect to come back for three or four years; and when he said fare-well to Ma-ry he gave her a fine lock-et, with some of his hair in it and set round with gold and pearls. It was but a use-less pres-ent for such a lit-tle girl. Ma-ry tied it round her neck with a black rib-bon and tak-ing up her rope she be-gan to skip, but then the lock-et jump-ed up and down on her neck, and once hit her on the mouth. Ma-ry tied it tight-er, and then it made her too warm. "What shall I do with it?" said Ma-ry. "Oh! Muff shall wear the lock-et, and then I can al-ways see it." So she call-ed Muff, and tied the lock-et round his neck. Muff shook his head a-gain and a-gain; he rub-bed his paw o-ver his ear, he could not think what was the mat-ter with his neck; then as the lock-et hung down be-low his breast, he pat-ted it from side to side, first with one paw and then with the o-ther, which made Ma-ry laugh ve-ry much. Ma-ry's mam-ma was that day go-ing out to din-ner and while Ma-ry was laugh-ing to see Muff pat a-bout the lock-et, her mam-ma came in to kiss her be-fore she went out. See-ing Muff with the lock-et she told Ma-ry to take it from him as it would be spoil-ed by Muff, and it was too good a lock-et to be made a play-thing. It would be best, she said, to wrap it in pa-per till Ma-ry was old e-nough to wear it her-self. Ma-ry took off the lock-et from Muff's neck and mam-ma went a-way to pay her vis-it.

Aft-er din-ner Ma-ry wish-ed she could show the maids how pret-ty Muff look-ed when dress-ed in the lock-et, so she for-got to mind what her mam-ma had said, and a-gain put the lock-et round the cat's neck. Muff was soon tired of play-ing with it ; he then be-gan to bite it with his teeth, so Ma-ry tied it tight un-der his chin where he could not get at it to bite it, and she and the maids all laugh-ed to see what odd tricks he play-ed as he tried to get rid of a thing he was not used to, and which teas-ed him ve-ry much. At last some per-son came in whom Ma-ry was glad to see, and she for-got the cat and the lock-et.

That per-son gave her a new book, and she read the book till it was time to go to bed, and still she nev-er thought of the cat and her un-cle's pres-ent.

When Ma-ry got up the next morn-ing, Muff did not come to purr a-bout her feet as he used to do. Ma-ry went down-stairs, and there was no Muff in the par-lour. No one had seen Muff that day. Ma-ry went up-stairs into the bed-rooms and into the gar-rets and look-ed in-to the kit-chen and the cel-lars, and the wash-house and the brew-house but Muff was not to be found in any of these places. Ma-ry went sob-bing in-to the gar-den and call-ed *Muff ! Muff ! Muff !* but Muff was not to be found in the sum-mer house, or green-house, or coach-house or sta-ble.

When Ma-ry went back to the par-lour, her mam-ma ask-ed her if she had a-gain tied on the lock-et to Muff's neck ? Ma-ry blush-ed, but she al-ways told the truth, and she said, " Yes, mam-ma, I did."

LITTLE MARY.

"You did very wrong," said her mam-ma; "you see what mis-chiefs hap-pen when lit-tle girls will not o-bey their mam-mas or those who are wis-er than them-selves. Some bad people have found Muff out of doors and have sto-len him for the sake of the locket. The cat you lov-ed so well may be ill-used or ev-en kill-ed, and the lock-et is lost which your un-cle gave you to keep for his sake when he was go-ing a-way for man-y years and might per-haps nev-er see you a-gain."

Ma-ry was read-y to break her heart with grief. She had made her mam-ma an-gry, she had lost her un-cle's pres-ent; she had caus-ed poor Muff who had been Nurse Brown's cat, and who was so fond, so gen-tle and so good a cat, to be stol-en, per-haps starv-ed, or beat or kick-ed if not kill-ed for she could not sup-pose that an-y per-son who was so wick-ed as to steal Muff and the lock-et would use him well. Ma-ry's mam-ma sent to all the hous-es round a-bout to en-quire for Muff, but no news could be heard of him. One day, two days, three days pass-ed a-way and Muff was not found. " I shall nev-er, nev-er see him a-gain," said Ma-ry; "oh! that I had mind-ed what my mam-ma said to me—then poor Muff would have been sit-ting on his stool be-side me here, and I should have been good and hap-py."

At the end of the week a poor ragg-ed boy of the vill-age to whom Ma-ry had oft-en giv-en her cakes and her fruit, be-cause she had been told he was ver-y kind to his sick fa-ther and work-ed hard to get mon-ey for his mo-ther to buy bread for his lit-tle bro-thers and sis-ters, came with some-thing un-der his coat and asked to see Miss Ma-ry. Ma-ry's mam-ma told the ser-vant to bring Ro-bert (for that was the boy's name), in-to the par-lour. He came in and pull-ing off his cap and mak-ing his best bow he said "Miss, I have found your cat!"

Ma-ry jump-ed up, and so did her mam-ma but they

LITTLE MARY.

look-ed very sad when they saw poor Muff al-most starv-ed to death and so weak that when Ro-bert put him on the floor he could scarcely stand up-on his legs.

Ro-bert work-ed hard at a farm-house, and had been sent that day by his master to sweep out an old sta-ble which had a hay-loft o-ver it. While Ro-bert was sweep-ing the sta-ble he thought he heard a cat cry. He look-ed a-bout and saw no cat, but still he thought he heard it cry. So, at last, he climb-ed up and push-ed o-pen the door of the hay-loft, and there he saw poor Muff ly-ing on the ground, and faint-ly cry-ing *mew*, *mew*, just as if he were dy-ing. Ro-bert call-ed him by his name for he knew it was the cat that Nurse Brown had giv-en to Mary; but Muff was so weak he could not get up to come to him. Ro-bert had his din-ner in his pocket; it was only a small bit of brown bread and a lit-tle bot-tle of milk and water, for his pa-rents were ve-ry poor; but he had a kind heart, and he broke his bread in-to ve-ry small pieces and wet-ted it with the milk-and-water and put them bit by bit in-to Muff's mouth. When Muff had eat the bread he seem-ed bett-er and Ro-bert was so glad that he took him in his arms, jump-ed down from the hay-loft and ran as fast as he could to car-ry him home to Ma-ry. The black string was still round Muff's neck but the lock-et was gone, and the bad man who stole the lock-et must have shut the cat up in that empty hay-loft where but for Ro-bert he would have died of hun-ger.

With good care and good food Muff grew well and fat a-gain, and was as happy and as mer-ry as ever; and Ma-ry's mam-ma was so pleas-ed with Ro-bert's giv-ing up his own din-ner to feed a starv-ed cat that she said she was sure a kind boy would make a good man, and she sent him to school that he might learn to read and write. She gave him new and warm clothes, and was kind to his fa-ther and mo-ther, bro-thers and sis-ters, for his sake. Ma-ry lent Ro-bert all her books as soon as he had learnt to read, and she used to di-vide her mo-ney with him that he might buy o-ther books and o-ther play-things for his lit-tle sis-ters. She nev-er for-got that Ro-bert had sav-ed her dear Muff from death, and that it was the wis-est and best thing she could do ev-er aft-er to o-bey her mam-ma and nev-er to do an-y-thing which her mam-ma bid her not do.

EMILY BARTON.

[From *Mrs. Leicester's School: or The History of Several Young Ladies; related by themselves.* Fourth Edition. London : Printed for Mr. J. Godwin, at the Juvenile Library, No. 41 Skinner Street. 1814.]

WHEN I was a very young child, I remember residing with an uncle and aunt who live in ——shire. I think I remained there near a twelvemonth. I soon found that it was a very dull thing, to live in the country with little cousins who have a papa and mamma in the house, while my own dear papa and mamma were in London, many miles away.

I have heard my papa observe, girls who are not well managed are a most quarrelsome race of little people. My cousins very often quarrelled with me, and then they always said, "I will go and tell mamma, cousin Emily;" and then I used to be very disconsolate, because I had no mamma to complain to of my grievances.

Though I often thought of my papa and mamma, by de-grees the remembrance of their persons faded out of my mind.

EMILY BARTON.

One morning my uncle and aunt went abroad before breakfast, and took my cousins with them. They very often went out for whole days together, and left me at home. Sometimes they said it was because they could not take so many children; and sometimes they said it was because I was so shy, it was no amusement to me to go abroad.

That morning I was very solitary indeed, for they had even taken the dog Sancho with them, and I was very fond of him. I went all about the house and garden to look for him. Nobody could tell me where Sancho was, and then I went into the front-court and called "Sancho, Sancho." An old man that worked in the garden was there, and he said Sancho was gone with his master. O how sorry I was! I began to cry, for Sancho and I used to amuse ourselves for hours together when every body was gone out. I cried till I heard the mail coachman's horn, and then I ran to the gate to see the mailcoach go past. It stopped before our gate, and a gentleman got out; and the moment he saw me he took me in his arms and kissed me, and said I was Emily Barton, and asked me why the tears were on my little pale cheeks; and I told him the cause of my distress. The old man asked him to walk into the house, and was going to call one of the servants; but the gentleman would not let him, and he said, " Go on with your work, I want to talk to this little girl before I go into the house." Then he sat down on a bench which was in the court, and asked me many questions; and I told him all my little troubles, for he was such a goodnatured-looking gentleman that I prattled very freely to him. Then he called to the old man, and desired him to fetch a post-chaise. The old man looked in a sad fright, and said, " O Sir, I hope you are not going to take the child away." The gentleman threw out a small card, and bid him give that to his master, and calling to the post-boy to drive on, we lost sight of the old man in a minute.

The gentleman laughed very much, and said, "We have frightened the old man, he thinks I am going to run away with you ; " and I laughed, and thought it a very good joke ; and he said, " So you tell me you are very shy ; " and I replied, " Yes, sir, I am, before strangers : " he said; " So I perceive you are," and then he laughed again, and I laughed, though I did not know why. We had such a merry ride, laughing all the way at one thing or another, till we came to a town where the chaise stopped, and he ordered some breakfast. When I got out I began to shiver a little ; for it was the latter end of autumn, the leaves were falling off the trees, and the air blew very cold. Then he desired a waiter to go and order a straw-hat, and a little warm coat for me ; and when the milliner came, he told her he had stolen a little heiress, and we were going to Gretna Green in such a hurry that the young lady had no time to put on her bonnet before she came out. The milliner said I was a pretty little heiress, and she wished us a pleasant journey. When we had breakfasted, and I was equipped in my new coat and bonnet, I jumped into the chaise again, as warm and as lively as a little bird.

When it grew dark, we entered a large city; the chaise began to roll over the stones, and I saw the lamps ranged along London streets.

I was sorry when the chaise stopped, and I could no longer look at the brilliant rows of lighted lamps.

Taken away by a stranger under pretence of a short ride, and brought quite to London, do you not expect some perilous end of this adventure ? Ah ! it was my papa himself, though I did not know who he was, till after he had put me into my mamma's arms, and told her how he had run away with his own little daughter. " It is your papa, my dear, that has brought you to your own home." "This is your mamma, my love," they both exclaimed at once. Mamma cried for joy to see me, and she wept again when she heard my papa tell what a neglected child I had been at my uncle's. This he had found out, he said, by my own innocent prattle.

My mamma ordered tea. Whenever I happen to like my tea very much, I always think of the delicious cup of tea mamma gave us after our journey. I think I see the urn smoking before me now, and papa wheeling the sofa round, that I might sit between them at the table. I thought to myself, "O dear, my cousins' papa and mamma are not to be compared to mine."

Papa said, "What makes you bridle and simper so, Emily?" Then I told him all that was in my mind. Papa asked if I did not think him as pretty as I did mamma. I could not say much for his beauty, but I told him he was a much finer gentleman than my uncle, and that I liked him the first moment I saw him, because he looked so good-natured. He said, "Well then, he must be content with that half praise; but he had always thought himself very handsome." "O dear!" said I, and fell a-laughing, till I spilt my tea, and mamma called me Little awkward girl.

The next morning my papa was going to the Bank to receive some money, and he took mamma and me with him, that I might have a ride through London streets. Every one that has been in London must have seen the Bank, and therefore you may imagine what an effect the fine large rooms, and the bustle and confusion of people had on me, who was grown such a little wondering rustic, that the crowded streets and the fine shops alone, kept me in continual admiration.

As we were returning home down Cheapside, papa said, "Emily shall take home some little books. Shall we order the coachman to the corner of St. Paul's Churchyard, or shall we go to the Juvenile Library in Skinner Street?" Mamma said she would go to Skinner Street, for she wanted to look at the new buildings there. Papa bought me seven new books, and the lady in the shop persuaded him to take more, but mamma said that was quite enough at present.

We went home by Ludgate-hill, because mamma wanted to buy something there; and while she went into a shop, papa heard me read in one of my new books, and he said he was glad to find I could read so well; for I had forgot to tell him my aunt used to hear me read every day.

My papa stopped the coach opposite to St. Dunstan's Church, that I might see the great iron figures strike upon the bell, to give notice that it was a quarter of an hour past two. We waited some time that I might see this sight, but just at the moment they were striking, I happened to be looking at a toy-shop that was on the other side of the way, and unluckily missed it. Papa said, " Never mind: we will go into the toy-shop, and I dare say we shall find something that will console you for your disappointment."

A large wax doll, a baby-house completely furnished, and several other beautiful toys, were bought for me. My mamma invited a little girl to spend a few days with me, to see, as she has since told me, if I should not be liable to fall into the same error from which I had suffered so much at my uncle's.

As my mamma had feared, so the event proved; for I quickly adopted my cousins' selfish ideas, and gave the young lady notice that they were my own playthings, and she must not amuse herself with them any longer than I permitted her.

A lady was sitting with mamma, and mamma said, "I believe I must pardon you this once, but I hope never to see such a thing again. This lady is Miss Frederica's mamma, and I am quite ashamed that she should be witness to your inhospitality to her daughter, particularly as she was so kind to come on purpose to invite you to a share in her *own* private box at the theatre this evening. Her carriage is waiting at the door to take us, but how can we accept of the invitation after what has happened?" The lady begged it might all be forgotten; and mamma consented that I should go. I had never seen a play; but when I got there, after the curtain drew up, I looked up towards the galleries, and down into the pit, and into all the boxes, and then I knew what a pretty sight it was to see a number of happy faces.

Just as the coach stopped, Miss Frederica said, "Will you be friends with me, Emily?" and I replied, "Yes, if you please, Frederica;" and we went hand and hand together into the house.

I shall never forget how delighted I was at the first sight of the house. My little friend and I were placed together in the front, while our mammas retired to the back part of the box to chat by themselves, for they had been so kind as to come very early, that I might look about me before the performance began.

She gave me a charming description of the king and queen at the play, and shewed me where they sate, and told me how the princesses were dressed. It was a pretty sight to see the remainder of the candles lighted; and so it was to see the musicians come up from under the stage. I admired the music very much, and I asked if that was the play. Frederica laughed at my ignorance, and then she told me, when the play began, the green curtain would draw up to the sound of soft music, and I should hear a lady dressed in black say,

"Music hath charms to soothe a savage breast:"

and those were the very first words the actress, whose name was Almeria, spoke. When the curtain began to draw up and I saw the bottom of her black petticoat, and heard the soft music, what an agitation I was in! But before that we had long to wait. Frederica told me we should wait till all the dress boxes were full, and then the lights would pop up under the orchestra; the second music would play, and then the play would begin.

The play was the Mourning Bride. It was a very moving tragedy; and after that when the curtain dropt, and I thought it was all over, I saw the most diverting pantomime that ever was seen.

A

JOURNEY TO LONDON;

OR, THE

DISAPPOINTMENTS OF A WEEK.

London:

Published by GEORGE WALKER, 106 *Great*

Portland Street ;

and sold by all other booksellers.

1815.

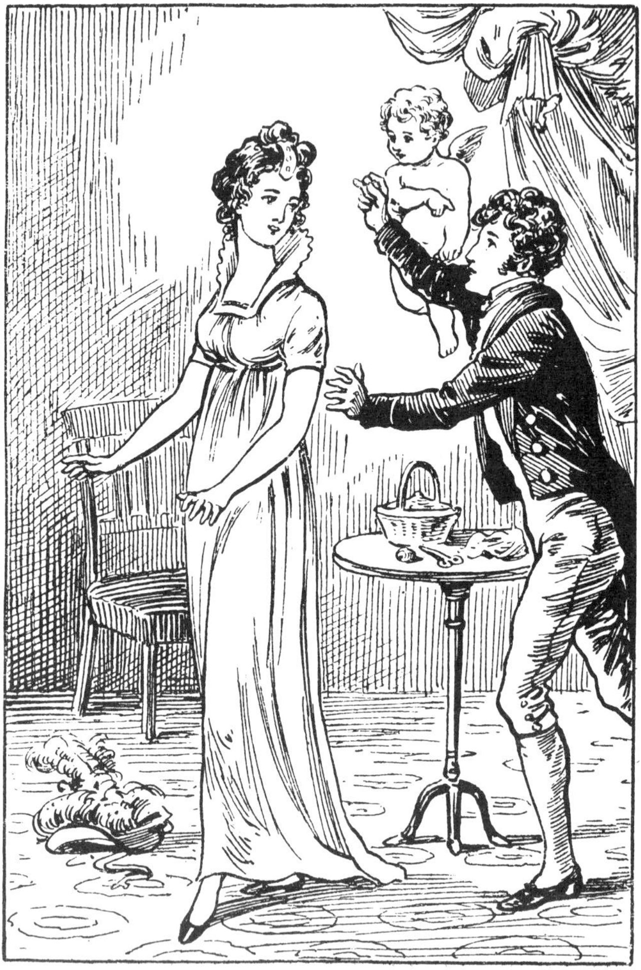

A JOURNEY TO LONDON.

A JOURNEY TO LONDON.

MRS. SUMMERS accompanied the two children to London in the stage, a journey of only forty miles, which was easily performed in one day. They set off in excellent spirits, and were highly delighted with the various prospects and objects along the road; amusing the rest of the passengers with

their remarks, and their expectations of what they should do and see in London. Though George wished the journey would last a week, they had not, however, travelled more than two hours before the closeness and motion of the coach turned them both sick; after which Ann laid down and fell fast asleep, and George having lost his spirits sat like a mope in a corner for the rest of the day. When they quitted the stage they were as glad to be released as they had been to enter it; and a large currant pie their Aunt Brown had provided for their supper soon made them forget their sufferings in the journey.

As they passed along Swallow Street they were alarmed by a prodigious uproar and shouting behind them of "Mad bull, mad bull!" They had not time to recover their surprise when the mob began to rush pell-mell round the corner, urging forward a poor over-driven ox, which could scarce stand for fatigue and fright. Not less than five hundred people were in full pursuit, headed by a band of butchers, labourers and boys, who took more delight in the mischief and fear they caused to the passengers than even in the sufferings of the poor beast, whom the butchers had goaded into a fever: women and children ran screaming up to the sides of the houses and into the shops; many had their clothes torn by the rush of the mob. Mrs. Brown seized George's hand, whilst Ann clung to her mother. They ran to get into a shop, but a great butcher's dog, covered with mud and animated by his master to the hunt, rushed forward, regardless of what it ran against, knocked down poor George and his Aunt, who were, however, immediately raised by some very well-dressed men in the stile of grooms who, notwithstanding they were turned round by the pressure of the mob, conducted Mrs. Brown and George to the door of a shop and then mingled with the throng now nearly passed.

Both George and his Aunt had been trod upon, and Mrs. Brown had suffered much in her dress, which was torn in a way which seemed purposely done; but when they recovered from their first fright, George missed his parcel of books

A JOURNEY TO LONDON.

and ran into the street to find them, but that was useless; he however saw his mother coming along with little Ann crying for the loss of him, for they had been parted by the mob and luckily got into a shop. They hastened to join Mrs. Brown whom they found lamenting the loss of her gold watch which there was no doubt had been taken by those officious gentlemen who assisted them, and who are always to be found in this sort of mobs, set on foot for the sole purpose of mischief: nor is it uncommon for these outrages of public peace and safety to be continued through half the town for hours, to the distress of thousands of women and children, and often producing the most serious accidents. . . .

As it is a fine day we will go to St. Paul's Cathedral. Being dressed and ready, Betty was called to fetch a coach —but not coming immediately, George, impatient as usual to be moving, proposed to call one himself, as the coach-stand was at the end of the street, and Ann joined her request to go too. After some time Mrs. Brown not hearing a coach coming and thinking the children stayed too long, looked out at the window, and seeing a little crowd at a distance, made no doubt they had met with some misfortune, and away she flew to see what could be the matter.

She found Ann standing crying, with her frock covered with mud, and George fighting with a boy a head taller than himself, while several idle fellows were urging them on, and almost forcing them to fight, instead of interposing and protecting the injured party. Mrs. Brown immediately went between the two combatants, and a gentleman coming out of the house interposed, or most probably she would have been insulted for interrupting the diversion of the mob.

"How did all this happen?" said Mrs. Brown.

"This boy," said George, "and another that is run away,

came along—this boy with a whip in his hand all over mud, and the other driving a hoop: we tried to get out of the way by crossing from side to side of the pavement; but he would drive his hoop against Ann, on purpose to spoil her clothes. I told him he was a very wicked boy for doing it, and the other gave me a cut in the face with his dirty whip, which made me very angry, and I gave him a punch; two men going by, cried out, 'that's right, young one, fight him! fight him!' and taking my arm they held me up to him, so I was obliged to fight."

As the mob always highly enjoy the distress of people who have been dirtied either by accident or design, not a few observations of wit were passed on little master and miss as their aunt hurried them, crying, home; and the little miscreant who had so grossly insulted them, was the loudest in shouting after them.

This misfortune completely interrupted the arrangements of the day, and to entertain them, Mrs. Brown sat down to the pianoforte which she played extremely well.

Little Ann said she should like to learn, and that she was to begin very soon, for her mamma had taught her the keys.

"That is well thought of," said Mrs. Summers, "we must have some music; and as our journey into the city is spoiled for to-day we will go and buy some."

"The best shop that I know," said Mrs. Brown, "is at Walker's in Great Portland Street, where you have all sorts of divertimentos for young performers."

* * * * * *

Thursday morning being remarkably fine it was determined to visit the Tower.

"Now we are going to see living lions, tygers, and other savage animals, and you must take care not to approach their dens, nor put your hands beyond the rail set up to keep incautious people at a distance. Many very shocking

A JOURNEY TO LONDON.

accidents have happened by people teazing the animals out of the keeper's sight."

. . . "I wonder what curiosity there is in that large dog with the flattish head," said George: "give me a biscuit, Aunt, for he looks hungry."

"That dog as you call him," said the keeper, "is a savage and fierce wolf; he looks so quiet only to catch you within reach of a snap: the wolf is a species of the dog, as the tiger is of the cat—all their habits, actions, and cries are similar. Take care of that white bear; he is so fierce that even looking at him puts him in a rage—his eyes flash—he shews his teeth and flies at the rails of his cage to get at you. This is an hyaena, from the interior of Africa; he is an animal never known to be tamed; he inhabits hot and desert climates, and destined by nature to prevent putrefaction from dead animals in those countries where all flesh turns to corruption in a few hours after death; he delights in putrid substances, and will tear open graves to devour the bodies; his eye is remarkably sly, and the outline of his figure is disgusting, though not so much so as that of the vulture, a bird whose propensities are similar, and which can go farther in search of the carrion, which it smells in the wind."

From the Tower they went to a pastrycook's in Cornhill for refreshments; their journey having given them good appetites. Whilst they sat in the shop they were alarmed by loud screams, and running to the door they saw a poor boy taken from behind a hackney coach with one of his arms torn and mangled in a dreadful manner; he was carried to St. Bartholomew's Hospital. They learned that this thoughtless boy, who had excellent legs to carry him, got up behind a coach, as foolish boys often do. The coachman, not liking to carry any that did not pay him, and finding the boy seated behind, without calling to him to get

A JOURNEY TO LONDON.

down as a man of any humanity would, began to lash him most savagely with his whip, cutting him over the face without mercy; this flurried the boy so much that in his haste to descend his arm slipped between the spring and the spokes of the wheel, and he would have been killed on the spot if a gentleman had not seized the horses and stopped them.

As they came up Holborn, George walked on a little way leading his sister Ann, though with difficulty they made their way through the crowds. Some fine pictures in a window were an irresistible attraction; and having first looked to see that there were no rails to tumble over, they ventured to admire the prints. A mischievous dirty vagabond who was also looking at the pictures very intently, slyly watching an opportunity for mischief, suddenly dashed George's head against the glass (see frontispiece) which was shivered to pieces; he was across the street in a minute, and the two ladies were too much engaged with the accident to pursue him, so that he escaped without the punishment he deserved.

Fortunately George's hat saved his head, or he might have been dangerously wounded with the glass; indeed had his face been dashed against the window, he might have been blinded or disfigured for life. Mrs. Summers paid for the window.

"The mischief of boys in the streets," said Mrs. Brown, "is truly insufferable, and really ought to be attended to by a judicious police. Thousands of errand boys from the nature of their employ, are the greater part of their time in the street, and they spread corruption amongst each other. All sorts of mischief and petty outrages they inflict upon women and children, which would make a very extensive catalogue of crimes: little children, clean and going to school, are the particular objects of their power—dirtying

A JOURNEY TO LONDON.

their clothes, striking them and teazing them in various ways, so that it is quite unsafe to let children go out without attendants. It is the duty of every man who sees any of these petty outrages, to interfere and punish the offender.

"I would have the beadles disperse the knots of idle boys which we see gambling, and wasting their master's time in the streets; it is in these assemblies they teach each other every sort of vice—swearing, lying, cheating, disobedience and insolence to parents and masters. These nests of young gamblers are more pernicious in society than those higher meetings of gamblers which are sought after by the police. No boy who idles his time in the streets playing with such characters, can be a good servant; he is robbing his master by wasting the time for which he receives victuals and wages, and those idle habits but too commonly attend him in every stage of life."

These reflections Mrs. Summers made upon the very serious mischief they had met; and little Ann was so much frightened that when she saw a dirty boy coming near her, she shrank to her aunt or mother for protection.

They had had enough of sights for that day, and felt not a little comfortable when they reached Mrs. Brown's.

* * * * * *

"Hark, I think the guns are firing—there must be good news—Lord Wellington I suppose has again beaten the French."

The guns were indeed firing; they proclaimed the defeat of the French by the great Wellington and his brave companions. The visit to the Panorama was forgot in the general joy of the victory, and the preparations for a grand illumination at night.

* * * * * *

"Ah," said George, "let me tell you of a very sad accident which happened to myself. I was on a visit to

Farmer Hall's: in the yard where they kept their wood for winter was a deep well with a folding-door over it; I had never seen a well of that sort and I wanted to know what was under the trap-doors. I raised up the trap by the ring with great difficulty, and the weight of it in going down drew me over and I fell into the well. The water and mud did not reach above half way to my mouth or I should have been drowned, for it was a great while before I could make anybody hear where I was and they then put down a ladder and took me up."

"That providential escape," said Mrs. Summers, "always makes me shudder. If any one circumstance had varied, you would certainly have been lost: if there had been foul air in the well; if the water had only been a foot deeper; if you had struck the side in falling; if you had fallen upon your head; if the trap-door had shut over you, you would certainly have been lost; and as long as you live never forget that God who protected you when none else could have changed one circumstance in the accident."

They had tea early, that they might prepare for their excursion in the evening.

It was proposed to take a coach, but Mrs. Brown objected to it, because they would be hours in creeping along the streets, and open to all the mischiefs of the mob, who amuse themselves with throwing squibs into carriages where they see ladies and children, frequently setting their clothes on fire and burning them in a most barbarous manner.

They proceeded to the bottom of Bond Street with much difficulty, but there the carriages entirely cut off the passage into St. James's Street, and rendered it dangerous to turn in any direction. Poor Ann was so pressed and squeezed that she begged to return; but this was as difficult as to go on. The people took little regard of children, and they were repeatedly trod upon; so that Ann began to cry and George begged to go home. After many efforts, they at length cleared the corner into Piccadilly, and by creeping under the noses of the horses they got into St. James's Street. Could they have enjoyed the sight free from danger they would have been extremely delighted with the profusion of lamps in all sorts of devices which the subscription houses displayed. On the south side of Pall Mall they contrived by taking time and caution, to approach within view of the superb decorations of Carlton House, where thousands of lamps formed a mass of light almost too brilliant for the eyes to look at: here the Prince Regent, to please the public, had spared no expense; and a company of artillerymen, with field-pieces on the top of the colonnade, highly delighted the people.

They went into St. James's Square, where there was more room; and they were very much pleased with Lord Castlereagh's house, particularly as they could stand to admire it; but they had not stood many minutes before a gentleman's servant, delighted with an opportunity of displaying his courage, slyly slipped behind little Ann and her mother, and clapping a blunderbuss close behind them, fired it off.

Mrs. Summers, fortunately, was not a nervous woman, or the consequences might have been fatal. She, however, turned sick with the fright, and little Ann screamed so that she could not be pacified, and was so deafened with the stunning noise that she did not hear for some hours afterwards. The hero of this exploit enjoyed the terror he had caused, and Mr. Wilmot in vain attempted to seize him, as he escaped in the mob. The visible consternation of the party, instead of exciting pity, only spirited the mischievous to hunt them with squibs, from which they ran as fast as possible, and were only rescued by the higher gratification which these people found in the shrieks of a young woman

A JOURNEY TO LONDON.

whose clothes they had set on fire with a squib, and who was so seriously burnt as to be carried to an hospital.

* * * * * *

"If we go to the play," said Mrs. Summers, on Saturday, "I should like to know what is to be performed."

"I can run and let you know in a minute," said Ann. "I know where I saw the play-bills stuck in a shop window; it does not rain now, and it is only down Rathbone Place into Oxford Street."

Ann, in high spirits, set off upon her commission, but she had not got half way down Rathbone Place when she was overtaken by a plain-dressed woman, who cried out when she came up to her—

"Dear me, what a beautiful child! Sure my pretty miss you are some nobleman's daughter; you are as handsome as an angel and dressed like a cherub: is not your father a Lord?"

"No," replied Ann, simply, "my papa is a country gentleman, and my aunt is Mrs. Brown."

"And are you indeed Mrs. Brown's niece?" said the deceitful hypocrite. "Come, my darling, and let me kiss you: I am going to drink tea with your Aunt this very afternoon. I am only going first to the jeweller's to buy a necklace for a little niece of mine—will you go along with me? I should like one the same pattern as that cornelian one you have about your neck."

"I can't go with you," said Ann; "I am going to see what the play is to-night, and must not stop, or my mother and aunt will be frightened."

"Aye, you are a good child now," replied the impostor; "never stop on your errands, my dear; I shall tell your Aunt when I come this afternoon, what an obedient little lady you are—yet I should like to have just such a necklace for my niece. She is a pretty girl, though not so pretty as

A JOURNEY TO LONDON.

you; near about your size," continued she, putting her hands round Ann's neck, and unclasping a fine cornelian necklace with a gold snap; "I wonder, my dear, you had not lost it—the snap is broke; well, but let me consider—how lucky I am going to the jeweller's—I will take your necklace and get it mended, match one like it for my niece, and bring it back when I go to tea. Tell your Aunt Brown that Mrs. Fertile has got it. Good-bye, my sweet little poppet."

Poor Ann was in too much confusion to know how to act; she did not like the woman's taking her necklace and yet she did not dare refuse her; she made haste to learn the name of the play—and when she arrived at home the first question she asked was if her Aunt knew a Mrs. Fertile that was to come there to tea that afternoon.

Her Aunt replied that she knew no such person, nor was anyone coming to tea that day. Poor Ann burst into tears.

"Then Mrs. Fertile told a story," cried she, "and I shall never get my necklace again."

"You foolish child," cried Mrs. Summers, "could anything be more stupid than to suffer a strange woman that you did not know, to take your necklace?—Have I not told you that such women watch for children, and by all manners of lies decoy them into some dark court and strip them?"

"Ha! ha! ha!" said George, "what a goose you must have been: do you think I should have been cheated in that manner? Nobody should cheat me; poor Ann!"

"You have no necklace to lose," said Ann. "I am sure I could not help it."

* * * * * *

"Well," said Mrs. Brown, "George shall go the baker's just round the corner and ask him the name of the play which Ann has forgotten—and at the same time bring me change for a pound note, as I do not like changing with coachmen, who frequently give bad money, particularly to ladies."

George could not refrain from whispering to Ann, as he passed her, that if he saw Mrs. Fertile with her necklace he would get it from her.

"Take care of yourself," said Ann.

George was so careful of the one-pound note that he kept his hand in his pocket with it all the way: he learnt the name of the play and received the change, but just as he turned the corner of Percy Street from Tottenham Court Road, a man came running up to him—

"Stop! stop!" said he—"you are the little boy my master gave the silver to just now; he does not like the note —here it is—if you have not got another you must give me the silver and get this changed."

The man held the note to him, which George believed to be the same he had given to the baker, and without any suspicion immediately returned the silver, though he had reflection enough to ask, if he brought another note, if they would not then give him the change?

"To be sure," replied the man, "I think myself it is a very good note, but master is very particular."

George ran home with the note in his hand, which he gave to his Aunt, saying it was a bad one.

"A bad one indeed, child," said Mrs. Brown, "this a decoy note for *one penny;* how came you by it? I gave you a one-pound note."

George was ready to drop with vexation and shame; but he told the whole story just as it happened—and there was no doubt he had been cheated by one of those sharpers who are too idle to work and live by cheating others.

"But how could he know I had changed a one-pound note?" said George; "I am sure I kept my hand in my pocket all the way I went, and held the note tight."

A JOURNEY TO LONDON.

"Most likely," replied his Aunt, "he judged you had something of value by that very action—and he followed you to the baker's, where he had seen your business through the window: those tricks are practised every day in every possible form to suit the circumstances of the moment. We will, however, send to the baker to see if he can describe the man. Let it be a warning to you never to listen to any kind of story from strangers in the streets—and never to laugh at the misfortunes of others, for the next moment you may be in the same case, or worse."

As was to be expected the baker could give them no information. To relieve them both from their vexation, their Aunt hastened their preparation for the play; and the town being all alive with the victory, and a new little piece being brought forward for the occasion, it was necessary to go early to the play; but though they were there almost as soon as the doors were open, the pit was so full it was with difficulty they got any place to sit down in, and that quite at the edge of the seats, where they were incommoded the whole evening by those who were obliged to stand.

The performance and performers could not but entertain those who had never seen a play; it was Othello—and George observed that it was a very stupid and savage action of the ranting fool of a black to murder a lady for a pocket-handkerchief not half so good as the shawl his Aunt lost the night before in the mob. They were very much annoyed by the pelting of orange-peel and nut-shells from the gallery; and a new bonnet which Aunt had on was quite spoilt by the stains of orange, and looking up once to see who had thrown it, she received a severe blow in the face with a piece of apple.

"It is a very vexatious thing," said Mrs. Brown, "that every dirty apprentice boy or servant can, by paying a shilling, enjoy the liberty of pelting their superiors for a whole evening. I am astonished such are tolerated ; for if you are well dressed you sit in pain for your clothes—and if you look up to see who are thus amusing themselves, you may receive a very unwelcome blow in the face."

When they reached home and sat down to supper, Mrs. Brown asked George how he liked the play.

"It's just like everything else, Aunt," said George ; "I don't know a single thing we have seen, but one way or other we have been disappointed. I am quite tired of London."

THE KIDNAPPED CHILD.

[From *Tales of The Hermitage; written for the Instruction and Amusement of the Rising Generation.* A New Edition. London : J. Harris, corner of St. Paul's Churchyard. 1815.]

IN a beautiful villa, on the banks of the Medway, resided a gentleman whose name was Darnley, who had during the early part of life, filled a post of some importance about the Court, and even in its decline preserved that elegance of manners which so peculiarly marks a finished gentleman.

It was Mr. Darnley's wish that the young folks should rise early, and take a long walk every morning before breakfast, but they were strictly ordered never to go beyond their own grounds, unless accompanied. This order they had frequently endeavoured to persuade Nurse Chapman to disregard ; but faithful to the trust reposed in her, she always resisted their urgent entreaties.

Mr. Darnley went away to Rochester, and next morning the poor woman found herself incapable of rising at the accustomed hour. The children, however, were dressed

THE KIDNAPPED CHILD.

for walking and the nursemaid charged not to go beyond the shrubbery and they all sallied out in high humour.

"Now Susan," said Sophia (as soon as they entered the garden) "this is the only opportunity you may ever have of obliging us: do let us walk to the village, and then you know you can call and see your father and mother."

"La, Miss!" replied the girl, "why you know 'tis as

much as my place is worth if Nurse Chapman should find it out."

"*Find it out, indeed*," said Amanda; "how do you think she is to find it out. Come, do let us go, there's a dear good creature."—"Yes, dear, dear Susan, do let us go," said Eliza (skipping on before them) "and I'll shew you the way, for I walked there last summer with papa."

THE KIDNAPPED CHILD.

Whether it was the wish of obliging the young ladies, or the desire of seeing her parents, I cannot pretend to say; but in a luckless hour Susan yielded and the party soon reached the village.

Susan's mother was delighted at seeing her, and highly honoured by the young ladies' presence.

"Oh, sweet, dear creatures!" said the old woman, "I must get something for them to eat after their long walk, and my oven's quite hot, and I can bake them a little cake in a quarter of an hour, and I'll milk Jenny in ten minutes." The temptation of her hot cake and new milk was not to be withstood; and Susan began taking down some smart china cups which were arranged in form upon the mantelpiece, and carefully dusted them for the young ladies' use.

Eliza followed the old woman into the cow-house and began asking a thousand questions, when her attention was suddenly attracted by the appearance of a tame lamb who went bleating up to its mistress with a view of asking for its accustomed breakfast.

"You must wait a little, Billy," said the woman, "and let your betters be served before you—don't you see that we have got gentlefolks to breakfast with us this morning?"

Eliza was so delighted with the beauty of the little animal that she wanted to kiss it, and attempted to restrain it for that purpose, whilst Billy, ungrateful for her intended kindness, gave a sudden spring and frisked away. Eliza followed in hopes of being able to catch him, but he ran baaing along into the high road.

A woman whose appearance was descriptive of poverty, but whose smiling countenance indicated good nature, at that moment happened to pass, and accosting Eliza in a tone of familiarity said, "That's not half such a pretty lamb, Miss, as I have got at home and not a quarter so tame."

THE KIDNAPPED CHILD.

" Oh, the pretty creature !" replied Eliza, " how I should like to see it ! "

"Well, come along with me, Miss, for I only lives just across the next field, but you must run as fast as you can, because my husband is going to work, and he generally takes Bob with him."

" Well, make haste then," said Eliza, " for I must not stay half a minute."

" Give me your hand, Miss," replied the woman, "for we can run faster together, but there goes my husband, I declare ; and there's Bob as usual skipping on before."

" Where, where ?" exclaimed Eliza, stretching her little neck as far as she possibly could, to see if she could discern the lamb.

" You are not tall enough," said the artful creature, " but let me lift you up, Miss, and then I dare say you'll see them," and instantly catching her up she cried : " Look directly towards the steeple, Miss, but I'll run with you in my arms, and I warrant we'll soon overtake them."

Eliza looked, but looked in vain ; and perceiving the woman had soon carried her out of sight of the cottage begged she would set her down as she dare not go any farther.

The vile creature was absolutely incapable of replying, for her breath was nearly exhausted by the rapidity of the motion, and Eliza continued entreating her to stop, and struggled violently to elude her grasp. At length after a quarter of an hour's exertion, the woman found herself incapable of proceeding, stopped suddenly, sat down on a bank, keeping tight hold of Eliza's arms, who cried dreadfully, and besought her to let her go.

" Let you go ! " she replied, " what, after all the plague I've had to knap you ? "

" Oh, my sisters ! my sisters ! let me go to my sisters," cried the child.

THE KIDNAPPED CHILD.

"I'll find plenty of sisters for you, in a few days," said the vile creature, "but they won't know you in them there fine clothes, so let's pull them off in a minute, and then we'll have another race after Bob."—So saying she stripped off the white frock, hat and tippet; the rest of the things shared the same fate, and she was compelled to put on some old rags which the inhuman creature took out of a bag which she carried under her petticoat; then taking a bottle of liquid from the same place, she instantly began washing poor Eliza's face with it, and notwithstanding all her remonstrances, cut her beautiful hair close to her head. Thus metamorphosed it would have been impossible even for Mr. Darnley to have known his child, and they proceeded onward until her little legs would carry her no farther.

At this period they were overtaken by the Canterbury waggon, and for a mere trifle the driver consented to let them ride to London. Eliza's tears continued to flow, but she dared not utter a complaint, as her inhuman companion protested she would break every bone in her skin if she ventured to make the least noise.

When they arrived in town she was dragged (for to walk she was unable) to a miserable hole down several steps, where they gave her some bread and butter to eat, and then desired her to go to bed. The bed, if such it might be called, was little else but a bundle of rags thrown into a corner of the room with a dirty blanket spread across it, and there she was left by the inhuman woman to mourn her misfortune, and to lament having disregarded her papa's injunctions. The next morning she was forced to rise the moment it was light, and to walk as far as her little legs would carry her before they stopped anywhere to take refreshment. The second night was passed in a barn, and about five o'clock the third afternoon they knocked at the

THE KIDNAPPED CHILD.

door of a neat looking cottage where nine or ten children were sitting in a little room making lace.

"Why, Peggy," said the woman, as she opened the door, "I thought you would never have comed again! however, I see you have got me a hand at last, and I'm enough in wants of her: for two of my brats have thought proper to fall sick, and I've more to do than ever I had in my life." On the following day Eliza's filthy clothes were all taken off, and she was dressed in a tidy brown stuff gown, a nice clean round-eared cap, and a little coloured bib and apron; and she was ordered, if any person asked her name, to say it was *Biddy Bullen*, and that she was niece to the woman who employed her. The severity with which all this wretch's commands were enforced wholly prevented any of the helpless victims who were under her protection from daring to disobey them; and though most of them were placed under her care by the same vile agent who had decoyed Eliza, yet they were all tutored to relate similar untruths.

While the family at Darnley Hall were a prey to unavailing sorrow, the lovely little girl who had occasioned it was beginning to get more reconciled to the cruelty of her destiny. She had acquired such a degree of skill in the art of lacemaking (which was the business her employer followed) as generally to be able to perform the tasks which were allotted her; and if it so happened she was incapable of doing it, Sally Butchell, a child about two years older than herself, of whom she was very fond, was always kind enough to complete it for her.

The cottage in which the vile Mrs. Bullen resided, was situated about a quarter of a mile from High Wycombe; and whenever she was obliged to go to that place either to purchase necessaries or to dispose of her goods, she always went either before her family was up or after they had retired to rest, locking the door constantly after her, and putting the key in her pocket, so that the poor little souls had no opportunity of telling their misfortune to any human creature.

One intensely hot afternoon in the month of August, as the children were sitting hard at work with the door open for the sake of air, an elderly lady and gentleman walked up to it, and begged to be accommodated with a seat, informing Mrs. Bullen their carriage had broke down about a mile distant, and they had been obliged to walk in the heat of the sun.

The appearance of so many children, all industriously employed, was a sight peculiarly pleasing to the liberally minded Mrs. Montague, and she immediately began asking questions about them; but there was something of confusion in her manner of replying that called forth Mrs. Montague's surprise and astonishment.

"They really are lovely children, my dear," said she, turning to Mr. Montague, who had stood at the door watching the approach of the carriage, which he perceived coming forward: "and as to that little creature with the mole under her left eye, I declare I think her a perfect beauty." Mr. Montague turned his head, and regarded Eliza with a look that at once proved that his sentiments corresponded with those of his lady.—"What is your name, my love?" said he in a tone of kindness which poor Eliza had long been a stranger to. The child coloured like scarlet, and looked immediately at her inhuman employer, who, catching the contagion, replied with evident marks of confusion—"Her name is Biddy Bullen, Sir: she's my niece; but 'tis a poor timid little fool, and is always in a fright when gentlefolks happen to speak to her: go Biddy," she continued, "go up into my bedroom, and wind that thread which you'll find upon the reel."

THE KIDNAPPED CHILD.

"You should try to conquer that timidity," said Mr. Montague, "by making her answer every stranger who speaks to her, but by taking that office upon yourself you absolutely encourage the shyness you complain of. Come hither, my little girl," continued he, observing she was retiring upstairs, "and tell me boldly what your name is."

Encouraged by the kindness of Mr. Montague's address, the agitated child obeyed the summons, although Mrs. Bullen attempted to frown her into resistance. "Well," continued the old gentleman, patting her on the cheek, "and where did you get that pretty mole?"

"My mamma gave it me, sir," replied the blushing child, "but I did not see her do it, because Nurse Chapman told me she went to Heaven as soon as I was born."

"Your mamma! and what was your mamma's name!" said Mr. Montague.

"*Darnley*, sir," and suddenly recollecting the lesson that had been taught her, "but my name is Biddy Bullen, and that is my aunt."

"*Darnley!*" exclaimed Mrs. Montague. "The very child that has been for these twelve months past advertised in all the papers," then turning to convince herself of the fact, "and the very mole confirms it!"

Mr. Montague immediately attempted to secure the woman, but her activity eluded his grasp, and darting out at the back door she was out of sight in a few moments.

"*Is she really gone?* Is she really gone?" all the little voices at once demanded; and upon Mr. Montague assuring them that she was really *gone for ever*, their joy broke out in a thousand different ways—some cried—some laughed—and others jumped. In short, there never was a scene more completely calculated to interest the feelings of a benevolent heart.

Mr. Montague's carriage at this period arrived, and the

THE KIDNAPPED CHILD.

footman was desired to fetch a magistrate from Wycombe, whilst the worthy clergyman resolved to remain there until his arrival, and began questioning all the children. Two had been there from so early a period that they could give no account of their name or origin; but all the rest were so clear in their description that the benevolent Mr. Montague had no doubt of being able to restore them to their afflicted parents.

The magistrate soon arrived, attended by the worthy rector of the place, who hearing from Mr. Montague's servant that a child had been stolen came with an intent of offering his services. All but Eliza were immediately put under his protection, but Mrs. Montague was so anxious she should be their earliest care, that she begged her husband to order a post-chaise immediately and set off for town. This request was willingly complied with, and by three o'clock the next afternoon the party arrived at Darnley Hall.

The aunt was standing at the window when the carriage stopped, and looking earnestly at her niece suddenly exclaimed, in a tone of rapture, "My child! My child! My lost Eliza!"

Mr. Darnley, who was reading, sprang from his seat, and flew to the door in an extasy of joy; in less than a minute he returned, folding his Eliza to his throbbing heart. The joyful intelligence ran through the house, and the other children impatiently flew to this scene of transport. To describe their feelings, or express their felicity, would require the aid of the most descriptive pen, and even then would be but faintly told; and therefore had much better be passed over.

From that moment the children unanimously agreed strictly to attend to their father's orders, and never in the slightest instance act in opposition to his will.

TALES

FROM THE

MOUNTAINS:

The Glutton.

The Hero of Romance.

LONDON:
DARTON, HARVEY & CO.,
Gracechurch Street.

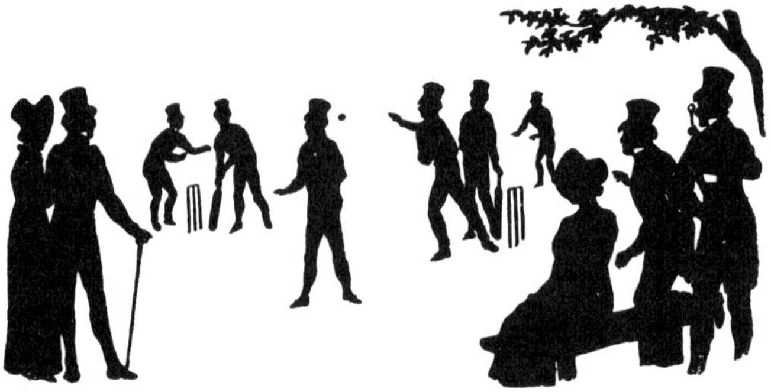

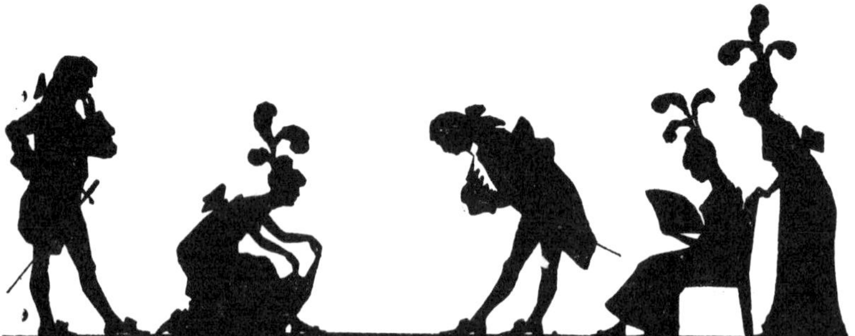

TALES FROM THE MOUNTAINS.

THE GLUTTON.

JAMES HANWAY was the only surviving child of his parents, and unfortunately had a mother so weakly indulgent towards him that she would never allow him to be contradicted. Like other spoiled children he was fond of eating improper things. Mamma could not bear to have him cry, and it was hard for him to sit at table and not partake of the same things as others did. Restraint, therefore, was at an end; and he not only eat sweet things, but rich soups and high-seasoned dishes, with which his father's table was daily supplied, as he kept a great deal of company, living near a county town. He not only drank wine but guzzled ale, and at night had his glass of brandy and water. He would at any time give an amusing book for a plum cake, or a humming-top for gingerbread.

James was too indolent even to play: yet he had his amusements, but they had their source in his passion for eating. He would wander through the garden—not to admire the powers of vegetation, nor to regale his sight and smell by the perfume of beautiful flowers: he would not hesitate to trample those into the earth, to snatch off the peach or nectarine. He would spend whole hours in pinching them to discover which were soft; and the golden pippin and the nonpareil exhibited the marks of his teeth as they still hung on the trees. He would search the farmyard for eggs merely that he might have some newly-laid for his breakfast. He would even feed a brood of young ducklings, that they might be fat and nice when they came to table. He would empty the gamekeeper's bag with peculiar satisfaction; not to examine and admire the form and plumage of the birds, but to anticipate the delicious meal he should have; and from the same motive he would attend his father to the river and hold the basket while he angled for trout.

Constantly engaged in self-gratification he paid no attention to others, and knew not the rules of common civility. If spoken to by strangers, he would hang down his head in stupid silence or mutter some unintelligible answer. At table he would be sulky to see others helped before him, and if requested by his mother to wait for his favourite dish till the company were ready to partake of it, he would express his discontent so audibly that some lady present would beg that he might at once be indulged; and mamma would not refuse the request of her kind visitor. As soon as his own greedy meal was finished, without waiting for others, he would push away his chair and leave the room to seek some new gratification.

Too ignorant to read, too stupid to benefit by improving conversation, he never offered his prayers and his praises to the Almighty, and he had imbibed all the weak and silly notions of the common people, so that he was afraid to be in the dark or go to bed by himself, for fear of a black dog coming down the chimney, or some ghost undrawing his curtains. He would therefore spend the whole evening snoring on the sofa; and if his father attempted to rouse him he would still more annoy the company by roaring. In vain did his mother whisper the promised reward and the indulgence of a servant sitting by him if he would go to bed; for he was resolved not to retire before she did, as he had a bed in her dressing room and he did not choose to go to it till she was in hers. To this mother, so blindly indulgent, it may be supposed he was very kind and attentive. On the contrary he delighted in tormenting her, although the greater part of her time was devoted to his amusement. He was dissatisfied with everything she did, disobedient to her wishes and often so saucy and so violent that she would faint away. He would laugh at as a trick, and this wicked boy could see the tears of a parent without sorrow or remorse. If company came he was sure to shew his contempt of her authority by behaving worse than usual. She was extremely neat in her person : he would go with uncombed hair and unwashed hands, and clothes as filthy as possible. But a glutton is always idle and a sloven, and a sloven is always contemptible.

He had one friend ; it was Henry Barnett ; yet he was a very opposite character, for he was active, lively and good humoured, and could make as good a dinner of milk and potatoes as with fish and turtle. . . .

People at last began to be tired of James's humours, and fearing that their own children might suffer from his evil example, no longer allowed them to visit him. Gluttony, and its constant companion, indolence, produced the most painful diseases and medicine became necessary ; but James who had never been used to taste anything but was agreeable refused to take the bitter and nauseous draughts which were now offered him. His life being in danger they were administered by force, and this threw him into such fits of passion as threatened to kill him. In time he recovered, and his father feeling the necessity of sending him from home would no longer suffer the mistaken fondness of a mother to prevail ; but sent him to a school where the boys were well treated and where they had plenty of plain and wholesome food.

James was wretched. He did not think there had been such misery in the world. What could he do ? He could not write, and none of the boys would do it for him. They were so well used and so happy that they disdained to be the bearers of complaints. At length he found means to let his father know : but he, having once made his resolution, was inflexible. James was therefore obliged to make the best of it. But how shocking it was to get up at seven o'clock in the morning ; to wash his hands and face in cold water before breakfast ; and then to have nothing but bread and milk instead of coffee and hot cakes. Dinner was still worse : he could never bear boiled mutton and rice pudding ; yet no greater luxuries were to be procured. Had it not been for the pastrycooks, he could not have existed. He visited them at every opportunity and when he could not get out he hired the servant boy to go for him. But his mother often sent him cakes, tongues, and whatever she knew he liked best. He would never share them with his companions, but shutting himself in his own room he would devour them so greedily that he made himself sick ; and yet he dared not complain or medicine would have been ordered, and at school resistance was vain.

Henry Barnett was at the same school, and he also would write to his mother for a cake. He did not want it rich, but it must be of such an enormous size that his schoolfellows must each have a bit. No sooner was it unpacked, than placing it on a table before him he flourished his knife over it and with a loud shout called all the boys about him. His own share was not larger than theirs ; nor would he leave out James who never gave him any in return. He would next sell the basket and the string by auction, and say so many droll things in their praise that the school was in a roar of laughter. He always found a purchaser, for schoolboys if they have money are silly enough to buy things which they do not want. The money thus raised was given to the servant lad who waited on them. Thus Henry Barnett, innocently merry and good humoured to all about him, was a general favourite, and lost nothing by his generosity, for he shared in every boy's presents. But James was generally excluded, for as they justly observed, he who would not give ought not to receive.

James now began to find his supplies run short; for his father by the advice of his master had contrived to restrict his pocket allowance unknown to his mother. It was still ample, but pastry was very dear, and a shilling would scarcely procure him a meal. He was once when at the pastrycook's so reduced as only to have one penny left to buy him a tart. Some nice cheese-cakes were at that moment brought into the shop. It was in vain to ask the woman to trust him, for she had strict orders never to do so. She was called away for an instant, and he contrived to slip two of them into his pocket. It was the first crime of that nature he had ever committed, and his countenance and manner betrayed him. She was moved by his tears and promised not to tell. She kept her word, but he never ventured to that shop again.

The next pastrycook's which he frequented was kept by an old woman who was almost blind. He pretended to want something at the further end of the shop, and he put some gingerbread nuts in his pocket. She did not miss them. Success made him bold. Swift is the progress of vice if not early checked. He now seldom went to her shop without bringing away nearly double what he paid for. The old woman wondered how the things went, but as the boys of two schools frequented her shop it was not possible to fix the thief.

The vacation was spent in excess and unrestrained indulgence. It was a length of time before James could be got to school again, and it was only effected by a stratagem at last. He roared and raved so much that the master was quite disgusted, and nothing but the respect he bore his father could have induced him to let him remain. James now began to be tired of sweet things, and to sigh for greater luxuries. Unfortunately he became acquainted with a boy who was at the other school, of the same turn as himself. He told him of a woman who roasted chickens, and procured punch and other things for those who had money to pay for them. He also instructed him in the means of getting out when the other boys slept. The scheme succeeded, and James sat and drank until he had spent all his money, and contracted a debt of some pounds. The woman knew it was in vain to apply to his master; but she sent the bill to his father, who paid it, but severely reprimanded his son, and unfortunately concealed it from the master; for James promised to amend, and every parent hopes well of his child.

He had no longer any money when he heard of the arrival of some lobsters. A feast of them was to be prepared for his friends who invited him to partake, that was, if he could pay. He knew not how to raise any money. Friends he had not one in the school excepting Henry Barnett, who was too thoughtless and too generous ever to keep any. A little boy who was just come was possessed of a crown, which, as he had shared the bed of James, he gave him to keep for him. No sooner was the unsuspecting child asleep than James joined his companions, and the five shillings barely paid the expenses of the evening. The little boy, anxious to display his riches, asked in the morning for his money. James said he had lost it; but the little fellow was not to be imposed upon. He sobbed and cried and threatened by turns. He was then assured that he should have it the next day with a shilling for the loan of it; but even this failed to pacify him, and he ran and made his complaint to the master. An enquiry now took place and the culprit was discovered and proclaimed. He was obliged to submit to a most severe flogging, and not a creature would associate with him or even sit at the same table, but as they passed him they called him thief, robber, and swindler.

Henry Barnett was moved for him and took him to his own room. He was a stranger to crimes himself and he detested them in another, but he remembered James when surrounded by luxury and indulgence in his father's house, and comparing his present with his past situation his heart bled for him. He reasoned with him and read to him, but he was sorry to see that he was more mortified than penitent.

It was not long after this that Henry had a one-pound note given him. Never had he been so rich—never so elevated. Not that he cared about money for himself, but a great holiday was approaching and he would be able to treat all his schoolfellows with strawberries and cream at a house kept in the country for that purpose. That day he thought he would try to prevail on them to forgive James and restore him to society. Locks and keys he had none, but what was his consternation a few days after on discovering that the bank-note was gone! The boys declared that James was the thief; but he solemnly denied it, and Henry was so convinced that such ingratitude and baseness could not exist that he entreated and prevailed on them to suspend their judgment for a short time. But to be disappointed in treating his friends cost him some tears.

Soon after this some linen belonging to Henry was discovered by the mistress to have been taken away. She found also that the stock of James was much reduced. Dishonesty is never long concealed. If no human eye sees it, God sees it, and will bring the culprit to light. This was soon found to be James. When the bank-note was gone, he had given those things to the woman who provided the hot suppers. A dreadful flogging was his first punishment.

His crimes were then declared in the presence of all his schoolfellows, and a great number of their friends who had assembled. He was then pronounced a disgrace to the school, and publicly expelled from it.

On receiving this intelligence James's father was nearly broken-hearted, and he refused to admit him into his own house; he was therefore conducted to one belonging to a friend, where he was confined in a dark garret, chained by the leg, with straw for his bed, and bread and water his only food. A relative who was going to the West Indies was prevailed on to take James with him. From his confinement he was released by his father, who did not reproach him. He spoke not of the past; but his sunken eyes and his pale face showed what he had suffered. James was informed of his destination, and when the chaise drove off in a contrary direction to that which led to his home, he cried, "Oh, my mother, my mother, shall I not see you again?" "Your mother," faltered his father, "is nearly dying of a broken heart, and you, on whom she so doated, she now refuses to behold—she cannot bear it." James threw himself back in the carriage and sobbed with agony.

They now crossed the country to Exeter, where Mr. Hanway had heard that a lad about the age of his own son was condemned to die for robbery. He was the only child of his mother who was a widow, and this was to her a death-blow. He was a youth of good sense and had been instructed by a clergyman. He appeared to be a real penitent and resigned to his fate. James was not told to what place he was going, and he shuddered as he entered the gloomy gaol, and saw the immense fetters, and heard the heavy closing doors of the dungeon. To one of those dismal places he was conducted, and left alone with the condemned robber. When he returned to the inn, he spent the night in tears and in prayer.

After a few days they again proceeded on their journey. He was placed by his father in an open carriage, and they drove out of town. They soon after entered a vast crowd. James now looked up and on a raised platform he saw the young robber. The fatal cord was already round his neck, and in a few minutes James was compelled to behold his dying convulsions. In imagination he heard his last shriek, and he sunk lifeless by his father. "My boy," his father exclaimed on his recovery, "had the laws been impartially administered, your fate had been like his; for your crime was greater. He robbed a stranger to serve his poor mother; you stole from the friend of your bosom: not to satisfy the wants of others—not to satisfy your own, for you had none —but to gratify a passion which levels you with the beast. The future is before you; atone for the past, and may your Heavenly Father forgive you as I do."

THE HERO OF ROMANCE.

SEVERAL circumstances combined to give to the mind of Horatio Alderney great delicacy of feeling. He had been a very weakly child from his birth, and was unable to join the noisy sports of his hardy brothers. He was always with his mother or his old nurse, to whose silly stories of ghosts and fairies, although so often repeated, he would listen with mute attention. As he was not thought able to contend with the boys of a large school, he was placed under the care of a clergyman who was an elegant scholar, but lived entirely excluded from the world.

Here Horatio recovered his health, made great progress in the classics, and discovered a very ingenious turn for drawing and mechanics. His person was handsome, and his manners so gentle and obliging that he was greatly beloved. At the vacations he returned to his father's, and from good nature, rather than inclination, he would join his brothers and sisters in the noisy game of *blind man's buff* or *puss wants a corner*, but he would gladly leave them to steal to his mother's closet to read poetry and romances.

Horatio had often visited alone a ruined abbey or castle; but now he began to tremble at the solitude of his own chamber, and gladly accepted the offer of a servant sleeping in his room, when he might indulge himself in the most delightful horrors until the hour of repose.

They were visited by a Mr. Grenville, the godfather of Horatio, and the most esteemed friend of his father. He was greatly attached to Horatio, and was a very sensible and humane man. He remarked, without seeming to do so, the employment he had been following and his state of mind in consequence. He engaged him to spend the approaching Christmas with him, in Staffordshire, where he was to meet some lads of his own age. Horatio promised with reluctance, for there he should have no novels, and he was more averse than ever to mix in any rude sports. He was to ride a few miles to meet the coach which would convey him to a town not far distant from Mr. Grenville's, one of whose servants was to be in waiting.

He did not find the company in the coach such as could dispel the discontent of mind which he felt. In silence he pursued his journey, and when he arrived at the inn he found it so crowded with company that he could get no one to attend to him, and he found that there was no person from Mr. Grenville's. As the evening was fine and the distance only three or four miles he determined to proceed on foot. He had walked nearly two miles when striking into a deep glen, sounds the most appalling met his ear. From buildings of uncouth form arose large volumes of flame, whilst the ponderous hammer was heard, and immense wheels looking like the works of giants, performed their

TALES FROM THE MOUNTAINS.

wondrous evolutions. He knew that ironworks were very common in this part of the country but their effect in the stillness of a winter's evening was very striking.

As he entered the village, the dirty black children tumbled and gambled before him. He struck with a switch which he had with him, a little yelping cur at his heels, which brought out the mistress who loaded him with the most abusive language, and the children to whom he had refused some half-pence began to pelt him with dirt and stones. Eager to escape from this savage crew, he rushed down a lane and soon found that he had lost his way. A light issuing from a distant window he hastened towards it; but started with horror as he saw suspended from the walls, handcuffs and various manacles for the human form. At the farther end was the hideous figure of a man employed in this dreadful work, and the glare of the fire gave a fuller view of his dark features. Horatio hardly able to articulate, requested information respecting the way to Mr. Grenville's house. He suspended the thundering hammer for an instant, and called a woman whose appearance was as forbidding as his own. He heard imperfectly her direction and hastened forwards.

He soon lost sight of habitations and darkness reigned around, for the evening was closed in. He now entered on a vast heath, bleak and desolate. The wind howled dismally over it, and in the pauses of the blast a great bell tolled heavily. He knew not how to proceed, but the moon appearing for an instant he thought he saw a gate at a distance. He passed through it and descended into a deep and hollow way. Soon after he appeared to be entering on the mazes of a vast forest.

He had not gone far when the sound of voices in rude mirth met his ear. Suddenly a light gleamed on the trees: he started on finding himself at the entrance of a large cave with rude rocks piled about it   He approached near enough to distinguish a group of people singing and drinking round a table at the further end; and in the pauses of the song he heard one of them in reply to some question, exclaim, "It has been a bad day with me; they all escaped me, except one old fellow whose blood is on my clothes." "Murderous wretch," thought Horatio, and with trembling steps he retraced his way and again found himself on the heath, and with a desperate resolution he moved forward. A faint light glimmered from afar : he found it proceeded from a window in a distant building of immense size; but whether an old castle or abbey he could not determine. The light again disappeared, and he was left in total darkness. Which way must he turn? Could he find his way across the heath? or would it not be better to seek some shed until the morning's dawn should enable him to escape? But this was a strange want of courage, and how unlike a *Hero of Romance* not to finish the adventure.

His spirit returned, and he approached the door and raised the massy knocker. The sound reverberated through the vast pile, and again all was still as death. He once more raised it, and soon after heard approaching steps and the falling of chains. The door slowly opened, and a man of a singular aspect appeared, bearing a light. To Horatio's enquiry if the mansion belonged to Mr. Grenville he replied not, but retired leaving the light.

Horatio surveyed the place : it was a large hall, and the windows of painted glass still remained entire. Suits of armour added to the solemnity, and some banners waved over them. Presently another man appeared whose look was not more prepossessing than the other; but he said it was the house of Mr. Grenville who was from home. He then led the way to a large oak room, and brought some wine and biscuits; Horatio refusing anything else and

TALES FROM THE MOUNTAINS.

desiring to be shewn to the compartment he was to sleep in. The female who came to conduct him to it wore a dress of uncouth form, and her feet and legs were bare. She spoke in language entirely unknown. Astonishing! Was he not in Staffordshire? Whence then this foreign dress and dialect? Surely the days of witchcraft were returned, and he was transported to the wilds of Calabria.

He boldly followed her through long passages to a remote part of the building. She closed the door upon him and went away; when taking up the lamp, for lamp it certainly was, he surveyed the room. It was large and gloomy: a high canopied bed stood in a remote corner. The walls were covered with tapestry, representing warriors of a gigantic size, preparing for battle. But what most appalled his senses was a large black curtain which was drawn before what seemed to be a recess: a dead body, or a skeleton was perhaps concealed there. He grasped the curtain; yet again shrunk, trembling, from the daring attempt.

He now seated himself at the foot of his bed pondering the means of escape from what he had no longer any doubt was the abode of the banditti. He remarked a kind of chasm across the neck of one of the warriors; and raising the lamp to examine further, discovered a low door concealed beneath the tapestry. He opened it with some difficulty, and beheld a flight of decayed steps. He was determined to explore the dungeons to which they must lead; all was still as death; no sound was heard but that of his own steps, until by opening another door he entered on a long passage. Soon he heard sounds, as of talking and laughing. The banditti then were returned.

Concealing his light beneath his coat, Horatio crept softly to a low window, which enabled him to observe those within without being himself seen. Several women as well as men were seated at supper, and he was more hurt than surprised to see the forger of the fetters and the murderer from the cavern among their number. The captain he concluded was not returned, for a woman of unwieldy size presided at the board. "Peter," she cried, "take care that your knife be sharp, and do you Bet," turning to another female, "see that no blood is spilled on the ground."—"Let me alone," replied the wretch, "I have been used to such jobs."

"It is my blood," inwardly groaned Horatio, "which is to flow. It is for my throat that the murderer's steel is preparing." He hastened onwards, but soon found his way impeded by a flight of steps. He descended, and expected every instant that the damps of the caverns would extinguish his light. He came to one of greater extent, and found the ground moist beneath his feet. He lowered his lamp and beheld a stream of blood. In ghastly horror he looked around for the poor victim, but it was already removed. Perhaps it was that which the dark curtain might conceal. He leaned against the wall, nearly fainting, when he was revived by a stream of air which seemed to come from an opening in the wall, but it was from a low, open door. He had just power to crawl into the court to which it led. He soon saw two men approach: one of them wore a kind of loose coat; the other carried a light. He had only time to conceal himself behind a projection of the building. As they passed, he heard one of them say: "The mother suffered a good deal, and I think I did right by cutting her throat and putting an end to her misery. As for this young one, I warrant we shall take care of her."

At this instant a suppressed cry like that of an infant was heard, and deeply affected the tender heart of Horatio. Soon after a sound still more dismal met his ear: it hardly seemed to proceed from one of human kind, but what strange expression will not distress assume. It appeared as if someone were trying to escape from confinement; and he determined on his release. Directed by the sound to the spot, he loosened a chain with a large stone, and a door burst open. Something instantly rushed out, with such force that he was thrown into the mud and his lamp extinguished.

When he recovered he endeavoured to make his way out of the court; in doing so, he struck against a low door which giving way he concluded himself precipitated into a dungeon, for it was so deep that he was bruised by the fall and could not again reach the door. He must, therefore, once more explore the caverns beneath this horrible abode with but faint hopes of escaping.

The dungeon was so filled with rubbish that it was with extreme difficulty he made his way over it. At length he appeared to enter on a larger space and a faint light glimmered at a distance. With trembling steps he approached and beheld a scene from which he recoiled with horror. A large fire was blazing, and over it was suspended a kind of cauldron. Near it sat a wrinkled old woman. Over her shoulders was fastened a piece of red blanket and something of the same material was bound round her head. Her shrivelled hands were spread and she muttered her incantations in an unknown tongue. He remembered having read of such a scene, where an enchantress was thus employed; and what dreadful preparation could this be?

He now endeavoured to make his way in another direction, and was soon lost in darkness. He groped, however, till he came to the bottom of a flight of stairs, which he determined to ascend; and on pushing open a door at the top he was convinced that he had once more entered his chamber.

Terrified and exhausted he threw himself on the bed to await his doom. Presently his ears were assailed by a deep and hollow groan; it either came from behind the black curtain or from some place adjoining his own room. The hero was no more, and he had not courage to search out the sufferer.

The midnight storm arose, and poured over the heath. The screech-owl flapped his wings against the casement, and the distant yellings of dogs were heard. In the pauses of the blast he still listened to the hollow groans of a distressed human being.—A horn was sounded and he distinguished the trampling of horses' feet. The massy knocker resounded, the doors opened and a large party entered below. The gang, then, were returned; and the chief, for one voice only now was giving orders for his death.

The murderer, with heavy steps, ascended the stairs;— the door was thrown open.—Horatio shrieked:—But it was Mr. Grenville he beheld. "Are you, also," exclaimed the terrified youth, "fallen into the hands of the banditti? and is your murder to be added to that of the victim who is now expiring?"

"My dear boy," said Mr. Grenville, "what can you mean by banditti and murders? Surely you are suffering from the delirium of a fever?" Then seeing him nearly fainting he went for a cordial which he desired Horatio to drink. Revived by this, and encouraged by the presence of his friend, he was able to repeat the whole of his adventures.

Mr. Grenville listened with astonishment, and left the room. He was some time absent, and when he returned he seated himself by the bedside, and burst into so long and so violent a fit of laughter that Horatio was both hurt and surprised at it. Mr. Grenville at length said, "My dear fellow, I am sorry to offend you, but a perverted taste has made you give to common family concerns such horrible features that I would rather deprive you of your rest than let you remain a prey to such terrors.

TALES FROM THE MOUNTAINS.

"I regret that a mistake as to time prevented your being met at the inn, but the walk is neither long nor perilous. We who are familiar with public works, survey those vast machines without surprise or emotion; though to persons unused to them they must have an extraordinary appearance. I grant also that the people employed in those works are not so pleasing in their appearance or manners as your father's peasantry. The forger, as you term him, certainly has plain features which were rendered more so by his sooty dress and skin; yet he is an honest and ingenious man and at all times has access to my kitchen. He was making fetters; as my friend, to whom those works belong, lately had a large order from the keeper of Newgate.

"You were right in both roads by which you attempted to reach my house, which is large and ancient. The side towards the heath, which has not yet been cultivated, remains in its original state. The front is modern, and the road to it lies through extensive plantations, and I own my pride gratified that you should mistake trees of the growth of a dozen years for an extensive forest.

"The tolling of the bell was the curfew from the next village, for the custom of ringing it at eight o'clock is still practised in many places.

"The cavern forms the entrance to my porter's lodge: some rocks of a singular form being found there, I suffered them to remain, and their effect, as you see, is very striking. The master was celebrating the christening of his child, and the company no doubt were jovial. One of them was my keeper, who knowing my desire for some game at this time, might regret that he had only been able to kill one hare.

"The massy knocker, the casement windows, and the bannered hall, are common in such ancient mansions. Ugliness, I have observed, is often in common life, treated with ridicule and insult. Feeling pity for such, I have never rejected servants who have applied to me, on that account; still, not supposing they would be taken for murderers. The man who opened the door for you is deaf. The girl who conducted you to your chamber is from my house in Wales, where you know I reside some months in the year. She retains her country dress, and in a great degree its language also, for as most of my servants understand hers, she does not try to learn theirs.

"You ought to have been better attended, but my housekeeper is lame with the gout. Your sable curtain in this tapestry room is one of dark green damask, and is drawn across the recess to preserve some books from the dust. This was the work of my housekeeper whose portly figure you saw presiding at the supper table, and sorry as I am to degrade the dignity of Romance, yet I am obliged to declare that the murderous steel was to butcher a poor pig, and the blood of which she was so careful was to form for me those vulgar things called black puddings.

"The many underground places in this large mansion were well suited to your nocturnal rambles, where scenes of bloodshed were still to await you. When you deplored the poor victim, had you but raised your eyes to the rafters you would have seen that the blood issued from the headless body of a goose.

"The infantine cry proceeded from a lamb whose mother, suffering from accident, my shepherd who is a most humane fellow, had killed. The prisoner you set at liberty was a fatted calf, which rejoicing in its freedom rudely bounded off to its native fields.

"The dungeon into which you were precipitated was the coal-hole which leads to the last dreadful scene. The sorceress in a red blanket is an honest old Welsh woman, mother to the girl before named. It is the dress of her country, where the women always brew, and their malt liquor is superior to ours. What you term a cauldron is a brass pan which they use instead of our furnaces. I suppose she was singing one of the mountain ditties, and such were the incantations of the witch.

"The dismal groans which you heard came from my butler who is suffering from the toothache. The horn was sounded in frolic by a young gentleman whom I have brought for your companion; and the captain of the banditti is the friend who is now addressing you. And now, my dear boy," he added, "you see the evil effects of reading romances which by weakening the mind render it alive to every fear and unfit for any exertion. You had forgotten the strong power of British laws which suffers no horde of banditti to inhabit the mansions of our ancestors. It was only in ruder times, and in countries where ignorance and superstition reign, that such lawless wretches could exist."

Horatio was now left to his rest, if rest he now could have taken; but shame and vexation kept him waking, and he dreaded the mortification which would await him at the breakfast table. But Mr. Grenville had kindly taken care not to have the adventure known, and did all he could to cheer and encourage Horatio who found the companions who had been selected for him very pleasant.

When the weather was fine they had their out-door amusements, or various games in the Bannered Hall.

Mr. Grenville was soon after obliged to visit the North of Europe for a few years. He took Horatio with him and they were accompanied by a gentleman who perfected the young traveller in the classics. His mind was expanded by seeing other countries, and observing the inhabitants and customs. Horatio never lost his modest demeanour or amiable disposition: This made him a general favourite. He was happy himself and desirous of rendering others so; but he never again aspired to be *The Hero of Romance*.

LUCY AND HODGE.

[From *The Juvenile Tell-Tale—Embellished with Eighteen Coloured Engravings.* By J. Smith. London: Dean & Munday, Threadneedle Street. Price Sixpence.]

LITTLE HODGE knocked one morning at Lucy's cottage door—" Pray give me a light," said he, " for our tinder is so bad, mother has been trying in vain for twenty minutes to strike one." Lucy very kindly gave him a light, but he had not got three yards from the cottage door before the wind blew it out; so he returned and knocked again. Lucy was very good-natured and lighted his candle a second time, but advised him another time not to forget to bring his hat to hold over it, to prevent the wind from blowing it out.

TOM AND THE OLD MAN.

"Hollo, Tom," said the old man in the picture, "are you turned gardener? I thought you had been a carpenter."

"Yes," replied Tom, "that I was once, but I had an accident and hurt my leg, and so I was obliged to go away, and here I am in the midst of turnips and carrots; but

come in now with me and taste them, my wife and I are just going to dinner." That the old man did very willingly; and if one can judge by the quantity that was eaten, they proved excellent, for of all that great load that Tom had got in his apron there barely remained enough to feed one little pig.

THE DUTIFUL SON.

MR. AND MRS. VINCENT were sitting in the drawing-room (it was Mrs. Vincent's birthday) when their son George, a boy about ten years old, entered with a book in his hand, and making a graceful bow, thus addressed his mother:—
"My dear mamma, this is prize day with us at school, and my master awarded one to me, giving me the choice of a number that lay on the table; now I had heard you wish to read 'Elizabeth, or the Exiles of Siberia,' and I looked and hoped it might be found among them: luckily it was one of them, and I have brought it for you to read; at the same time allow me to wish you many happy returns of this day." I think this was a very clever address for so young a boy.

THE ELDERLY GENTLEMAN.

(TITLE PAGE MISSING.)

The elderly Gentleman's here
  With his Cane, his Wig and his Hat,
A good-humoured Man all declare
  But then he's o'erladen with fat.

THE ELDERLY GENTLEMAN.

By the side of a murmuring stream
   This elderly Gentleman sat;
On the top of his head was his Wig
   And on top of his Wig was his Hat.

THE ELDERLY GENTLEMAN.

The Wind it blew high and blew strong
    As this elderly Gentleman sat,
And bore from his head in a trice
    And plunged in the river his Hat.

THE ELDERLY GENTLEMAN.

The Gentleman then took his Cane
　Which lay on his lap as he sat,
And dropped in the river his Wig
　In attempting to get out his Hat.

THE ELDERLY GENTLEMAN.

Cool reflection at length came across
While this elderly Gentleman sat,
So thought he would follow the stream
And look for his fine Wig and Hat.

THE ELDERLY GENTLEMAN.

His breast grew cold with despair
    And full in his eye Madness sat
So he flung in the river his Cane
    To swim with his Wig and his Hat.

THE ELDERLY GENTLEMAN.

His head being thicker than common
 O'erbalanced the rest of his fat,
And in plumped this Son of a Woman
 To follow his Wig, Cane and Hat.

THE ELDERLY GENTLEMAN.

A Newfoundland Dog was at hand,
  No circumstance could be more pat
The old man he brought safe to land
  Then fetched out his Wig, Cane and Hat.

THE ELDERLY GENTLEMAN.

The Gentleman dripping and cold
    Seemed much like a half-drowned rat
But praised his deliverer so bold
    Then adjusted his Cane, Wig and Hat.

THE ELDERLY GENTLEMAN.

Now homeward the Gentleman hied
    But neither could wear Wig nor Hat
The Dog followed close at his Side
    Fawned, waggled his tail and all that.

THE ELDERLY GENTLEMAN.

The Gentleman filled with delight
    The Dog's master hastily sought;
Two guineas set all things to right
    For that sum his true friend he bought.

THE ELDERLY GENTLEMAN.

From him the Dog never would part
  But lived much caressed for some years
Till levelled by Death's fatal dart,
  When the Gentleman shed many tears—

Then buried poor Tray in the Green,
  And placed o'er his grave a small stone,
Whereon a few lines may be seen
  Expressive of what he had done.

Marmaduke Multiply's

Merry Method

of

Making Minor Mathematicians;

or, the

MULTIPLICATION TABLE

Illustrated by

SIXTY-NINE APPROPRIATE ENGRAVINGS.

London:

Printed for J. Harris,
Corner of St. Paul's Church-yard

1816

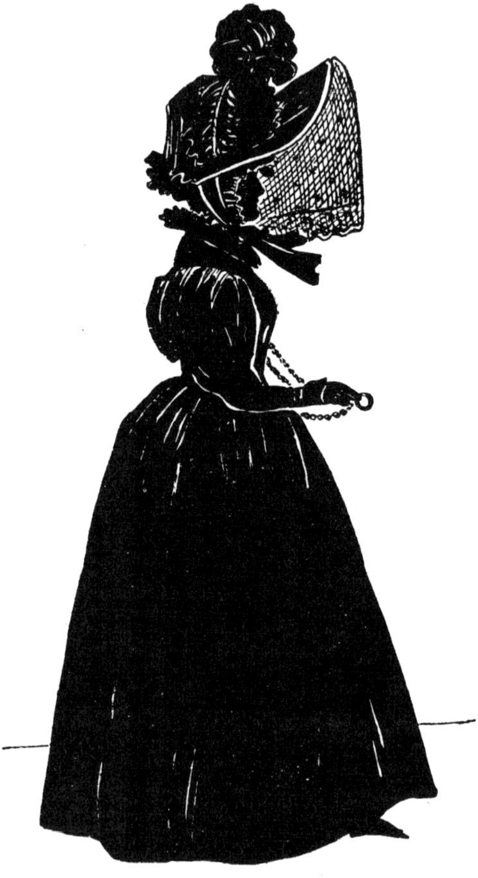

MARMADUKE MULTIPLY'S MERRY METHOD.

Twice 1 *are* 2
I know that as well as you.

Twice 2 *are* 4
Pray hasten on before.

MARMADUKE MULTIPLY'S MERRY METHOD.

Twice 3 *are* 6
You're always playing tricks.

Twice 4 *are* 8
Your bonnet is not straight.

Twice 5 *are* 10
Look at my gallant Men.

Twice 6 *are* 12
I cannot find St. Elve.

Twice 7 *are* 14
They're dancing on the Green.

Twice 8 *are* 16
Yonder are Lions to be seen.

Twice 9 *are* 18
My Cow is very lean.

Twice 10 *are* 20
My Purse is almost empty.

Twice 11 *are* 22
We'll drink to the Hero of Waterloo.

MARMADUKE MULTIPLY'S MERRY METHOD

Twice 12 *are* 24
Pray haste and open me the door.

3 times 1 *are* 3
My darling come to me.

3 times 2 *are* 6
The Man has brought some bricks.

MARMADUKE MULTIPLY'S MERRY METHOD.

3 times 3 *are* 9
This Man's a friend of mine.

3 times 4 *are* 12
I find no rhyme but delve.

3 times 5 *are* 15
We soon shall change the Scene.

3 times 6 *are* 18
We'll draw for King and Queen.

3 times 7 *are* 21
Dear Ma'am pray see my Dog and Gun.

3 times 8 *are* 24
Be sure I will do so no more.

MARMADUKE MULTIPLY'S MERRY METHOD.

3 times 9 *are* 27
My Babes and I are going to Devon.

3 times 10 *are* 30
My face is very dirty.

3 times 11 *are* 33
Jack and Bill are gone to Sea.

3 times 12 *are* 36
We'll hide our Cakes behind the ricks.

4 times 4 *are* 16
The Air is very keen.

MARMADUKE MULTIPLY'S MERRY METHOD.

4 times 5 *are* 20
Jack says his purse is empty.

4 times 6 *are* 24
I think I've seen your face before.

4 times 7 *are* 28
Come with me and see me Skate.

4 times 8 *are* 32
I once could dance as well as you.

MARMADUKE MULTIPLY'S MERRY METHOD.

4 times 9 *are* 36
Your Medicine I soon will mix.

4 times 10 *are* 40
Monsieur! I come from Malta.

4 times 11 *are* 44
Pray make this noise my dears no more.

4 times 12 *are* 48
I hope that I shall get some Bait.

5 times 5 *are* 25
I thank my stars that I'm alive.

MARMADUKE MULTIPLY'S MERRY METHOD.

5 times 6 *are* 30
She's tall as any Fir tree.

MARMADUKE MULTIPLY'S MERRY METHOD.

5 times 7 *are* 35
The Chicks are safe beneath the Hive.

5 times 8 *are* 40
My little Beau escorts me.

5 times 9 *are* 45
We're going with Tom to take a drive.

5 times 10 *are* 50
Dear me! they're very thrifty.

5 times 11 *are* 55
I see the Chaise, they'll soon arrive.

5 times 12 *are* 60
The House is like a Pig's sty!

MARMADUKE MULTIPLY'S MERRY METHOD.

6 times 6 *are* 36
This pretty Bird is Cousin Dick's.

6 times 7 *are* 42
This is the road which leads to Looe.

6 times 8 *are* 48
Dear Aunt! your dress is out of date.

6 times 9 *are* 54
Dear Ma'am I'll ne'er deceive you more.

6 times 10 *are* 60
This pretty cap will fix me.

MARMADUKE MULTIPLY'S MERRY METHOD.

6 times 11 *are* 66
We're four by Honours, and three by tricks.

6 times 12 *are* 72
Methinks I hear the loud Curfew.

7 times 7 *are* 49
You'll say, I think, this is good Wine.

7 times 8 *are* 56
That fellow merits twenty kicks.

7 times 9 *are* 63
Come pray, Sir, give that Hat to me.

MARMADUKE MULTIPLY'S MERRY METHOD.

7 times 10 *are* 70
We're sailing very pleasantly.

7 times 11 *are* 77
I always make my bread with Leaven

7 times 12 *are* 84
Oh, happy little tawny Moor.

8 times 8 *are* 64
A baron bold in days of yore.

8 times 9 *are* 72
Come here, I'll shew you where they grew.

8 times 10 *are* 80
I think she's pretty weighty.

MARMADUKE MULTIPLY'S MERRY METHOD.

8 times 11 *are* 88
If you fall down you'll break your pate.

8 times 12 *are* 96
My wandering thoughts I cannot fix.

9 times 9 *are* 81
I'll bet five pounds on Wellington.

9 times 10 *are* 90
Now you shall taste my fine Tea.

9 times 11 *are* 99
See Sophy, how my ear-rings shine.

MARMADUKE MULTIPLY'S MERRY METHOD.

9 times 12 *are* 108
See what a noble, fine first-rate.

10 times 10 *are* 100
How he got there, she wondered.

10 times 11 *are* 110
A Lion's surely in that Den.

MARMADUKE MULTIPLY'S MERRY METHOD.

10 times 12 *are* 120
I laugh and sing and live in plenty.

11 times 11 *are* 121
Come here little Boy and buy a nice Bun.

MARMADUKE MULTIPLY'S MERRY METHOD.

11 times 12 *are* 132
How do you, Miss Hannah? Oh, Sir, how are you?

12 times 12 *are* 144
They're all going out to hunt the Boar.

THE COMICAL GIRL.

[From *Jingles, or Original Rhymes for Children.* By M. Pelham. London: Printed for Richard Phillips, 7 Bridge Street, Blackfriars. 1811.]

THERE was a child, as I have been told,
Who when she was young didn't look very old;
Another thing, too, some people have said,
At the top of her body there grew out a head;
And what perhaps might make some people stare
Her little bald pate was all covered with hair:
Another strange thing which made gossipers talk
Was that she often attempted to walk.
And then, do you know, she occasioned much fun
By moving so fast as sometimes to run;
Nay, indeed, I have heard that some people say
She often would smile and often would play;
And what is a fact, though it seems very odd,
She had a monstrous dislike to the feel of a rod.
This strange little child sometimes hungry would be
And then she delighted her victuals to see;
Even drink she would swallow, and though strange it appears,
Whenever she listened, it was with her ears.
With her eyes she could see, and strange to relate,
Her peepers were placed in the front of her pate.
There, too, was her mouth and also her nose,
And on her two feet were placed her ten toes:
Her teeth I've been told were fixed in her gums
And besides having fingers she also had thumbs.
A droll child she therefore most surely must be
For not being blind she was able to see.

THE CROCUS.

One circumstance more had almost slipped my mind
Which is, when not cross she always was kind.
And strangest of any that yet I have said
She every night went to sleep on her bed,
And what may occasion you no small surprise
When napping she always shut close up her eyes.

THE PARLOUR GUESTS.

[From *The Crocus; or Useful Hints for Children, being Original Poems on Popular and Familiar Subjects.* London: R. Harrild, 20, Great Eastcheap. 1816.]

> MAMMA gave James a glass of wine,
>   And Julia had one too,
> For when they in the parlour dine,
>   'Twas usual so to do.
>
> But Julia drank no health at all,
>   And James no thanks return'd,
> To see them growing up so tall,
>   I felt myself concern'd.
>
> Now when they both retired to rest,
>   This precept I enjoin'd,
> When each became a parlour guest,
>   Good manners they would mind.

THE ADMONITION.

How very warm you are, my dear,
    Do pray pull off your tippet,
Your hat untie, and bring it here,
    And take your tea and sip it.

THE CROCUS.

Where is it you have been, my love,
   I wish you would be seated;
You know how much I disapprove,
   Your being over-heated.

You dearly love to run about,
   And exercise is good;
But when the sun is out so hot,
   You should not be so rude.

Perhaps a fever may ensue,
   And then you'll need a nurse,
And you must have the doctor too,
   Or you'll grow worse and worse.

A rash indeed may all come out,
   Upon your face and skin,
Ah silly child, to run about,
   You'll wish you'd stayed within.

Then be advised, my dearest Ann,
   E'er yet it be too late,
To keep in health do all you can,
   And seek a cool retreat.

THE YOUTHS.

How many little boys are found
   Who love to dive in water,
Three times they rise, and then are drown'd,
   Calamitous disaster.

THE CROCUS.

O have you never seen the men
  Their lengthened cords throw in,
And strive with all their might and main,
  To drag them up again.

What a variety of means,
  Are used to bring them to,
And while a spark of life remains,
  What methods they pursue !

But ah, alas ! 'tis often vain,
  And numbers yield their breath,
Nor can they purchase health again,
  For mines of glitt'ring wealth.

Then be forewarn'd, ye giddy youths,
  Who float upon the water,
Store well your minds with sacred truths,
  Prepare for an hereafter.

THE ROOM.

SEE the cobwebs round the room,
Betty, come and bring your broom,
Sweep them all away, I pray,
Leave them not from day to day.

Parlours should look clean and neat,
Ev'ry slab and ev'ry seat,
Ev'rything around should tell
They've been swept and dusted well.

THE CROCUS.

But, alas, we seldom see,
Servants what they ought to be,
Now they rove from place to place,
Is it not to their disgrace?

Betty, do you wish to stay,
Meditate on what I say,
Serve with rev'rence and delight,
Act as in your Master's sight.

And my children recollect,
Servants claim all due respect,
You pursue the Saviour's plan,
Do them all the good you can.

MARIA.

Maria was a pretty girl,
But she could neither read nor spell,
And tho' she had so sweet a face,
She often got in sad disgrace.

She loved within the glass to look,
Rather than take her spelling-book.
To decorate and curl her hair,
Oft to the mirror she'd repair.

Soon she became exceeding tall,
And did not go to school at all,
Now she begins to feel her need,
And wishes she could spell and read.

THE CROCUS.

Does she attempt to write a line,
How sadly do her letters join,
Her diction is so incorrect,
Alas! she mourns her past neglect.

Nor will that season e'er return,
In early days ye children learn,
Strive to repeat your lessons well,
And ten to one but you excel.

COUGHING.

AMELIA, what a cough you've got,
  You are exceeding hoarse:
To-night you take a something hot,
  Or else it may get worse.

Remember that you go to bed
  Too, at an early hour,
And when your ev'ning prayer is said,
  Do not commence a roar.

Some candied horehound you shall have,
  Some gruel sweetened nice:
And if you really well behave,
  We'll mix in wine and spice.

There's many little girls I know,
  That do not mind what's said,
And when they're ill they will not go
  Upstairs into their bed.

NURSERY MORALS.

THE PIG.

[From *Nursery Morals; chiefly in Monosyllables.* London: J. Harris, St. Paul's Churchyard. 1818.]

How we all turn with scorn from the Pig.
His skin is thick in dirt.
He lies on damp musty straw, and rolls in mud and mire.
He lives to eat and drink, and will perhaps die because he is too fat.
How sad to look on so dirty a brute.
But, oh! how much more sad to be like him.
To eat all day long.
To eat much more than ought to be eaten,
And to be sick with greediness.
Then to lie down in the dirt, and sleep in the mud.
This is all most shocking.
Boys and girls are not quite so bad.
But, sometimes, they are *almost* as bad.
Have you seen children devour sweets and delicates without end?
Tarts, and cakes, and fruits?
Then with greasy face and dirty hands fall asleep on the ground.
Their clothes all spoiled
Their limbs all twisted.
Well, are not such children as bad as pigs?
Aye, and worse, much worse,
For they know better.
They have the choice to be clean if they please.

We can all wash ourselves when we chuse.
We can keep our clothes neat and tight.
We should scorn to be seen with hair uncombed and our dress in rags.
Girls can sew and mend the rents in their coats and frocks
And take care to be at all times neat.
Or else in truth they will be no better than the
Pigs we all look on with scorn.

THE SWEEP.

ONE day I fell down a long chimney and broke my leg,
But no one felt for me.
I have a wound in my side, but I have no salve to heal it.
You pity me, little girl!
But hush! I must not even hear the kind words of pity, for my master is near, and he will say I complain,
And he will beat me the more.
Oh, I cannot look upon this boy. His pains wring my heart.
Can nothing be done to save him, to ease him,
To snatch him from his hard, hard fate?
Little girl, dry your tears. I have some good news for you.
There will soon be a law, a blessed law that shall stop the pangs of the poor sweep.

NURSERY MORALS.

THE PROUD BOY.

THERE was once a boy who was proud, because his papa kept a fine coach.

He would look with scorn on boys that had to walk.

Those boys would at the same time laugh at him for his weak airs

And say, among themselves,

That proud boy loses much pleasure; for while he rides shut up in a coach,

We run in fields and woods, jump in the mead,

Pick lilies from the pond, and cull the furze from the heath.

We grow strong and brisk, and laugh more in one day than he does in one year.

Poor boy, he scorns us, but we pity him!

Come—one more dip !

Come—all alone !

A VISIT

TO

THE BAZAAR.

By the Author of
THE LITTLE WARBLER OF THE COTTAGE;
JULIET, OR THE REWARD OF FILIAL AFFECTIONS;
PORT FOLIO, ETC., ETC.

London:
Printed for J. HARRIS,
Corner of St. Paul's Church Yard;
And may also be had at Several Shops in
THE BAZAAR, SOHO SQUARE.

1818.

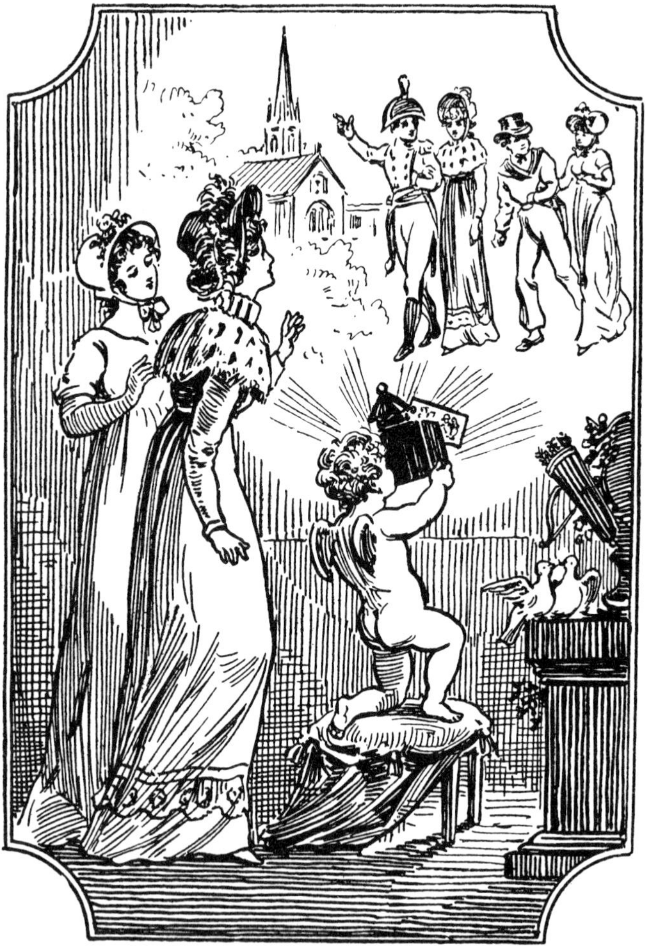

THE BAZAAR.

"My Dear," said Mrs. Durnford to her husband on his return from a long walk, "I this morning received a letter from poor Susan Boscawen, full of the most lively expressions of her gratitude, for the kind assistance which you gave to her on the death of her father. She has established herself at the Bazaar, in Soho-square, which I understand is a most respectable institution, founded by a gentleman of considerable opulence residing in the place, and by this means, she is enabled to support her aged mother and her two helpless brothers. The one you know is a cripple, and the other was born blind. If you have no objection, I should like to take the children to town some morning, when it would be convenient to you to accompany us, and shew them the interior of our English Bazaar."

"Our Bazaar in Soho-square, was founded by Mr. Trotter, on premises originally occupied by the store-keeper general, consisting of several rooms which are conveniently fitted up with handsome mahogany counters, extending not only round the sides, but in the lower and upper apartments, forming a parallelogram in the middle. These counters, having at proper distances flaps or falling doors, are in contiguity with each other, but are respectively distinguished by a small groove at a distance of every four feet of counter, the panels of which are numbered with conspicuous figures, and these are let upon moderate terms to females who can bring forward sufficient testimonies of their moral respectability. The person who from strong recommendation obtains a counter in our bazaar, pays daily, three-pence for every foot in length, and is not required to hold her

THE BAZAAR.

situation more than from day to day. I have been told, that at present, there are upwards of a hundred females, who are employed in these rooms, and a more pleasing and novel effect can hardly be imagined, than is here produced by the sight of these elegant little shops, filled with every species of light goods, works of art and female ingenuity in general."

Early the next morning Mr. and Mrs. Durnford, with Maria and Emily, who were twins, and just turned of twelve years of age, and Caroline, a sweet little girl about seven, accompanied by Theodore, proceeded with light hearts and buoyant spirits to town, which was only two miles from the residence of their father, a gentleman of large independent fortune. They had frequently visited the metropolis, had been once to a play, and had seen several other places worthy of their inspection, but they all felt their curiosity strongly excited to view the Bazaar.

They stopped at the Pastrycook's, where a young lady was eating a jelly, and laughing archly at a little boy who greedily endeavoured to force a whole cake into his mouth at once.

"Why, you silly little fellow," said she, "what are you stretching your mouth so wide for? Why don't you eat it properly? You might choke yourself if you did get it in all at once. Bite a piece off, and don't do as you did the other evening at tea, fill your mouth so full that you would have been suffocated, had not Sally relieved you by turning out the toast as fast as you had put it in."

"Dear mamma," said Caroline in a low voice, "what a sad thing is greediness. I dare say that little boy would not give his sister a morsel for all the world, and I should not enjoy the finest thing that ever was made, unless my brothers and sisters shared it with me."

"That I will answer for, Caroline," replied her mother. "And now my dear children take whatever you please, as it is necessary that you should have some refreshment after your walk."

They now turned towards the Milliner, where little Caroline again saw something to excite her laughter, and to call forth the smile of her father. A lady, long past the prime of life, but dressed in a style of girlish fashion, with short sleeves which shewed her shrivelled arms, and still shorter petticoats, was viewing herself with much complacency, as she placed on her head, the grey hairs of which were concealed by the flowing tresses of an auburn wig, a large straw hat, loaded with flowers and feathers, and only fit for a young woman under thirty.

"Surely, mamma," cried Emily, "that old lady can never intend to buy that hat? It is too gay for one of her years."

THE BAZAAR.

"She certainly does," said Maria, "and I dare say believes that it will make her look twenty years younger than she really is."

"She thinks wrong then, sister," exclaimed Theodore. "For unless she can hide the wrinkles in her face and neck, and the loss of her teeth, and the leanness of her body, she will only the more expose her age, by dressing so ridiculously."

"Mamma! mamma!" cried Caroline, "there is the very same old lady looking at that beautiful crape dress, at the Dressmaker's, who was trying on the large straw hat with such a profusion of feathers and flowers."

"Hush! my lovely girl," said her mamma, "if you are not more silent I must take you home."

"It is just the thing, Mrs. Tasteful," screamed out the

old lady. "It will suit my figure exactly. Square bosom, and off the shoulders, why with a lace frill I shall look delightful. A saucy fellow had the impudence to tell me, as I was getting out of my carriage, that I had better wear my petticoats a little longer to hide my legs, and put a shawl on to conceal my neck. The fool had no more taste than a Hottentot. Well, my dear woman, you will let me have

this dress immediately. I am going out to a ball this evening, and I shall want to put it on. Primrose coloured crape over white sarsenet. Charming, I declare!"

"Come on, my dears," said Mr. Durnford, hastily, "I have no inclination to listen any longer to such disgusting vanity and folly. The age of that lady ought to have enabled her to set good examples to the younger and inexperienced part of her sex, instead of which she is only a disgrace to it. Come on, my dears, I will not stay a moment longer, lest another burst of weakness should offend my ear. You all know what is the province of a dressmaker, therefore it requires no explanation."

"Now for the Bookseller," cried Theodore, with delight, as his eyes rested upon a parcel of books neatly bound, which were placed on the next counter.

"I have no objection to your selecting one book apiece," said his father, "but you remember, Theodore, that I always make a point of buying all your books at the corner of St. Paul's Church-yard. You may, however, purchase a few of this person, who appears to have got a very good selection."

"I had them, Sir, of Mr. Harris, in St. Paul's Churchyard," said the woman. "He was so good as to choose for me what he thought would sell best."

VISIT TO MELVYN LODGE.

[From *Inducements to Virtuous Habits; Exemplified in a Series of Original Letters, Between A Father and Son during the absence of the latter at school.* London: printed for J. Bysh, 52 Paternoster Row. 1818.]

WHEN we arrived we accompanied Sir James Melvyn to a walk over the grounds that surrounded the house: it is a very pretty place with a fine view of the river; we entered a beautiful field slightly paled all round, leaving a space the breadth of a narrow road round the paling, which took us to a large barn; but, think what was my surprise at seeing the barn filled with company; not the ladies and gentlemen of the neighbourhood, but the poor farmers and labourers, old

VISIT TO MELVYN LODGE.

and young sitting at a long table where they had dined, and were now enjoying their pipes and fine October beer. Our friend, old Dennis, sat at the head of the table, his two grandsons attending to the company.

When we entered the barn they all stood up, and bowing to Mr. Frederick Melvyn, begged leave to drink his honour's health: this being agreed to, they filled their tumblers and with looks of gratitude to their good master they wished his son to enjoy long life and happiness. Mr. Frederick thanked them, saying it would always be his greatest pleasure to see them and their families in comfort. "And now, Dennis, as you are master of the ceremonies here, will you give a health for your companions to follow?" Dennis immediately stood up, and putting his hand to his breast said, "I will be happy, sir, to shew my regard to a gentleman who in taking notice of my poor boys and teaching them their duty, has given their old grandfather the greatest of blessings, content and cheerfulness; I mean, sir, Mr. Franklin." He then desired Patrick and Dick to drink the health of their best friend; and thus was Mr. Franklin honoured by this happy company.

We were now joined by many ladies and gentlemen whom Lady Melvyn took to see the rustic party.

After staying a short time in the barn, Sir James asked the company if they would proceed with him to the paddock; they all consented, and we went to the field I mentioned before.

There we were met by four young men, dressed in blue silk jackets and hunting caps; each of them leading a donkey nicely trimmed and ornamented with blue ribbon roses, and bridles of the same; who looked so conceited and vain of this finery, that they appeared quite different from any donkeys I had ever seen. The ladies went to a marquee prettily fitted up for the purpose. Mr. Frederick then desired the young men to mount, telling them that they were to run their donkeys three times round the paling, and the first that reached the starting post would obtain the donkey he rode on. A trumpet then sounding

they all set off together, and you would be surprised to see how quick these little creatures cantered round. I thought of my pretty poney and how far he would have left them all behind.

In the first round one had got a great deal before the

VISIT TO MELVYN LODGE.

rest, and it was thought Jack would win the prize; the second round he was still the first, but the others were almost up to him. In the third Jack began to tire, and Dick got before him; but Jerry who had been hindmost now got forward and won the race; while poor Jack unable to keep up any longer, though encouraged by his rider, made a full stop and would not proceed a step further.

The victory was proclaimed by the loud shouts of the people, all eager to shake hands with William Cowslip the young farmer who won the donkey, and who was promised a nice cart to fit him by Mr. Frederick Melvyn.

Cowslip looked delighted; and making an awkward bow thanked Mr. Melvyn for his kindness. Everyone seemed happy but the young man who rode on Jack: him I perceived at the further side of the field sitting under a tree seemingly in trouble. I went to him, and asked him why he sat there by himself, while everyone else is so merry?

"Oh, sir," said the poor lad; "I have lost the donkey which would have made my poor mother quite comfortable."
"How can the loss of the donkey make you so sad," said I, "when you know it was all a chance whether you would win him?"

"Oh, my dear young gentleman," said he, "that is very true; but I had other reasons than amusement to try my chance. I am a wood-cutter; and had an ass and cart to carry my wood through the country, and was able to support myself and sickly mother very well; for we did not want anything; but my poor ass died about three months ago, and I am not able to buy one. I can now only sell my wood in the neighbourhood, and we begin to feel great want. I could shift for myself very well, but cannot leave poor mother." "Don't make yourself so unhappy, my good fellow;" said I, and gave him what money I had : "this small sum may be of a little use to your mother; perhaps I may be able to get you an ass—think no more of it, but come and be happy with your companions." The gratitude of the poor lad quite distressed me: he raised his eyes and hands to Heaven praying for blessings on me. After a little while we both recovered and walked together to the cheerful party.

"Where have you been, Sydney?" said Sir James; "and who is it you have with you? Why this is honest Ben Trayford who rode on Jack." "Yes, sir," I answered, and I told him what trouble Ben was in.

"Well, my dear Charles," said Sir James; and he pressed my hand with the same warm affection that you often do, "your friend Ben shall not have cause for so much grief: he is as worthy a lad as any on my estate. Come to the Lodge, Ben, to-morrow morning, and I will speak to you: but now make yourself easy; I must not see an unhappy countenance among my friends to-day."

CURLING, OR HOCKEY.

[From *School Boy's Diversions: with Proper Directions for playing them.* Second Edition. Engravings from designs by R. Stennett. London: printed and sold by Dean & Munday, Threadneedle Street. Price One Shilling.]

HOCKEY is a game much practised in the northern parts of Great Britain, particularly during severe weather. A number of persons, each with a stick curled at one end, pursue a large ball or round piece of cork, over the frozen ground or

SCHOOL BOY'S DIVERSIONS.

ice. Nimbleness and agility are the chief requisites of this game, the main diversion lying in your being able to keep the ball at play for some time against the combined efforts of all your playfellows. Of course this is much more difficult on the ice than on the ground: those therefore should only join it on the ice who can stand well in their skates.

SKIPPING.

THIS is performed either by one or by several children; if the former, it is either with the rope crossed or extended; if the latter, two hold the rope while a third (or a couple at once) leap over it. This a most charming exercise for cold weather and proper for either sex.

SCHOOL BOY'S DIVERSIONS.

PRESSGANG.

To play at this one of the boys represents an officer, and four or six others the gang. They catch their companions one at a time and on catching one, say to him—

> "High ship, or low ship;
> King's ship, or no ship?"

If he chooses one of the ships, they send him as a prisoner in the custody of two of their gang, to any place they may agree upon, where he must stop a prisoner; but if he say, "No ship," they must take him by force, by his hands, legs and arms to their rendez-vous for pressed men. When they are all pressed, the pressed men and volunteers, by turn become pressgang and officer.

HUCKLEBONES.

HUCKLEBONES can be played with more or fewer bones, but five in general are used. Particular names are given to almost all the different ways of playing. This is what is called the first. Take five bones, throw one into the air and lay the others on the table; take up one again; and then another before the first falls and so on to the last. Here is the second way: take up two at a time, and as they are falling, take up three; throw them up;—then four.

There are many others: first, the Kisses—kiss the bone while the other is in the air; or strike your breast with one bone.

This game is played a hundred different ways, and so long invented that it was played by the Greeks at the siege of Troy.

The tricks are these: make a bow with your thumb and forefinger, and every bone passes through while the others

SCHOOL BOY'S DIVERSIONS.

are in the air; or make a well with your hand and put them all in one after the other. Make the Change by putting one bone in the place of the other;—the Raffle in taking up all the bones together. You may play the Hollow or Reverse by turning them all one after the other on the marked side. The most difficult, because it must be light, is to gather them up successively, one after the other; that is what they call the shoots. The Square is made by arranging the four bones in a quadrangle; before taking them you must first have one; then two, which you must throw up in taking the third, and still retain two, and so on.

JAMES MANNERS.

[From *James Manners, Little John, and their dog Bluff.* By Elizabeth Helme, jun. Fifth Edition. London: Darton, Harvey & Darton. 1818.]

JOHN ran back regardless of the affront he had received, grasped the dog by the throat and disengaged the terrified James.

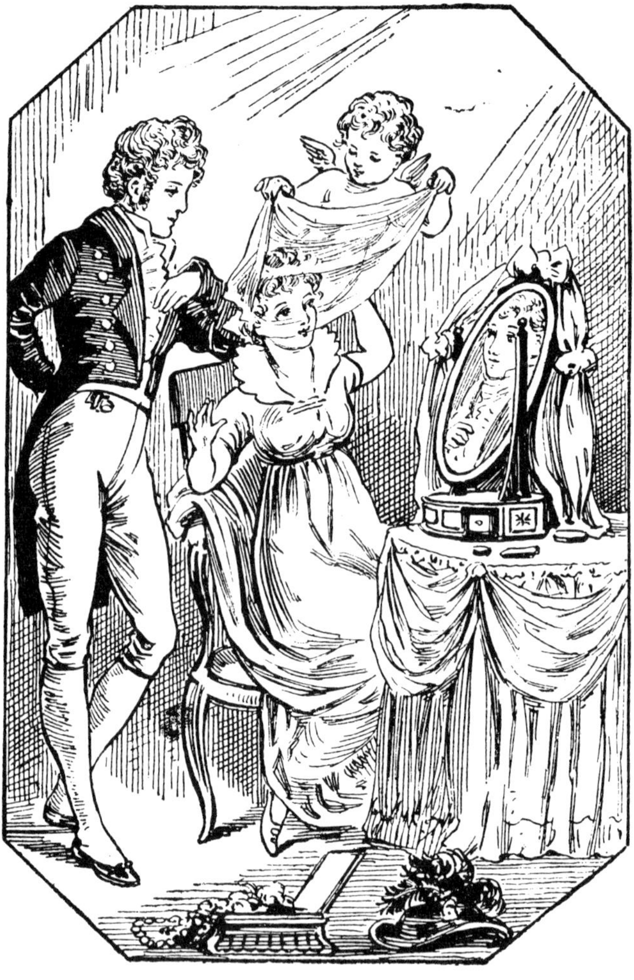

The Mint;

OR

Shillings Transformed into Pounds.

BY

PEREGRINE PROTEUS, *the Younger*,

A NEAR RELATION OF THAT CELEBRATED CHARACTER

MARMADUKE MULTIPLY

J. HARRIS & SON
Corner of St. Paul's Church-yard.
1819

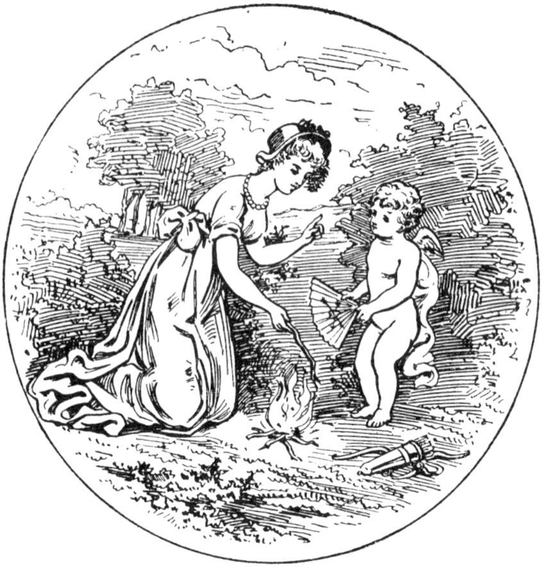

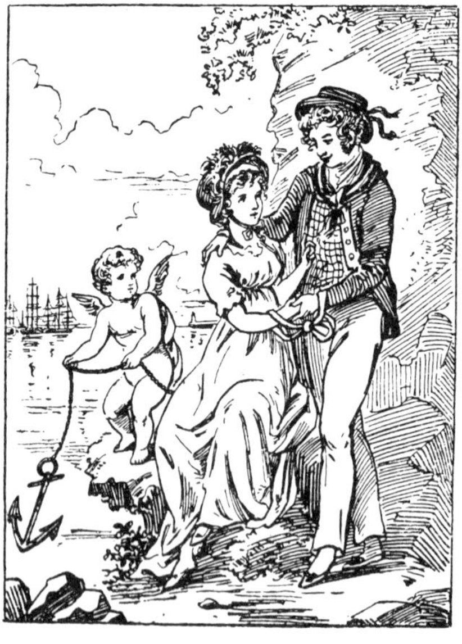

THE MINT.

THAT Twenty shillings are a Pound
Is known full well the World around.

And Thirty shillings, One Pound Ten
The Poet's fortune, now and then.

With Forty shillings, just Two Pounds,
I think I'll purchase yonder grounds.

With Fifty shillings, Two Pounds Ten
Grand Ma oft pays our Husbandmen.

THE MINT.

Here's Sixty shillings or Three Pounds
Then who's afraid of Fortune's frowns.

The Wages given to our boy Ben
Is Seventy shillings—Three Pounds Ten.

Eighty shillings is Four Pounds
Which Master gave for these fine hounds.

Ninety shillings is Four Pounds Ten
The Bounty giv'n to NELSON's Men.

THE MINT.

One-hundred shillings is Five Pounds
You'll want it in your market rounds.

AVOIRDUPOIS WEIGHT.

In all things you sell and whatever you buy,
To justice and honour keep steady your eye.

THE MINT.

Come trip along my Girls and Boys
We'll have fair weight AVOIRDUPOIS.

Of your best snuff for my Aunt Flounce
Give Sixteen drams which make One ounce.

Sixteen ounces just One pound
I've got of Coffee ready ground.

Twenty-eight pounds of Butter I gave to your Daughter
Though it is better known in our Trade by a Quarter.

This Bale is Four quarters or One hundredweight
Which I bring from yon ship by desire of the Mate.

O dear, what delight 'tis to have such a Son
Who of Sugar has sent Twenty hundreds, One ton.

Harris's Cabinet

—

PENCE TABLES

ONE SHILLING.

J. HARRIS & SON
Corner of St. Paul's Churchyard
1819

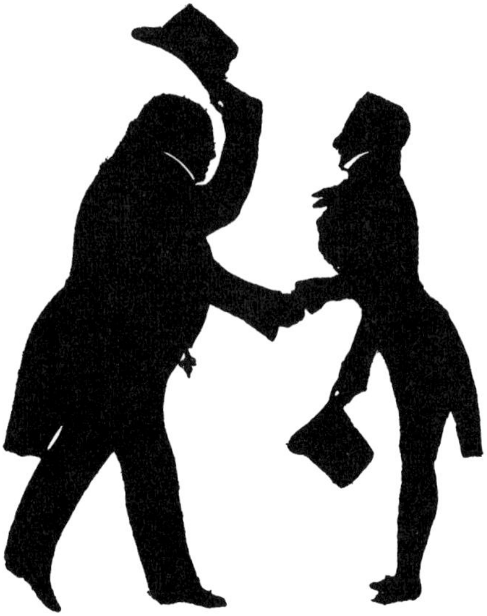

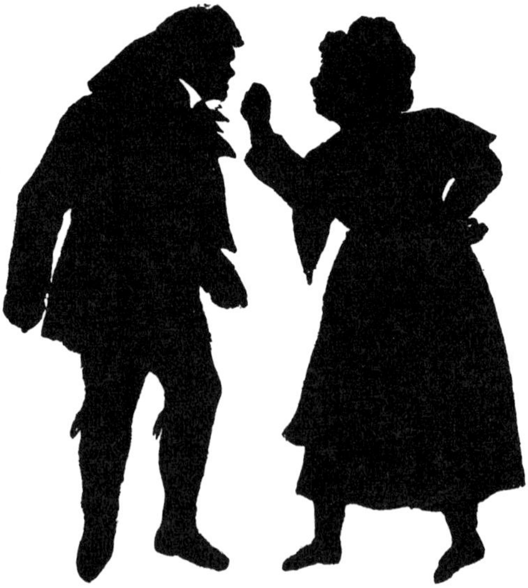

HARRIS'S CABINET.

Twelve Pence is just 1sh.
  This I gave to buy a Whip.

Fourteen Pence is 1sh. and 2d.
  Which I paid for my New Ship.

Sixteen Pence is 1sh. and 4d.
  The price of this fine flying Toy.

Eighteen Pence is 1sh. and 6d.
  This I gave the Negro Boy.

Twenty Pence is 1sh. and 8d.
  This in paper out I laid.

HARRIS'S CABINET.

Thirty Pence is 2sh. and 6d.
   Which I for a Grammar paid.

Forty Pence is 3sh. and 4d.
   This I spent in going to School.

Fifty Pence is 4sh. and 2d.
   And with this I bought a rule.

Sixty Pence is just 5sh.
   Master this in entrance got.

Seventy Pence is 5sh. and 10d.
   Who dares say that it is not.

Eighty Pence is 6sh. and 8d.
   This is just a Lawyer's fee.

Ninety Pence is 7sh. and 6d.
   Which you all may plainly see.

PETER THE GREAT.

One-hundred Pence is 8sh. and 4d.
  This I lent to Cousin Ben.

And as he wanted 9sh. and 2d.
  I sent him the other Ten.

He wrote to have it made 10sh.
  And then I gave him ten pence more

And begg'd hereafter he'd not teaze me
  Nor borrow thus to make me poor.

PETER THE GREAT.

[From *Æsop in Rhyme, with some Originals. By Jefferys Taylor, Author of Harry's Holiday.* London: printed for Baldwin, Cradock & Joy, Paternoster Row. 1820.]

A CERTAIN man, as some do say,
  Who liv'd in peace and quiet,
Did line his inside every day
  With most nutritious diet.

" For sure," thought he, as skilfully
  The mutton he did carve,
" 'Twould be exceeding wrong in me
  My body for to starve."

His body, measured round about,
  When his great coat was on,
Was four good yards there's not a doubt;
  His weight was forty stone.

*   *   *   *   *   *

PETER THE GREAT.

"Judith, I am not well at all,
  Within I'm sore distrest;
I fear I'm ill with what they call
  A load upon the chest."

"I know not when I've felt so bad;
  I think, say what you will,

That goose that yesterday I had
  Is in my stomach still!"

"Haste for the doctor ere he's out,
  For he may be of use:
Tell him my feet have got the gout;
  My stomach's got the goose."

PETER THE GREAT.

Said she, "I go; but it may be
   Some time I shall be gone;
So 'twill be better first for me
   To put the boiler on."

Water and fire with angry strife,
   A hissing dire did make;
Which Peter hearing, dreamed his wife
   Was broiling him a steak.

Then in his dream his sleepy poll
   With anger great did nod he;
When lo! the tumult of his soul
   Awoke his peaceful body.

Then loudly to his wife be called
   "Come hither dame, I pray!"
But vainly to the dame he bawled
   For she was far away.

At last he reached his walking stick,
   To shove the boiling pot;
When o'er his legs it tumbled quick!
   And water scalding hot!

No longer now he felt the gout,
   But roaring out amain,
Briskly he turned his legs about,
   And stood upright again.

With scalded feet and broken head,
   He danced upon the floor;
He had not done the like 'tis said
   For twenty years or more.

PETER THE GREAT.

At last the street door lock within
　　The key began to rattle;
Thought Peter, "now will soon begin
　　A most tremendous battle."

Then, with the doctor close behind
　　Entered the wife of Peter;
But how was she surprised to find
　　Her husband come to meet her.

Said she, "how's this, that thou *alone*
　　Canst walk along the path?"
Said he, "I've been, since thou wast gone,
　　In a hot water bath."

Then Peter he related quite
　　What we have told before;
Then did the doctor laugh outright,
　　With loud and lengthened roar.

"But, sir," said he, "now I suppose
　　That all this time you've fasted;
Pray tell me if your stomach's woes
　　The same till now have lasted."

"Why, no," said Peter, "I must own
　　That since from food I've rested;
The load is from my stomach gone,
　　And seems to be digested."

"Then," said the doctor, "I advise
　　When plagued with gouty pain;
Since that's removed by exercise
　　To scald your legs again."

FANNY AND MARY.

[From *Fanny and Mary, or Juvenile Views of Happiness.* By the Author of *Mamma's Pictures, &c.* London: Printed for Harvey & Darton, no. 55 Gracechurch Street. 1821.]

"I RAN down to the beach and filled my pockets with pebbles. I used to run and skip on the sand and shingles, and play at being a flying fish. I would always run on the

FANNY AND MARY.

wet sand and into the salt-water puddles, so at last mamma said that it spoiled my clothes, and I was forbidden to walk on the beach."

THE YOUNG REVIEWERS.

[From *The Young Reviewers, or, The Poems Dissected.* London: William Darton, 58 Holborn Hill. 1821.]

THE boys came running in from school calling out "A holiday this afternoon! a half-holiday to-day! Huzza! Is dinner almost ready; that we may take a walk and fly our kites this fine day?"

THE YOUNG REVIEWERS.

"Well, my dear children," said Mrs. Heathcote, as she presented each of them with a small reward, "you have been very quiet and diligent, and I hope these little Poems may be the means of impressing on your minds sentiments of far more value than this little reward of your exertion."

PICTURESQUE PIETY.

THE DOG GLAD OF A CRUMB.

[From *Picturesque Piety*. By the Rev. Isaac Taylor. London: printed for E. Butler, Bruton Street; and Longman, Hurst Rees, Orme & Brown, Paternoster Row. 1821.]

SEE how Jowler sits and begs,
    All the while my mess I'm eating;
How he holds his little legs;
    Whining, wagging, and entreating.

How he'd like to have my stool,
    Or to get upon the table;
Ah, you saucy little fool,
    I should beat you, were you able.

PICTURESQUE PIETY.

There's a tiny crumb of bread,
    Good enough for you, sir, truly;
Dogs should not like us be fed,
    But with scraps and crumbles, duly.

THE MOTH.

Now who has spoiled my pretty muff,
    And torn the fur, look here:
I'm sure I put it safe enough,
    'Twont do another year.

I do declare it is the moth,
    See, here are more and more;
They've eaten holes quite through the cloth
    And ruined all my store.

ORIGINAL POEMS FOR INFANT MINDS.

THE LITTLE FISHERMAN.

[From *Original Poems for Infant Minds. By Several Young Persons*. 2 vols. Twentieth Edition. London : Harvey & Darton, No. 55 Gracechurch Street. 1821.]

> THERE was a little fellow once,
>   And Harry was his name :
> And many a naughty trick had he—
>   I tell it to his shame.
>
> He minded not his friends' advice,
>   But follow'd his own wishes;
> And one most cruel trick of his,
>   Was that of catching fishes.
>
> His father had a little pond,
>   Where often Harry went;
> And in this most inhuman sport,
>   He many an ev'ning spent.
>
> One day he took his hook and bait,
>   And hurried to the pond,
> And there began the cruel game,
>   Of which he was so fond.
>
> And many a little fish he caught,
>   And pleas'd was he to look,
> To see them writhe in agony,
>   And struggle on the hook.

At last, when having caught enough,
    And tired too himself;
He hasten'd home, intending there
    To put them on a shelf.

But as he jump'd to reach a dish,
    To put his fishes in,
A large meat-hook, that hung close by,
    Did catch him by the chin.

Poor Harry kick'd, and call'd aloud,
    And scream'd and cried, and roar'd;
While from his wound the crimson blood
    In dreadful torrents pour'd.

The maids came running, frighten'd much
    To see him hanging there,
And soon they took him from the hook,
    And set him in a chair.

The surgeon came and stopp'd the blood,
    And up he bound his head;
And then they carried him up stairs,
    And laid him on his bed.

Conviction darted on his mind,
    As groaning there he lay,
He with remorse and pity thought
    About his cruel play.

"And oh," said he, "poor little fish,
    What tortures they have borne;
While I, well pleas'd, have stood to see
    Their tender bodies torn;

"O! what a wicked boy I've been,
   Such torments to bestow;'
Well I deserve the pain I feel,
   Since I could serve them so:

"But now I know how great the smart,
   How terrible the pain!
As long as I can *feel* myself,
   I'll never fish again."

J. T.

JAMES AND THE SHOULDER OF MUTTON.

YOUNG Jem at noon returned from school,
   As hungry as could be,
He cried to Sue, the servant maid,
   My dinner give to me.

Said Sue, it is not yet come home,
   Besides, it is not late:—
No matter that, cries little Jem,
   I do not like to wait.

Quick to the baker's Jemmy went,
   And ask'd "Is dinner done?"
"It is," replied the baker's man.
"Then home I'll with it run."

"Nay, Sir," replied he, prudently,
   "I tell you 'tis too hot,
And much too heavy 'tis for you."
   "I tell you, it is not.

" Papa, mamma, are both gone out,
    And I for dinner long;
So give it me—it is all mine,
    And, baker, hold your tongue.

" A shoulder 'tis of mutton nice!
    And batter-pudding too;
I'm glad of that, it is so good;
    How clever is our Sue!"

Now near the door young Jem was come,
    He round the corner turn'd!
But oh, sad fate! unlucky chance!
    The dish his fingers burn'd.

Low in the kennel down fell dish,
    And down fell all the meat;
Swift went the pudding in the stream,
    And sail'd along the street.

The people laugh'd, and rude boys grinn'd,
    At mutton's hapless fall;
But though asham'd young Jemmy cried—
    " Better lose part than all."

The shoulder by the knuckle seiz'd,
    His hands both grasp'd it fast,
And deaf to all their gibes and cries,
    He gain'd his home at last.

" Impatience is a fault," cries Jem,
    " The baker told me true;
In future I will patient be,
    And mind what says our Sue."

ADELAIDE.

SOPHIA'S FOOL'S-CAP.

Sophia was a little child,
Obliging, good, and very mild,
Yet, lest of dress she should be vain,
Mamma still dress'd her well, but plain.—
Her parents, sensible and kind,
Wish'd only to adorn her mind;
No other dress, when good, had she,
But useful, neat simplicity.
Tho' seldom, yet when she was rude,
Or ever in a naughty mood,
Her punishment was this disgrace,
A large fine cap adorned with lace,
With feathers and with ribbons too;
The work was neat, the fashion new;
Yet, as a fool's-cap was its name,
She dreaded much to wear the same.

A lady, fashionably gay,
Did to mamma a visit pay,
Sophia star'd, then whisp'ring said,
"Why, dear mamma, look at her head!
To be so tall and wicked too,
The strangest thing I ever knew;
What naughty tricks, pray, has she done,
That they have put that fool's-cap on."

ADELAIDE.

WASHING AND DRESSING.

Ah! why will my dear little girl be so cross,
   And cry, and look sulky, and pout?
To lose her sweet smile is a terrible loss,
   I can't even kiss her without.

You say you don't like to be wash'd and be drest,
    But would you be dirty and foul?
Come, drive that long sob from your dear little breast,
    And clear your sweet face from its scowl.

If the water is cold, and the comb hurts your head,
    And the soap has got into your eye;
Will the water grow warmer for all that you've said?
    And what good will it do you to cry?

It is not to tease you and hurt you, my sweet,
    But only for kindness and care,
That I wash you, and dress you, and make you look neat,
    And comb out your tanglesome hair.

I don't mind the trouble, if you would not cry,
    But pay me for all with a kiss;
That's right—take the towel and wipe your wet eye,
    I thought you'd be good after this.

Ann.

The Notorious Glutton.

A duck who had got such a habit of stuffing
That all the day long she was panting and puffing,
And by every creature who did her great crop see,
Was thought to be galloping fast for a dropsy;

One day after eating a plentiful dinner,
With full twice as much as there should have been in her
While up to her forehead still greedily roking
Was greatly alarmed by the symptoms of choking.

ORIGINAL POEMS FOR INFANT MINDS.

Now there was an old fellow, much famed for discerning
(A drake who had taken a liking for learning)
And high in repute with his feathery friends
Was called Dr. Drake: for this doctor she sends.

In a hole of the dunghill was Dr. Drake's shop,
Where he kept a few simples for clearing the crop;
Small pebbles, and two or three different gravels,
With certain famed plants he had found in his travels.

So taking a handful of suitable things,
And brushing his topple and pluming his wings,
And putting his feathers in apple-pie order,
He went to prescribe for the lady's disorder.

"Dear Sir," said the duck, with a delicate quack,
Just turning a little way round on her back,
And leaning her head on a stone in the yard,
"My case, Dr. Drake, is exceedingly hard.

"I feel so distended with wind and opprest,
So squeamish and faint, such a load at my chest;
And day after day, I assure you it *is* hard,
To suffer with patience these pains in my gizzard."

"Give me leave," said the doctor with medical look,
As her cold flabby paw in his fingers he took;
"By the feel of your pulse, your complaint I've been
 thinking,
Must surely be owing to eating and drinking."

"Oh! no, Sir, believe me," the lady replied,
(Alarmed for her stomach as well as her pride)
"I'm sure it arises from nothing I eat,
But I rather suspect I got wet in my feet.

"I've only been raking a bit in the gutter,
Where cook has been pouring some cold melted butter,
And a slice of green cabbage, and scraps of cold meat:
Just a trifle or two that I thought I could eat."

The doctor was just to his business proceeding,
By gentle emetics, a blister, and bleeding,
When all on a sudden she rolled on her side,
Gave a terrible quack, and a struggle and died!

Her remains were interred in a neighbouring swamp
By her friends, with a great deal of funeral pomp;
But I've heard, this inscription her tombstone was put on
"Here lies Mrs. Duck, the notorious glutton";
And all the young ducklings are brought by their friends
There to learn the disgrace in which gluttony ends.

The Spider and His Wife.

In a dark little crack, half a yard from the ground,
    An honest old spider resided;
So pleasant, and snug, and convenient 'twas found,
That his friends came to see it from many miles round:
    It seemed for his pleasure provided.

Of the cares, and fatigues, and distresses of life,
    This spider was thoroughly tired;
So leaving those scenes of distraction and strife
(His children all settled) he came with his wife,
    To live in this cranny retired.

He thought that the little his wife would consume
    'Twould be easy for him to provide her;
Forgetting he lived in a gentleman's room,
Where came every morning a maid and a broom,
    Those pitiless foes to a spider!

For when (as sometimes it would chance to befall)
    The moment his web was completed,
Brush—came the great broom down the side of the wall,
And perhaps carried with it web, spider and all
    He thought himself cruelly treated.

One day when their cupboard was empty and dry,
    His wife (Mrs. Hairy-leg Spinner)
Said to him, " Dear, go to the cobweb and try
If you can't find the leg or the wing of a fly,
    As a bit of a relish for dinner."

Directly he went, his long search to resume,
    (For nothing he ever denied her)
Alas! little guessing his terrible doom,
Just then came the gentleman into the room
    And saw the unfortunate spider.

So while the poor insect in search of his pelf,
    In the cobweb continued to linger,
The gentleman reached a long cane from the shelf,
(For certain good reasons best known to himself
    Preferring his stick to his finger :)

Then presently poking him down to the floor,
    Nor stopping at all to consider
With one horrid crash the whole business was o'er,
The poor little spider was heard of no more,
    To the lasting distress of his widow.

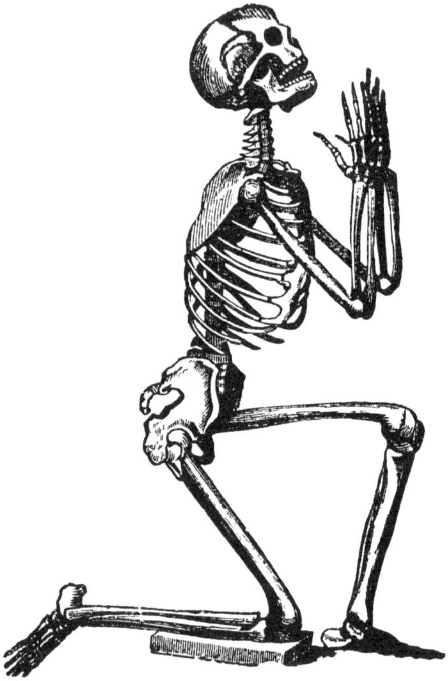

The

DANDY'S BALL;

or,

HIGH LIFE IN THE CITY

Embellished with Sixteen Coloured Engravings.

LONDON:
Printed and sold by
JOHN MARSHALL,
140 Fleet Street
From Aldermary Church Yard
1823

Price 1s. 6d,

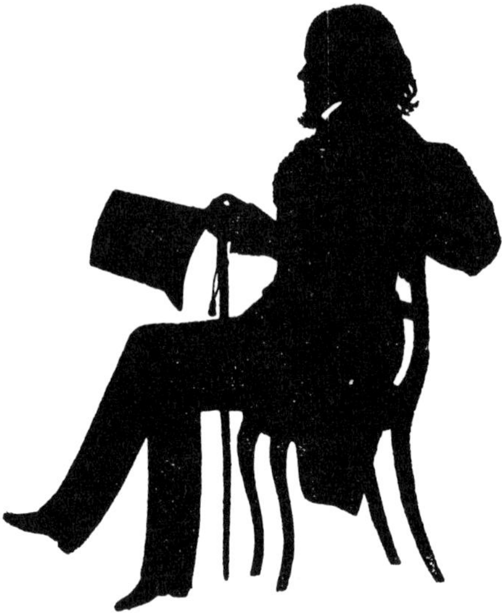

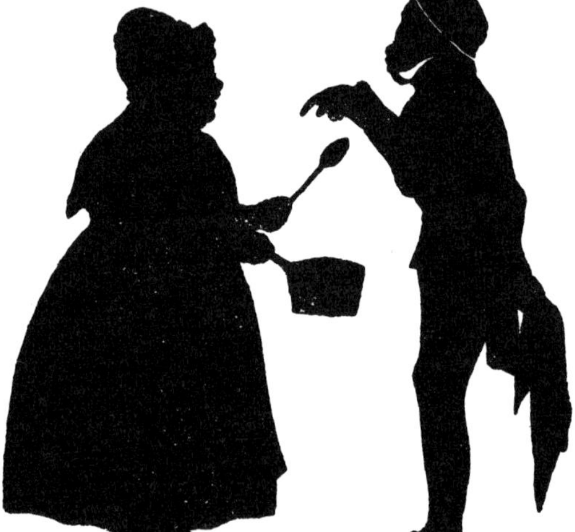

THE DANDY'S BALL.

Mr. Pillblister
And Betsy his sister,
Determin'd on giving a treat;
Gay Dandies they call
To a supper and ball
At their house in Great Camomile Street.

THE DANDY'S BALL.

Mr. Padum delighted
For he was invited
Began to consider his dress;
His shirt was not clean
Nor fit to be seen
So he wash'd it: he could not do less.

THE DANDY'S BALL.

Here's the stays from the tailor
For Mr. Mac Nailor
Oh, Jeffrey! lace it quite tight.
I'll hold by the post,
That no time may be lost;
At the Ball I'll outshine all to-night.

THE DANDY'S BALL.

At dinner so pleased
For his mind was quite eased,
As all his new clothes were just come,
Sat our dear Mr. Parrot,
Till carving a carrot,
He unhappily put out his thumb.

THE DANDY'S BALL.

A hole in my stocking
Now how very shocking!
Cries poor Mr. Mopstaff enraged;
It is always my fate
To be so very late
When at Mr. Pillblister's engaged.

THE DANDY'S BALL.

I'll dance with my charmer,
    Said Mr. Bob Palmer,
I'm determin'd to-night at the Ball.
I've dined on the fishes,
    And washed up the dishes,
And wait for the Barber to call.

THE DANDY'S BALL.

While sipping his tea
Mr. Frill you may see,
And his friend, both so gaily dressed out
For Mr. Pillblister's
And his polite sister's
Most splendid and elegant rout.

THE DANDY'S BALL.

Alas ! only think
When poor Mr. Pink
Had decked himself out in his charms,
When dressing was done,
With fatigue overcome
He faints in his Grandmother's arms.

THE DANDY'S BALL.

Mr. Cuff in a shower
Stood full half an hour,
In hopes some kind friend he should meet;
For his handkerchief fell,
I am sorry to tell,
When turning up Camomile Street.

THE DANDY'S BALL.

From the street called Threadneedle
Came gay Mrs. Tweedle,
And her Squire, in their Dennet so neat;
But when most delighted
Our prospects are blighted,
By accidents sadly complete.

THE DANDY'S BALL.

To be candid, I'll tell
To the Camomile smell,
Their horse took a prejudice small;
He reared up and pranced
And on his legs danced,
Till he overset carriage and all.

THE DANDY'S BALL.

When the company met,
They all bowed to Miss Bet,
Excepting poor Mr. Bob Palmer,
Who had the mishap
To knock off the cap
And tread on the toes of his charmer.

THE DANDY'S BALL.

When the dancing began
To their places some ran,
For when they came to the saloon
So stiffened and tight
As for dancing that night
They might as well rise to the moon.

THE DANDY'S BALL.

For their supper some wished
When they heard it was dished
In raptures they sat down to eat;
But so hard was their case,
For they could not unlace,
So few of them tasted the treat.

THE DANDY'S BALL.

>Many ordered their carriage
>And thought till their marriage
>They would never be in so much pain;
>Though I very much doubt
>But at the next rout
>We shall see all these Dandies again.

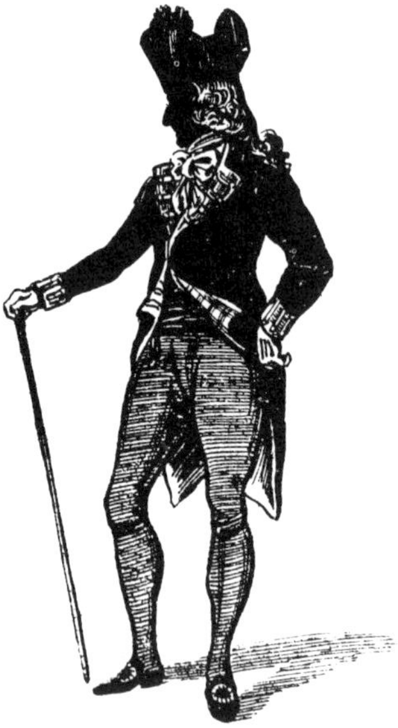

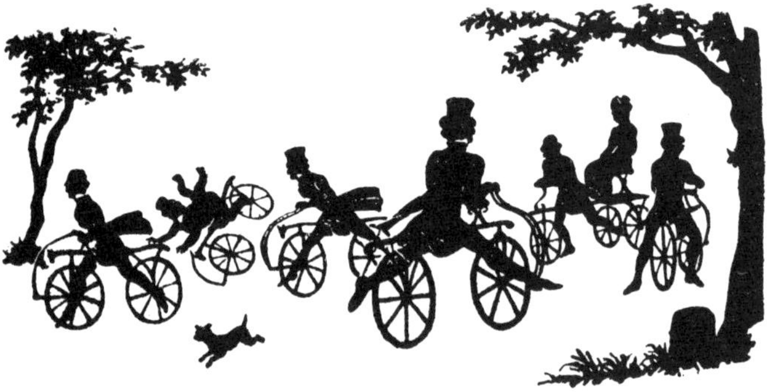

TOWN AND COUNTRY TALES.

Intended for the

AMUSEMENT

and

MORAL INSTRUCTION

OF YOUTH.

LONDON:
Printed for JOHN TERKITT, 62, Judd Street,
Brunswick Square;
And N. HAILES, 172, Piccadilly.

1824.

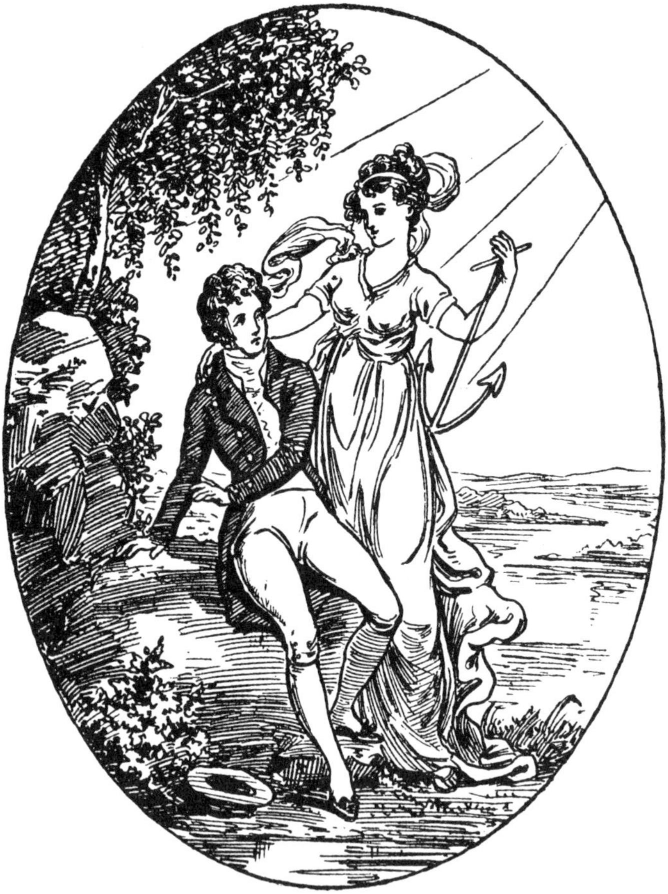

TOWN AND COUNTRY TALES.

THE YOUNG PROTECTOR.

Felix Dunmore was sent one day by his father on an errand of some importance. Although but fourteen years of age, the steadiness of his character, and the judgment and prudence he had shown on several occasions, had acquired him the entire confidence of his parent.

In passing through an unfrequented street, he perceived a young lady of about his own age, and very respectable in her appearance, in the midst of several young men, who seemed to amuse themselves with her evident embarrassment in finding herself thus alone and unprotected. She had lately arrived from the country, and had gone out on that morning with her mother, from whom she was separated in a crowd, and after wandering through several streets, she was now enquiring her way home. Without noticing the sneers of the spectators, he enquired of the young lady her address, and having learned it, he told her respectfully that as he was himself going to that part of the town where she lived, he would, with her leave, have the pleasure of seeing her home.

After some hesitation the young lady accepted his offer, and Felix having expressed, as they were walking together, his indignation at the unmanly conduct of the people whom they had just left, she felt reassured with regard to the character of her new companion.

At a short distance from her house, they met the mother of Olivia, (such was the young lady's name) who after fruitless researches and enquiries, was returning home in the greatest anxiety for her daughter's safety. Seeing her with a young man of respectable appearance, she enquired his name, at the same time expressing her warmest thanks for the care he had taken of her daughter. Felix wishing out of delicacy, to lessen the importance of the service he had rendered, said he was proceeding that way on business, and mentioned the person to whom he was taking a letter from his father. Olivia's mother perceived that in order to oblige her daughter, he had gone considerably beyond the place of his destination; she therefore repeated her thanks to him, and her excuses for his trouble and loss of time.

During this conversation they arrived at the lady's house, which was in one of the fashionable streets near Grosvenor Square. The lady was a person of rank, and kept her carriage and livery servants, but on that morning had walked out with her daughter, unattended by a footman, to call upon an intimate acquaintance; when meeting unexpectedly with a crowd of people at the turning of a street, her daughter had been suddenly separated from her, and they had lost sight of each other.

Lady Chalmers insisted upon Felix walking into the parlour to rest himself; at the same time she ordered her carriage, while she engaged him in conversation, asking him several questions about his family. Felix, with great candour, told her, he was the son of a retired officer without fortune, who had come to town to solicit a pension from government, on account of his long services and injured health, and that he was going that morning with a memorial on the subject addressed to a person in office.

At last Felix rose to take his leave:—the lady told him that her carriage was ready to convey him to the place of his destination, in order to make up for the time he had lost.

"Lost, Madam!" exclaimed Felix, "I shall always look upon *that* time as well employed, in which I shall have an opportunity of rendering any service to a lady, and make reparation for the brutality of some of my own sex." He left Lady Chalmers highly delighted with him, and desirous of shewing her gratitude in a more effectual manner.

A few days after Felix had delivered the memorial, his father received a letter from the minister, informing him that a liberal pension had been granted to him, with the additional promise, that his son would shortly be provided for. Captain Dunmore, full of satisfaction and gratitude, went to return thanks to the minister. The secretary who received him, did not conceal from him, that the granting his request had been hastened by powerful recommendations. The veteran testified his surprise at such an unexpected interest in his favour, of which he was totally unaware.

"Your pension," said the secretary, "would certainly have been granted to you, as you had proper claims to it, although from the pressure of business you would perhaps have been obliged to wait a little longer; but as to the favour which it is in contemplation to bestow upon your son, and which was unasked by you, it is entirely in consequence of his own handsome conduct to a lady, a near relation of a person high in office." He then related to the happy father the meeting of his son with Olivia, of which Felix, out of modesty, had not mentioned a word.

On returning home, the veteran commended his son for his manly conduct, and congratulated him on the happy results of it. They went together to the residence of their benefactress. On attempting to express their thanks, they were stopped short by Lady Chalmers, who observed, that the honourable spirit and the sense of delicacy of so young a man as Felix, fully deserved the interest that had been excited in his favour, and that it must be a satisfaction to those who are possessed of any influence to use it in bringing forward deserving persons.

Thus we see that even the world does not always let good actions pass unrewarded, although it is the secret approbation of conscience, that ought at all times to be considered as a sufficient recompense for them.

SELF-INFLICTED CORRECTION.

MR. WHARTON, a retired merchant, was left in his old age with only one daughter out of several children he had had. Katharine was the object of her father's tenderness, his companion, and the comfort of his declining years. Having been deprived of her mother at an early age, and left to the care of an old governess, she had contracted the pernicious habit of doing everything according to the whim of the moment, of following the dictates of her unruly imagination, and though hardly in her teens, she took upon herself the supreme command over all her father's household.

This overbearing propensity was increased by her father's indulgence, and grew at last to an intolerable extent. If a servant happened to forget some trifling commission, the young lady had entrusted to him, she upbraided him in the most humiliating terms. If another was a minute too slow in answering the summons of her bell, it was an unpardonable crime for which he received a thousand reproaches, and even was threatened with being turned away. If Katharine's maid, when lacing her stays, missed a single hole, her mistress, flushed with passion and stamping her feet, would cry out—"You are the most awkward creature —quite beyond bearing."

The frequent repetition of scenes of this sort at last tired out all the domestics in the house; most of them complained to Mr. Wharton, and expressed a wish to quit his service, however they regretted to leave so good a master. The latter, who grieved in his heart for his daughter's improper behaviour, wished to recall her to a more reasonable line of conduct, by an easy method, of which he had been thinking for some time. He told his domestics not to pay any attention to the clamour, nor to the rebukes of his daughter, but to answer her by an obsequious smile, and never to obey her orders, when given in a supercilious tone and manner. Mr. Wharton's directions were punctually obeyed.

When Katharine called for any of the servants in her usual overbearing manner, no one answered her; if she put a question to any of them, or gave orders with an imperious air, she saw everyone smile, turn round, and desert her. Overcome with vexation, unable to understand this mysterious behaviour, she complained of it to her father, expecting that he would discharge those who dared to fail in their respect to her; but Mr. Wharton replied to her coolly and pointedly: "I have also observed, my daughter, that all our servants are determined to obey you no longer; but is not this rather your fault than theirs?"

Katharine, in a fit of peevishness declared that she would not in future address a single word to the servants, and would dispense altogether with their services; "let those who will employ them, submit to their caprice; I will not allow any one of them, not even the old governess, to enter my apartment."

"This is the surest means of not being interrupted in your occupations," coolly replied Mr. Wharton.

"I shall do everything myself, make my bed, arrange my room, attend to my toilet, all by myself."

"In this manner you will have every thing done exactly according to your fancy," replied her father.

"I intend also, that none of the servants shall wait upon

me at table, and I will have a dumb waiter placed by me upon which I may find what I want."

"I willingly subscribe to your plan, my dear, and will give orders accordingly."

"How happy I shall be, to be able to shew to these people that I can manage without them, and that all masters might do the same, and save thereby the expense of feeding a crowd of idle fellows, giving them wages, and loading them with presents which are often repaid with ingratitude."

"I wish, Katharine, that you may succeed in giving them a lesson," replied Mr. Wharton composedly.

That very day Katharine began to act upon her new system. At dinner she changed her own plates, filled her glass, cut her bread, looking askance at the servants who stood near the table, and who seemed surprised at the novelty of the scene. Katharine, however, broke a decanter, and a china plate, and spilt some red wine on the table cloth. Her father merely observed with his accustomed kindness, "We must all go through an apprenticeship before we can get used to any new situation."

Returning from the theatre, in the evening, Katharine carefully folded her shawl, and put by her gloves and bonnet. The maid entered her room to assist her to put her hair in paper, and unlace her stays, as she used to do every night.

"I have no occasion for you," said Katharine sharply to her; "I have put on stays which are laced in front; I shall arrange all that is necessary for my toilette, and put on my curling papers myself; yes, I shall do it myself, however you may simper."

The good old governess appeared soon after, according to custom, in order to assist Katharine in undressing for the night. Katharine refused her assistance, and dismissed her bluntly, notwithstanding all the kind remonstrances of this affectionate attendant.

Next morning to the great surprise of the people of the house, and of Mr. Wharton himself, young Katharine was seen sweeping the floor of her apartments, dusting the furniture, making her bed, &c. In doing this, however, she broke a looking glass, tore some drapery, and upset a lamp on the carpet; but her father hearing of her mishap, told her, with his usual good nature, "In every thing we undertake practice is necessary to make us perfect."

Katharine tried afterwards to light her fire. She put up the coals and wood well enough; she struck a light by means of her flint and steel, lighted the tinder; and succeeded in making her fire burn. She did not do all this, however, without hurting her hand with the steel, and burning her fingers. She was also near setting fire to the rug, but her father coming into the room in time, condescended to assist her, and calmly repeated, "We must get used to a thing before we can succeed in it."

At dinner time, Katharine made her appearance in the drawing-room, where she found several guests already assembled who were struck with the disorder of her dress. Her frock was all on one side, her stays were too high up, her tippet was thrown upon one shoulder leaving the other bare, her sash was tied clumsily behind. But that which particularly struck those who were in the habit of seeing Katharine and admiring the taste of her usual head-dress, was now seeing her hair out of curl, hanging over her face, and before her fine eyes, which gave such an extraordinary appearance, that a general titter ran round the assembly. Mr. Wharton with great coolness explained to his friends the new plan of the young reformer, affecting an air of serious importance, which his hearers assumed likewise.

Katharine however had been deeply mortified at the

effect produced by her appearance, and in looking at herself in the glass, her vexation was increased. She could not conceal from herself that she looked frightful, and this was too great a trial even for her fortitude.

On retiring to her apartment for the night, Katharine in order to avoid a repetition of the same mortifying scene, put her hair carefully in paper, and then pressed the curls repeatedly with the irons. In doing this she burnt her forehead and one of her ears, but she comforted herself with the idea of showing, next day, that she could dress her hair better than any chamber-maid or hair-dresser. What then was her dismay next morning on taking off her cap, to see all her curling-papers fall on the floor, each with the curl of hair contained in it. In great trepidation she put her hand to her head, ran to the mirror and beheld! her beautiful locks singed by the too hot irons, and her once fine head of hair entirely spoiled. She uttered a shriek of despair, which brought to the room some of the servants and Mr. Wharton himself. The latter could not help smiling when he saw his daughter's head half shorn, with only a few tufts of hair here and there partly singed, forming a strange contrast with Katharine's pretty face, of which a few days before they were the principal ornament.

Katharine was obliged to have her head shaved, and wear a wig for more than six months. She then discovered that it is impossible to live in a state of society without the assistance of those who compose it. She confessed all the wrongs she had been guilty of, towards the persons belonging to her father's household, begged of them to forget the past, and became from that time as mild and indulgent, as she had been till then, fastidious and overbearing. All the servants resumed their accustomed services to her, and everyone of them, finding in Katharine's kind behaviour the reward of his zeal and assiduity, redoubled his

TOWN AND COUNTRY TALES.

eagerness to execute her orders, and to meet her least desires.

After a certain time, Katharine's hair grew again, and the wig was put aside; she soon became more handsome than ever, especially as an air of mildness and satisfaction added to her charms: the only trace of her former folly consisted of a slight scar on her forehead, made by the curling-irons, the mark of which remained during her life; every time Katharine saw herself in the glass and perceived this mark, she remembered her father's words: "We cannot ourselves do every thing we wish; in whatever situation we may be, we must depend upon our fellow creatures, for a thousand wants, and therefore we ought to repay their services by kindness and gratitude."

THE TAME STAG.—A FABLE.

[ILLUSTRATIONS DESIGNED AND CUT OUT IN SILHOUETTE
BY A. L. P. & M. G.: SEE INTRODUCTION.]

[From *The First Book of Poetry. For the Use of Schools.
By W. F. Mylius.* Ninth Edition. London: M. J. Godwin
& Co. no. 195 (St. Clement's) Strand. 1825.]

As a young stag the thicket pass'd,
The branches held his antlers fast.
A clown who saw the captive hung,
Across the horns his halter flung.

Now safely hampered in the cord,
He bore the present to his lord.
His lord was pleas'd; as was the clown,
When he was tipp'd with half-a-crown.

THE TAME STAG.

The stag was brought before his wife;
The tender lady begged his life.
How sleek's the skin! how speck'd like ermine'
Sure never creature was so charming!

At first within the yard confin'd
He flies and hides from all mankind;
Now bolder grown, with fix'd amaze
And distant awe, presumes to gaze;
Munches the linen on the lines,
And on a hood or apron dines.

THE TAME STAG.

He steals my little master's bread,
Follows the servants to be fed :
Nearer and nearer now he stands,
To feel the praise of patting hands.

Examines every fist for meat,
And, though repuls'd, disdains retreat ;
Attacks again with levell'd horns ;
And man, that was his terror, scorns.

Gay.

JUVENILE ANECDOTES.

EDWARD SEYMOUR; OR, A MODEL FOR LITTLE BOYS TO IMITATE.

[From *Juvenile Anecdotes, founded on facts, collected for the Amusement of Children. By Priscilla Wakefield.* Seventh Edition. London: Harvey & Darton, 55 Gracechurch Street. 1825.]

MRS. COURTLEY one day, at breakfast, happened to have some hot bread upon the table: it was offered to Edward, but he refused it, at the same time casting rather a wishful eye upon it, which she observed, and desiring to know the cause of it, asked him whether he liked hot bread? "Yes," replied he, "I am extremely fond of it." "Why then, my dear child, did you refuse to take any?" "Because, madam," said the excellent boy, "I know my papa does not approve of my eating it. Am I to disobey a father and mother that I love so well, and to forget my duty to them, because they are a great way off? I would not touch the cake, were I sure nobody could see me; I myself should know it, and that would be sufficient." "Nobly replied," exclaimed Mrs. Courtley; "act always thus, and you must be happy; for although the whole world should refuse you the praise that is your due, you must enjoy the approbation of your own conscience, which is beyond every thing else."

THE TUREEN OF SOUP.

HENRY was a little boy of high spirit, and did not readily submit to be contradicted; this disposition frequently led him into inconveniences that caused him severe repentance.

Being one day at table with the family, a tureen of soup was served up among other things; when his mother ladled it out into the plates, she observed a quantity of gravel-stones in it. " This is very extraordinary, indeed," said she, with some warmth; "let the cook be called in, that she may inform us how this dirt came into the soup." Henry coloured, but kept silent for some time; at length the cook entered, and his father being very angry with the poor girl, who had nothing to allege in her defence but that she was quite ignorant of the matter, he could keep the secret no longer, but rising from his chair, exclaimed, " Be angry with me, my dear father : I am alone to blame. When I was at play this morning, I put the gravel into the soup, while Ann was gone into the parlour to answer the bell." " You do very right to acknowledge the truth," replied his father : " I shall not punish you for this offence, since you confess it so generously."

THE GRATEFUL SCHOOL-FELLOW.

TALE-BEARING is an odious fault, and generally renders those who are guilty of it, not only disliked, but despised. But there is a proper distinction to be made between the tattler, who repeats every inadvertent action, with a malicious design to make mischief, and the boy of true courage, who dares appeal in an open manner to his master, at the risk of being scoffed at by his companions for a tale-tale, when he sees the weak oppressed by the strong, and is unable to redress the injury. The four sons of Mr. Milton were sent to a large school, in which were boys of all ages. It frequently happens at such schools that the bigger boys impose upon the younger ones, employing them in their errands, and making them what they call *fags;* a treatment which they are obliged to submit to, till they become old enough to assert their own independence, and tyrannise in their turn. In these numerous seminaries, friendships are likewise formed, which are maintained with a warmth of affection, and are productive of instances of generosity, worthy of a more advanced age. Similarity of taste and disposition united the Miltons in a close intimacy with a boy of the name of Danvers. The partiality of their sons introduced him to the notice of Mr. and Mrs. Milton, from whom he had received many testimonies of regard. With design to gratify their children, especially Roland, the youngest, who was particularly attached to Danvers, they sometimes invited him to pass part of the holidays at their house; on other occasions, they would send him a rich cake, or increase his stock of pocket-money by a present. The heart of Danvers was too grateful not to feel the value of these favours, and he returned them, by the only means in his power, an increase of attachment towards their sons. In every contest he sided with the Miltons, and fought many a battle in their defence; but one day he met with an antagonist who was above his match. As he was hastily passing across the play-ground, he was stopped by the cries of his young friend, Roland, suffering from the cruel behaviour of one of the great boys, who was hated as the tyrant of the school. Danvers, seeing that his oppressor used him excessively ill, by beating, kicking, and shoving him about, enquired what was the cause of such treatment. "What is that to you?" replied Fletcher: "mind your own business, or I will presently teach you the consequences of interfering in what does not concern you." Danvers expostulated, and endeavoured to convince him of the injustice and meanness of tyrannising over those who are unable to avenge themselves. But it was in vain to argue with one who was deaf to remonstrance, and he was conscious that he was no match in strength with Fletcher, who was as powerful as he was cruel and ill-natured; therefore he went directly to Dr. Stephenson, his master, and related the transaction. The doctor sent for Fletcher, and reprimanded him severely for fighting, but more especially for his dastardly conduct in beating a child of six years of age. "Had you possessed true courage," continued the doctor, "you would have scorned to have abused an adversary so unable to oppose you: retire to the school-room, and remain there during the whole of the playtime this day, for infringing the rule made against fighting." Fletcher withdrew with a sulky countenance, expressive of the revenge he meditated; for his haughty spirit could not brook the mortification of being punished upon the accusation of another; and to undergo a penance from the report of an inferior was insufferable. He was, therefore, no sooner released, than he collected all the boys of his age and class, and related the affair to them in such a light, as made Danvers appear like a mean tell-tale, whom it was their common interest to chastise. In consequence of this misrepresentation, they agreed to seize poor Danvers the first opportunity, and satiate their revenge upon him. Danvers sustained their blows with manly resolution, calling out whilst under their hands, "I scorn to tell tales for my own sake, however ill-used I may be; but *now* I suffer in defence of my friend, and for the gratitude I owe to my benefactors, Mr. and Mrs. Milton; therefore, you may beat me as much, and as long as you please."

JUVENILE ANECDOTES.

THE BLACK BOOK.

IN different schools there are different modes of regulating the behaviour of the pupils, according to the inclination of those who govern them. A better plan can scarcely be adopted than that of the school where the Miltons went. Dr. Stephenson formed a code of laws, as they might properly be called, enjoining certain penalties for certain faults, which gave every boy an opportunity of knowing the consequences of disobedience, before he committed the act. But, as it was impossible, from the multiplicity of offences, to remember the exact time when every boy was guilty of a fault, many would doubtless have escaped all punishment, who deserved as much as those who suffered, had there not been a book kept, called the Imposition-Book, in which a daily account was entered of the offences committed, and of the tasks imposed, by which it was easy to ascertain the time when each delinquent ought to be able to repeat his task. As an emblem of its melancholy office, this book was bound in black leather, and deposited, under lock and key, in Dr. Stephenson's own desk; which was a necessary precaution, as he had promised, that if ever it should be lost or missing, an act of grace should follow, and all punishments which were due, should be forgiven.

Charles Stephenson was about eleven years old, and of the most amiable disposition; his good temper, and desire of rendering others happy, made him the darling of the school. This promising child fell sick of a fever; the physicians pronounced him in great danger, and urged the necessity of his taking the medicines which they had ordered, regularly, as his recovery depended much upon it. Poor Charles was in an uncomfortable situation, his stomach loathed the nicest food, and the draught was very nauseous; his resolution failed, and he refused to swallow it. His mother entreated him, and even wept at the bedside, but without success. After every effort had been vainly tried, his father was called. "My dear Charles," said he, "I am sensible of the difficulty you feel to comply with my request, but the medicine must be taken: name any reward or indulgence which I can bestow, as the price of your compliance, and it shall be granted." Such an unlimited offer would have tempted many boys to have procured some gratification for themselves; but Charles Stephenson, after a moment's reflection, said, "Give me the cup, and burn the Imposition-Book, and I will drink up the draught without hesitation." It had a happy effect: Charles recovered, and the first day that he was well enough to play among the boys, the destruction of the black book was commemorated by a holiday, which all enjoyed, but none so completely as he who had procured this festivity, by preferring the happiness of others to his own.

THE CAUTIOUS MOTHER.

THERE are few books so pure in sentiment and expression as to be completely unexceptionable: even many of the publications that have been written expressly for youth, are defaced by exclamations, inconsistent with that simplicity which is the chief ornament of an unperverted mind. Mrs. Dennis was so particular with respect to the books she admitted amongst her children, that it was her constant practice to examine the most childish story-book, before she permitted them to read it; and as she considered instruc-

JUVENILE ANECDOTES.

tion as the chief object in reading, she never scrupled to sacrifice the beauty of a new purchase, by freely cutting out as many leaves as contained passages likely to give them false ideas, or to corrupt their innocence. So very exact was she in her correctness, that not an objectionable sentence escaped. Thus there were but few books in the library of her school-room, that did not bear the marks of her hand. The children, believing their mamma to be wiser than any person whatever, and being assured also that her love for them induced her to take this trouble, showed no desire to see those parts which she had effaced. In time they became so accustomed to her alterations, that they omitted the words through which she had drawn a line, as a thing in course. The sacred name of the Deity, they never were suffered to pronounce, but in the most reverential and serious manner, making a solemn pause when it occurred, even in the Holy Scriptures; but, if it was ever introduced in other books, by way of exclamation, they passed it over, and mostly marked it as a word not to be repeated.

At about seven years of age, she was obliged to relinquish Theodosius, her eldest boy, to the care of a gentleman who was engaged in the education of a few scholars. The day of his arrival passed so pleasantly, that he began to think that he should be quite as happy with Mr. Perrin, as he had been at home. The next morning he entered regularly into the order of the school, and in his turn was called up to read. Mr. Perrin, not supposing him to be well qualified, gave him a spelling-book by way of trial; but he presently found that he was capable of reading something of a superior kind; upon which he took another book from the shelf, and, making an apology for having offered him a lesson so much beneath his powers, desired him to read a speech in one of Madame Genlis' Dramas. The little boy began in a manner that convinced Mr. Perrin that the utmost diligence and judgment had been exerted, to prepare him for his future progress in more difficult studies. After advancing to the middle of the page, he suddenly stopped, and looking up with great innocency at Mr. Perrin, said, "Pray, Sir, where is your pencil?" "What occasion can you have for a pencil, my dear, whilst you are engaged in your lesson?" "Do not you see, Sir," said the little boy, "that there is the awful name which I dare not repeat; and my mamma used always to draw a line through those words which she did not choose we should say." Mr. Perrin apprehended his meaning in a moment, and complied with his request, The custom pleased him so well, that he adopted it ever after in those books which he appointed for the use of his scholars.

EMPLOYMENT.

[From *Employment, The True Source of Happiness; or The Good Uncle and Aunt. By Mrs. Bayley.* London: John Harris, corner of St. Paul's Churchyard. 1825.]

JOHN GREEN, the miller, was originally a small farmer and possessed a few acres of land, bequeathed to him by his father, and which he managed to the greatest possible advantage. At an early age he married an industrious young woman, and was doing as he thought, tolerably well. His family increased rapidly; in a few years he found himself father of seven children. By this time, his wife, who was naturally of a delicate constitution became very sickly and unable to attend to the domestic duties of her family; and as they could not afford to keep a proper person to look after the children they were much neglected, and everything in the house went wrong. This to, poor Margaret (the miller's wife) who was doatingly fond of her family was a heart-sickening reflection; and her grief had so great an effect upon her health that she gradually declined till her life was despaired of. At this time, to add to poor Green's misfortunes, a fire happened in an out-building adjoining his stable, which not only consumed his granary, containing the produce of his year's labour, but even his barn and stable were burnt to the ground; and in the latter perished his team of horses. This was a loss which his scanty means could not hope to replace; and to complete his distress he had some demands coming upon him of which he had anticipated the discharge by the sale of his corn. That resource being lost he had no alternative; and to enable him to pay his debts he was obliged to dispose of his few acres of land, together with the little tenement in which he dwelt. This was immediately done, and as far as the money would reach every one was honestly paid. Poor Green, with his disconsolate wife and children, repaired to a small hovel, a short distance from their former residence, where by daily labour he endeavoured to gain for them a subsistence. But, from depression of mind, his health had suffered and very few were disposed to employ a man who was not able to work hard. In this dreadful situation, they would probably all have perished, but for a very humane kind-hearted apothecary residing in the village who had formerly attended poor Margaret, and who called in during this season of distress, to inquire after her. He described the state he found them in as the most pitiable he had ever witnessed. The poor wife stretched on a bed of straw, apparently in the last stage of consumption, nursing one sickly infant at the breast, and another not eighteen months old was lying by her side crying for food.

The other five children, all under seven years, seated round a deal table were waiting for a scanty portion of potatoes which their father was preparing in the best way he was able for their dinner. The good-natured apothecary was much affected at the sight and enquired how they could have been reduced to so deplorable a state? "Have you no money?" said he. Green earnestly looked at him, and with a firm voice (though a big tear rolled down his manly but pale countenance) replied "*I have.*" "Have you money," said the doctor, "and yet allow your wife and family to remain thus miserable?" "*I have,*" said Green, "but though we perish it must not be touched." The apothecary rose hastily and indignantly from the wooden bench on which he had been seated; "Unfeeling wretch!" said he: "what! suffer your wife and children to perish, though you have the means of relief in your power? It *must* not; it *shall* not be." The tears rolling down his face, and his voice half-choked with grief and resentment, he hastened from the hovel and bent his steps towards the parsonage-house intending to consult with the clergyman, as to what could be done for the immediate relief of this poor family. They decided on returning instantly to the cottage, and insist on Green's explaining what appeared to them his inhuman conduct. As they opened the door, they found this affectionate husband kneeling by the side of his wife apparently in an agony of distress, but praying with great devotion. For some moments the visitors were unable to speak. They then emphatically enquired the reason why he did not with the money he acknowledged himself to be possessed of procure for his family the necessaries they so much required? The poor man burst into tears. "The money I have is *not my own*. Before my sad loss I was indebted to the miller on the heath twenty pounds, which sum I have not yet been able to pay. He has now consented to take it by instalments of two guineas per month; and the two guineas I have by me I must take to him on Monday next." The gentlemen were astonished; they strongly commended his virtuous principles; and giving him a guinea each, desired he would immediately procure necessaries and comforts for his wife and children. They then left him, and went to the miller intending to solicit his lenity towards this poor family. He was a good old man, and was greatly moved at the melancholy recital. After a few moments' reflexion, he said: "Gentlemen, I am, as you perceive, considerably advanced in life, and find my business more than I can well manage; I have been for some time thinking of a partner. An honest man is all I want, and one who will do the laborious part of the business. Green will answer the purpose; and I will immediately take him into my concern." He did so; and on his death, two years afterwards, left Green his mill, house and furniture, with two or three hundred pounds in money.

THE LITTLE CHIMNEY SWEEPER.

[From *Tales of the Cottage*. London: Vernor and Hood, 31, Poultry.]

I SAW a child sitting upon the grate, whilst its master, with a whip in one hand and a candle in the other, was vowing either to cut him in pieces or set him on fire unless he climbed the chimney. Bursting into tears the boy exclaimed: "Oh, sir, take me to my mamma, and never let me go with that nasty man again!" "God bless your honour," said the man in evident confusion, "he means his nurse at the workhouse." I pulled the bell and ordered my servant to take care the fellow did not escape, when he flew to the window, jumped out, and was out of sight in a moment. "Who is your mamma?" "My mamma's name is Melville, and she lives at a great white house near Windsor." I sent immediately to a tailor's, and the little chimney sweeper was soon converted into a gentleman. I sent my servant in advance, and ordered my carriage to follow. At length we reached the avenue, and saw a lady in deep mourning. "Oh, my dear, dear mamma!" exclaimed the child, and in less than a minute the happy parent pressed her lovely boy to her bosom. The happy, weeping servants came crowding round the child, who asked for Molly his nursemaid. "She is gone home, my darling," said Mrs. Melville, "for I could not bear the sight of so careless a person." "Indeed it was not Molly's fault; my cousin George went one way and I another, and so she could not catch us both; and just as I got outside the park gate that nasty man catched me up in his arms, and said 'A, ha! have I got you my young master?' and never stopped until he came to an old tumbledown house where he made me take off my nice blue jacket and put on a nasty sooty coat. Look at my shoulder, mamma," continued he, drawing out his little arm as far as he could.

Mrs. Melville shrieked when she beheld the results of the barbarian's inhumanity, and besought me to find out the wretch. But as little Edward could give no account of the place where he had been secreted, all our attempts were in vain.

TALES FOR ELLEN.

By the Author of
"*Ellen, the Young Godmother,*"
"*The Young Naturalist,*" &c.

VOL. I.

CONTAINING
HARRY THE PEASANT;
ELLEN & GEORGE, OR THE GAME AT CRICKET;
THE LITTLE BLUE BAG.

London:
PRINTED FOR H. R. THOMAS, JUVENILE LIBRARY,
HANOVER STREET, HANOVER SQUARE.

1826.

I *will* have a kiss!

THE GAME AT CRICKET.

George was up on the donkey's back in a minute; but with all the famed prowess of the butcher's boy as a donkey driver, and with all George's thumps and kicks the animal would not move from the spot where he had fixed himself. The butcher's boy was quite in a rage, and he was venting his spleen on the stubbornness of all donkeys and this donkey in particular, when the sudden sound of a horn made both the donkey and the pony prick up their ears. In a few moments a stage coach was in sight, and in a few more the horn and the rattling wheels approached with great velocity towards the two equestrians. George would have

THE GAME AT CRICKET.

jumped off to save himself from being run over, but the donkey saved him for the present the trouble. All his energies were suddenly aroused, and he darted forwards at a pelting gallop. The butcher's pony did the same. Away they both flew before the leaders of the stage, scarcely distancing them by a horse's length, and all the passengers thought that mischief was inevitable. A gentleman on the box begged the coachman to pull in, but the coachman seemed to enjoy the fun, and only whipped on his horses; the pony and the donkey were still galloping furiously, both their riders keeping their seats. Butchers' boys always seem glued to their saddles, so that there appeared nothing astounding in Jem Rattle's not getting a fall; but how George, without a saddle, and not much accustomed to riding, sat so long, was something more remarkable. Whether he might have got to the end of his race without accident if his father and mother had not appeared by the side of the road, it is impossible to say, but certain it is that the sight of them diverted the attention which had before been entirely given to keeping his eye steadily before him; —at the same instant the donkey gave a little curve out of the line in which he had been going, and most providential was it that he did so, for by this inclination George was thrown sufficiently aside to clear the wheels of the coach. The pony had given in some few minutes before, and the donkey having once checked himself stopped suddenly, and stood quietly by the road side as if nothing had happened. The gentleman on the box now insisted upon the coachman drawing up, to see if the young gentleman had sustained any injury; and Mr. and Mrs. Danvers, in a state of harassing alarm, also hastened to approach the spot.

Mr. and Mrs. Danvers were more alarmed than George was hurt; he certainly got a few bruises, but he received no serious injury. He immediately jumped on his legs, and relieved the anxiety of his parents, when, after Mr. Danvers

THE GAME AT CRICKET.

had thanked the gentleman on the box for his kind interference, and joined with him in condemning the coachman for not having before checked his horses, the coach drove on, and George joined his father and mother. The butcher boy was commissioned with the promise of a shilling to bring back the donkey to Mr. Danvers' field; and George looked not a little foolish as he went home.

* * * * * *

At length the day arrived on which Mr. Danvers had promised to join the lads at cricket. The boys were all in high spirits. George did not tire himself by rising early, and what was even of more consequence, he sat quietly down to his books as usual after breakfast, not perhaps with the fixed attention he sometimes gave to his studies, but with tolerable assiduity and diligence: neither had Ellen on this day any useless longings to leave her book or her work before the time prescribed. I do not say that she never suffered her attention to be diverted from either, for it is a long time before such active lively little girls as Ellen can sit down to their employments without sometimes thinking of other things. She thought a good deal of a pretty white flannel jacket edged with blue that her mamma had made for George; indeed at one time her mind was so intent upon this that when her mamma was questioning her upon her geography lessons, she spoke of some town on the white jacket instead of the White Sea.

"Even now, Ellen, I would not advise you to go out directly," said Mrs. Danvers; "wait till the gardeners have finished putting up the tent, and then we will go together."

It was at length completed, and Stevens and Wilson and the two Porters were all arrived, each in a white jacket trimmed with blue; and papa was ready; and what was better than all, papa had also a white jacket trimmed with blue. Oh, how Ellen also longed for a white jacket trimmed with blue; she almost wished to be a boy; but she

THE GAME AT CRICKET.

remembered that boys go to school and leave papa and mamma for a great many months together. Next week George was going to school—oh, she should not like to be going to school; she had rather remain at home without the white jacket. She had just come to this conclusion, when Mrs. Danvers entered the room with a little calico spencer trimmed with blue, which she invited Ellen to put on. The new garment was speedily adjusted, and then Ellen, her eyes glistening with delight, took her mother's hand and proceeded to the cricket field.

The game of cricket, and the day in general, went off as happy as could be wished. All engaged in it with good humour, and although George was beaten by Tom Fletcher he bore the loss of the game without loss of temper; and all the boys told him he would when as big as Tom be quite as good a player. The two boys afterwards played a game together against Mr. Danvers, who, when young, had been a first-rate player, and would have beat half-a-dozen such boys. The boys, however, found the advantage of having youth and agility on their side in getting up a good number of notches, and George's delight was great at twice bowling out his father. Mr. Danvers won the game, but it was a very hard run thing, and till the last it seemed very doubtful which party was to be successful.

Ellen was very active throughout all the games in handing fruit and milk to the players, and was much amused in watching the progress of all the games. She would have been better satisfied if George had won the game he played against Tom Fletcher: her little heart was in a flutter of agitation every time George took the bat; and when he gained a notch, she could not withhold a shout of delight. She was satisfied to look forward to some day of brighter success for him, and found as he did some compensation for the loss of the other games in having belonged to the party who won the last.

GENTILITY DEFINED.

[From *A Sketch of My Friend's Family, intended to suggest some practical hints on religion and domestic manners.* By Mrs. Marshall, Author of Henwick Tales. Fifth Edition. London: J. Hatchard & Son, Piccadilly. 1827.]

"MAMMA, what does the word *genteel* mean?" "You must consult your friend the dictionary, Jane, so soon as we have breakfasted," replied her mother. "I have, mamma, but I thought that could not give the right meaning, for it only says 'polite, elegant'; and I think *genteel* must mean something more than that." "No, Jane, it does not mean anything more; but tell me what makes you think it does?" Jane blushed, and hesitated, and at last said, "Why, mamma, the ladies I went to see yesterday seemed so anxious about gentility, and one of them said she should like to know you because she heard that you were *genteel* and not because you were *good* —so I thought it must mean something more."

EXCUSE FOR NOT VISITING POOR SUSAN.

MR. CLIFFORD inquired of Mrs. Hammond, whether she had yet had an opportunity of visiting the sick woman whose case he recommended to her? "No, really," she replied, "I have not had one moment of leisure since you named her to me. On Monday I was at a Bible Society's meeting; Tuesday, I went to hear Mr. —— preach; Wednesday, I dined at Mrs. Nelson's, where a select number of serious friends were assembled to meet the Rev. Mr. H——; all Thursday I was occupied in endeavouring to procure subscribers to our Dorcas society; and to-day I shall hardly have time to swallow my dinner, on my return home, before the arrival of a lady who has promised to go with me to hear a sermon for the benefit of our Sunday School." As Mrs. Hammond paused, I asked my friend, in a low voice, "Is it possible to be *religiously dissipated?*"

THE NEW PELISSE.

ON our way we passed the rooms of a fashionable dressmaker, when Emma, who had before remained unusually silent, stopped and exclaimed with earnestness, "This is where my aunt purchased Maria's new pelisse, papa. You cannot think what a contrast there was in hers and mine today. One looks so nicely and the other so old-fashioned and so shabby that I did not like to walk with her." "I am very sorry for that, Emma," said I, "yet I must confess, that had you not told me it was so, I should have discovered nothing so very obsolete or mean in your pelisse. However," I added, " since it exposes you to so serious a mortification in wearing it, I will make you a present of a new pelisse like Maria's, if your mamma have no objection."

The object of my walk was to seek out the residence of a little girl in our Sunday School, who had for some time been absent on a plea of illness. With some difficulty we discovered the house ; and entering found the child who a few weeks before appeared healthy, strong and cheerful, sitting by the side of a nearly extinguished fire, pale, emaciated and dejected.

"And where is your mother, my good girl?" I demanded. "Surely you are not in a condition to be left alone?" "Sir," replied my Sunday Scholar, bursting into tears, " my father's wages are very small, and my poor mother has already lost so many days in nursing me, that she was obliged to go to work to-day, or we should have had no fire and hardly anything to eat for the remainder of the week." "And how is your appetite?" I enquired of the poor little sufferer. "Not very good, Sir," said she, " and that makes my poor mother fret because she cannot get the things I fancy I could eat."

Whilst she spoke I looked at Emma, whose eyes, suffused with tears, were first fixed on the wan cheeks and sunken eyes of the child, and then on me, with an imploring earnestness.

On leaving the house I perceived that Emma, chilled with the unusual severity of the weather, shuddered as she took my arm. " Oh, my dear papa," said she, with a soft beseeching look, " will you not send these poor people in some coals before we return home? for I am sure I shall have no pleasure by the side of our own comfortable fire if that poor girl has none to warm her." "I cannot afford it, Emma," I replied, " you remember I have promised you a pelisse, like Maria's; it will therefore be necessary to refrain from giving to this poor family, and perhaps to several others, things which they greatly need."

The reproof was sufficient, and bursting into tears, she exclaimed " Forgive me, my dear papa; and since vanity can only be gratified by such cruel selfishness as this, I hope I shall never again be ashamed if my clothes are not so expensive or so fashionable as Maria's."

I then immediately complied with her request and we ordered in the coals, and purchased several little indulgences which sickness converts into absolute necessaries. And all these cost but a very inconsiderable part of the sum which must have been expended on a new pelisse.

[From *The Little Grammarian; or an Easy Guide to the Parts of Speech, in a series of Instructive and Amusing Tales.* By the Rev. W. Fletcher, St. John's College, Cambridge. London: John Harris, St. Paul's Churchyard. 1828.]

The following sentences are erroneous, therefore be pleased to correct them at pleasure.

He run well.
We has a dog.
The flowers grows.
I has slept.
Pigs squeaks.
She have a cat.
He hit she.
John beat I.
Jane struck we.
I see he.
This is he whom have done it.
Him here boy was lazy.
That there dog is mine.
Them who hide can find.
A dog who I found.

I has a boat.
We should not hurt no creature.
He does not know nothing.
John likes she.
Neither him nor she were there.
John and Betsy has a ball.
I will take these loaf.
You behaved foolish.
Good children never tell no lies.
Don't say nothing not to nobody.
One may deceive themselves.
John were very eager to go.
He always behave well.
The dog who I bought is better than the one whom you sold.

ODD CUTS.

Mamma at Romps.

The Darling Dancing.

The Darling Awake!

The Darling Asleep!

Give me a Kiss!

Clarissa.

Maternal Instruction.

Filial Attention.

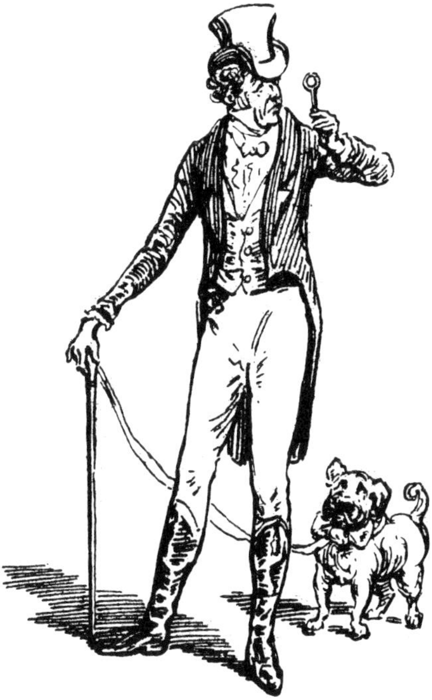

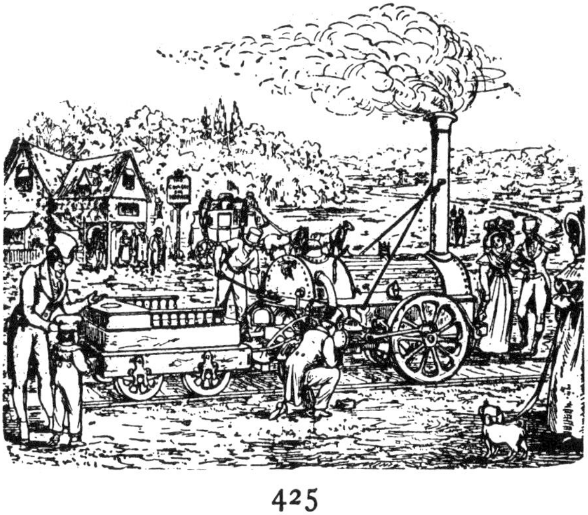

426

427

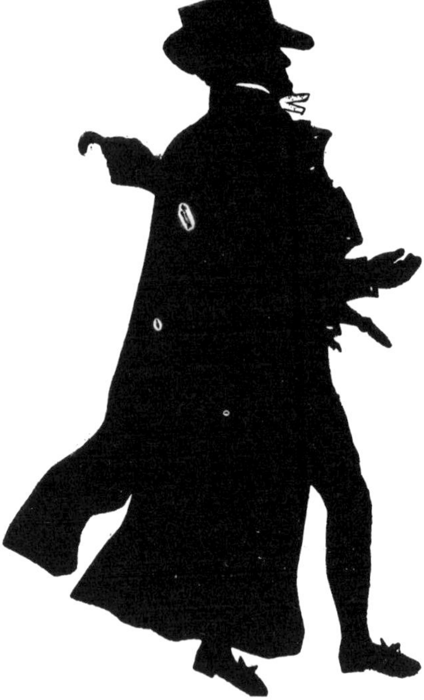

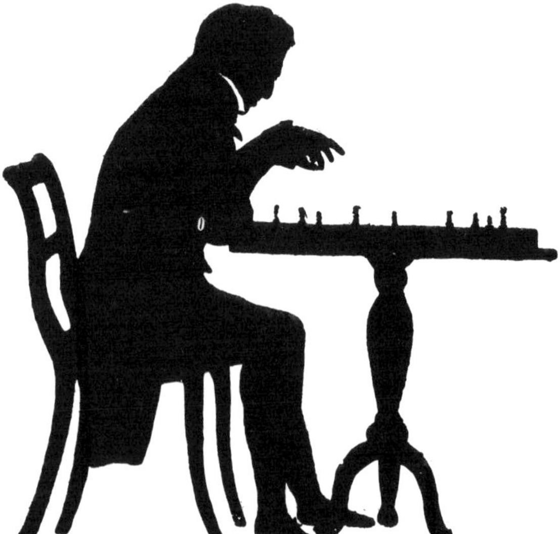

429

430

431

432

INDEX.

	PAGE
Admonition, The	306
Adventures of Joe Dobson	65
Æsop in Rhyme	343
Alphabet (Amusing) for Young Children	165
Amusing Alphabet for Young Children	165
Amusing Picture and Poetry Book, Harrison's	205
Anecdotes (Juvenile) Founded on Facts	395
Anecdotes of Mrs. Truegood's Scholars	91
Bad Family, The	148
Ballroom, Visiting The	138
Ball, The Dandy's	363
Bazaar, Visit to the	315
Beasts, Birds and Fishes	200
Black Book, The	399
Blaize, Mrs. Mary	95
Blind Child, The	27
Book of Games	163
Cautious Mother, The	400
Children, Original Rhymes for	305
Children's Magazine	31
Chimney Sweeper, The Little	405
Choice Collection of Pretty Songs and Verses	161
Christmas Holidays	91
Coach, The	134
Cobler, Stick to your Last	65
Cockchafer, The	92
Collection of Simple Stories	129
Comical Girl	305

INDEX.

	PAGE
Contrast, The	122
Conversations Instructive and Amusing	33
Coughing	310
Cricket, Game at	409
Cricket in 1812	163
Cries (London) for Children	109
Cries of London, as they are daily exhibited in the Streets	115
Crocus, The	306
Crowd, The	124
Cup of Sweets that can never Cloy	57
Curling	326
Curtesy, To make a	7
Dandy's Ball, The	363
Dangerous Sports	85
Dangers of the Streets	140
Delightful Tales for Good Children	57
Directions for Young Ladies to attain a Genteel Carriage	7
Disappointments of a Week	227
Disappointment, The	129
Discontented Child, The	119
Dog glad of a Crumb	351
Dr. Goldsmith's *Mrs. Mary Blaize*	95
Dutiful Son, The	274
Easy Lessons	50
Easy Guide to the Parts of Speech	416
Elderly Gentleman, The	275
Elegant Girl, The	183
Ellen's Fairing	207
Emily Barton	220
Employment	402

INDEX.

	PAGE
Evil of Going too near the Fire	208
Excuse for not Visiting poor Susan	414
False Alarms	21
Familiar Letter-Writer	25
Familiar Representations	208
Fanny and Mary	347
Fanny and Mary, History of	197
Fido	59
First Book of Poetry	392
Foolish Fears	158
Game at Cricket	409
Games, Book of	163
Gammer Garton's Garland	161
Generous Daughters, The	31
Gentility Defined	413
Gentleman, The Elderly	275
Ghosts and Apparitions, Spectres and Hobgoblins	21
Glutton, The	253
Going to School	133
Good Family, The	153
Good Manners, Rudiments of	148
Good Uncle and Aunt, The	402
Goldfinch, History of a	210
Grammarian, The Little	416
Grateful School-fellow, The	396
Harrison's Amusing Picture and Poetry Book	205
Harris's Cabinet	339
Henry	57
Hermitage, Tales of the	242
Hero of Romance, The	261
High Life in the City	363
Hockey	326

INDEX.

	PAGE
Honours of the Table	23
Hucklebones	329
Inducements to Virtuous Habits	322
Infant Minds, Original Poems for	353
James and the Shoulder of Mutton	355
James Manners, Little John and their Dog Bluff	331
Jingles	305
Joe Dobson, Adventures of	65
Journey to London	227
Juvenile Anecdotes founded on Facts	395
Juvenile Moralist	28
Juvenile Pieces	52
Juvenile Sports, History of	163
Juvenile Tell-Tale	272
Juvenile Views of Happiness	347
Kidnapped Child	242
Kind Tutor, The	171
Lessons for Children	148
Lilliputian Magazine	9
Lily, The	117
Lion, The	165
Little Children, Verses for	198
Little Chimney Sweeper, The	405
Little Fisherman, The	353
Little Grammarian, The	416
Little Mary and Her Cat, Story of	213
London Cries for Children	109
London, Journey to	227
London, Visit to	28
Lucy and Hodge	272
Mamma's Pictures	197
Manners (Jas.), Little John and their Dog Bluff	331

INDEX.

	PAGE
Maria	309
Marmaduke Multiply's Multiplication Table	287
Melvyn Lodge, Visit to	322
Mental Amusement, or the Juvenile Moralist	28
Mint, The	333
Mischievous Doctrine of Ghosts and Apparitions, of Spectres and Hobgoblins	21
Moral Playthings	62
Moth, The	352
Mrs. Leicester's School	220
Mrs. Mary Blaize	95
Mrs. Truegood's Scholars, Anecdotes of	91
Music	127
Music and the Bird	137
New Pelisse, The	414
New Riddle Book	43
Notorious Glutton	358
Nursery Morals	311
Nursery Parnassus	161
Old Man and his Calf	162
Original Poems for Infant Minds	353
Original Poems intended for the Use of Young Persons	92
Original Poems for Young People	206
Original Poems on Popular and Familiar Subjects	306
Original Rhymes for Children	305
Packet of Pictures for Good Children	137
Painter's Panegyrist, The	52
Parent's Offering	169
Parlour Guests	306
Parlour Teacher	50
Peep into the Country for Children	134

INDEX.

	PAGE
Pelisse, The New	414
Pence Tables (Harris's)	339
Peter the Great	343
Picturesque Piety	351
Pig, The	311
Pleasing Instructor	137
Poems Dissected	349
Poems on Popular and Familiar Subjects	306
Poetry, First Book of	392
Polite Academy for Young Ladies and Gentlemen	6
Polly Pert, History of	17
Poor Susan, Excuse for not Visiting	414
Pretty Book of Pictures for Little Masters and Misses	1
Primrose Prettyface, History of	45
Proud Boy, The	313
Pressgang	329
Remedy, The	125
Renowned History of Primrose Prettyface	45
Riddle Book, New	43
Riding the Donkey	131
Rod, The	119
Room, The	308
Rose, The	206
Rudiments of Good Manners	148
Rules for Behaviour at Table	23
Rural Scenes	134
Sally Spellwell, History of	13
Schoolboy's Diversions	326
School, Mrs. Leicester's	220
School, The	121
Self-inflicted Correction	386
Seymour (Edward), or a Model for Little Boys to Imitate	395
Shillings Transformed into Pounds	333

INDEX.

	PAGE
Simon Simple	11
Sketch of my Friend's Family	413
Skipping	328
Songs for Little Misses	32
Sophia's Foolscap	357
Spider and his Wife, The	360
Spinning Wheel, The	132
Stage Waggon, The	136
Summer Rambles	33
Sweep, The	312
Tales for Children	62, 169
Tales for Ellen	407
Tales of the Hermitage	242
Tales from the Mountains	251
Tales Uniting Instruction with Amusement	140
Tame Stag, The	392
Throwing Squibs	143
Tom and the Old Man	273
Tommy Trip's History of Beasts and Birds	1
Town and Country Tales	381
Truant Boy, The	166
True Source of Happiness	402
Tureen of Soup, The	395
Useful Hints for Children	306
Verses for Little Children	198
Visiting the Ballroom	138
Visit to London	28
Visit to Melvyn Lodge	322
Visit to the Bazaar	315
Washing and Dressing	357
Young Protector, The	383
Young Reviewers, The	349
Youths, The	307